INSIDE THE TUDOR HOME

DAILY LIFE IN THE SIXTEENTH CENTURY

BETHAN CATHERINE WATTS

PEN & SWORD HISTORY

AN IMPRINT OF PEN & SWORD BOOKS LTD.
YORKSHIRE – PHILADELPHIA

First published in Great Britain in 2023 by
PEN AND SWORD HISTORY
An imprint of
Pen & Sword Books Ltd
Yorkshire – Philadelphia

ISBN 978 1 39908 927 2

A CIP catalogue record for this book is available from the British Library.

Typeset in Times New Roman 11.5/14 by
SJmagic DESIGN SERVICES, India.
Printed and bound in the UK by CPI Group (UK) Ltd.

Pen & Sword Books Limited incorporates the imprints of Atlas, Archaeology,
Aviation, Discovery, Family History, Fiction, History, Maritime, Military,
Military Classics, Politics, Select, Transport, True Crime, Air World, Frontline
Publishing, Leo Cooper, Remember When, Seaforth Publishing, The Praetorian
Press, Wharncliffe Local History, Wharncliffe Transport, Wharncliffe True Crime
and White Owl.

For a complete list of Pen & Sword titles please contact
PEN & SWORD BOOKS LIMITED
George House, Units 12 & 13, Beevor Street, Off Pontefract Road,
Barnsley, South Yorkshire, S71 1HN, England
E-mail: enquiries@pen-and-sword.co.uk
Website: www.pen-and-sword.co.uk

or

PEN AND SWORD BOOKS
1950 Lawrence Rd, Havertown, PA 19083, USA
E-mail: uspen-and-sword@casematepublishers.com
Website: www.penandswordbooks.com

INSIDE THE TUDOR HOME

DAILY LIFE IN THE SIXTEENTH CENTURY

'Historians desiring to write the actions of men, ought to set down the simple truth...'

Sir Walter Raleigh

Contents

List of Illustrations

1. *Gathering Twigs*. Simon Bening [Illuminated Book of Hours]. (Bruges, c. 1550), MS. 5093., MS.19v. Image courtesy of The J. Paul Getty Museum, Los Angeles.
2. *Cosmeston Medieval Village, Vale of Glamorgan*. Unknown photographer. Image courtesy of Vale of Glamorgan Council.
3. *Wattle Fencing*. Item held at The Museum of London, Barbican. Author's photograph.
4. *Wattle and Daub*. Item held at The Museum of London, Barbican. Author's photograph.
5. *Tudor Farmhouse*, Jonathan Heggie (Pembrokeshire, c. 1400s). Image obtained with kind permission of Mr Heggie.
6. *Sopwell Priory*, Eleanor Grana (Hertfordshire, c. 1500s). Image obtained with kind permission of Miss Grana.
7. *Close-up of Sopwell Priory*, Eleanor Grana (Hertfordshire, c. 1500s). Image obtained with kind permission of Miss Grana.
8. *January*. Simon Bening [Illuminated Book of Hours]. (Bruges, c. 1540), MS 24098, f. 18v. Image courtesy of The British Library, London.
9. *Door and Doorway,* A.25:1, 2-1913. Unknown (England, ca. 1500 – 1530). Image courtesy of the Victoria and Albert Museum, South Kensington.
10. *Tudor Merchant's House*, Unknown (Pembrokeshire, c. 1500). Image courtesy of St Fagans National Museum of History, Cardiff.
11. *Mary Arden's Farm*. Robert Arden (Warwickshire, 1514). Image courtesy of Tudor History.org https://tudorhistory.org/
12. *Cutlery Set*, M.602 to C-1910. Unknown (France, c. 1550 – 1600). Image courtesy of the Victoria and Albert Museum, South Kensington.
13. *Armchair*, W.21-1965. Unknown (Salisbury, c. 1600 – 1620). Item held at the Victoria and Albert Museum, South Kensington. Author's photograph.

Acknowledgements

Many thanks are due to the wonderful people whose assistance and support were invaluable to me during my time in writing this book.

Firstly, to the team at *Pen & Sword Books* to who I am greatly indebted for offering me this opportunity. Their assistance in the publication of this book has been much welcomed and greatly appreciated.

To the curators at the *Mary Rose Museum* who kindly gave permission for the use of their image in this book. Also, many thanks are due to Miss Eleanor Grana and Mr Jonathan Heggie, who each offered their own images of sixteenth-century buildings when I was unable to get to them myself; thank you both so much again.

I researched and wrote this book whilst simultaneously studying for my Master's degree, and as such so many thanks are due to my wonderful lecturers, whose passions for history have inspired me more than I can adequately express.

To all of those who have followed my online historical blog from all corners of the globe. I will forever be immensely grateful for the support that you have shown me.

And finally, to my family and friends, who have all encouraged me in my passions for writing and for the past. For all the trips to historical sites and visits to dusty bookshops, for the hundreds of hours sat watching documentaries and listening to my spiels about long-dead people. I am so, so grateful for all the love, enthusiasm and cups of tea you have given me throughout the process of writing this book.

Money Conversion

In the sixteenth century, twelve pennies equated to one shilling. Twenty-eight shillings equated to one pound. This meant that one pound was made from two hundred and eighty pennies.

One pound in 1550 was around thirty-three days wages for a skilled tradesman, and comes to around £275 in sterling today.[1]

Preface

The moment Henry Tudor stepped off his ship and onto the beach at Milford Haven in 1485, life changed in England forever.

The years that followed brought wars, plague, religious condemnation and domestic policies that greatly impacted the lives of the entirety of sixteenth-century England for both better and for worse. Yet, it also brought prosperity, ostentation, power, and culture the country had never before seen. When we think of Tudor England, no one image comes to mind. We envisage Shakespearean black and white timber framed houses nestled amongst sprawling orchards and tilled agricultural fields; filthy street urchins begging on street corners, and city slums flowing with raw sewage. We think of the luxurious country estates of the rich and wealthy, all replete with plush, imported goods and expensive items from the New World. We picture country hovels, where entire large peasant families nestle around open fires in the only room in the house.

But how could these such hovels co-exist in a country where its monarchs and nobility lavished in excess and outrageous luxury? How did the Tudors truly live, and what was the Tudor home really like?

*

To what extent was it true that the Tudors bathed only on special occasions, and that there was no such thing as soap? Were the floors of dining halls really littered with discarded animal bones, and was it true that they lived off simple, flavourless diets consisting entirely of potatoes, cabbages, and gruel? Did the Tudors decorate their houses, celebrate birthdays, tend to flower gardens? How did they buy their clothes, keep food fresh, and care for their infants? Did they have exercise routines, or favourite cosmetics? What games did children play? How did women cope with their monthly menstrual cycles, and how did they bury their dead?

We have been conditioned to imagine the sixteenth century as a period of both stagnation and of progress; of insufficient medical practices and illiteracy and sanitation, but also of glorious cultural revolution and of the explosion of the arts. Some of the greatest literary, philosophical and mathematical minds came from the sixteenth century – William Shakespeare, Leonardo da Vinci, Amerigo Vespucci. So why do we continue to picture it as a provincial, stagnant place?

Close your eyes and imagine yourself in the sixteenth-century English countryside. Sounds of ploughs rattle in distant fields, and the delightful squeals of children at play fill the air. It is quiet, you think, quieter than you are used to, but loud and lively all the same. The air is pure, and it smells sweet with the natural floral fragrances of honeysuckle and apple blossom and lavender. There are no motors here, no planes in the sky, no pylons or wind turbines or television aerials. There is no suffocating smog, air or light pollution. There is little to obscure your view of wild, undulating fields, which, to your surprise, are sparsely inhabited by houses and instead occupied by droves of grazing cattle and sheep. In the distance you hear a horse neigh, and a washerwoman hum as she pegs out her laundry. The smell of woodfire fills the air, delicious aromas of crisping meats and yeasty dough, fresh, juicy fruits and the comforting, creamy smell of curds and whey. Soon will be the call for dinner, and hordes of tired labourers will return home to settle for the evening. Then will come nightfall, and the sounding of curfew bells. It is darker than you expected; much darker. There is no electricity here, and you are unaccustomed to the thin glow of candles as your only form of light. Soon these candles will stop burning, for the night has arrived, and the day has ended.

Welcome to the sixteenth century. Welcome to the Tudor home.

*

The prospect of writing a book about daily lives in a period that I had never – and will never – experience, seemed daunting. Tudor England, the *authentic* Tudor England, was an alien world, a place I was totally unfamiliar with. As a social historian, I had some decent understanding of the lives of our ancestors; but how little did I truly know?

To portray an accurate representation of daily life in the sixteenth century, I tried my best to get into the mindset of a Tudor. I thought of my own routines, of my diet, apparel, relationships. It seemed inconceivable that our ancestors five hundred years ago would wash daily, apply cosmetics, socialise with friends, and eat filling, satisfying meals just as we do today; but how wrong I was. Our forefathers and foremothers went about their daily routines in remarkably similar ways to how we do today. And in fact, should a twenty-first century person find themselves in the sixteenth century, I am willing to bet that they would soon settle down into a routine with which they would be relatively familiar. I learned throughout the process of writing this book that the centuries dividing 'us' from 'them' little mattered; in the Tudor age we see a reflection of us.

We often think of the sixteenth century as a period of social inequality, where the rigid feudal systems of the bygone Middle Ages still dictated a person's position in life. But, that was simply not the case. Grubby street urchins mingled with wealthy merchants who mingled with pious clergymen. Streets would have been filled with people from all walks of life; a lawyer could live next door to an illiterate fishwife, who could live next door to an adolescent apprentice. Cities were hubs of life, a microcosm of Tudor society. People flocked there in the hopes of a better life, an illustrious career, an advantageous marriage. Peasants were born and raised in the same villages, even houses, where they would die; city merchants were buried in the same graveyards where their forefathers had also been buried. People were born, got sick, celebrated achievements, argued with family, duelled with rivals, spent lavishly on gifts, married their sweethearts, and took their final breaths in cities and towns similar to our own. The ordinary people were, truly, the heart of Tudor society.

We have this misconception that the people of the past were not 'real', that they were instead just characters from a kind of storybook. We are all guilty of applying labels to the past – that it was dirty, that the people were flea-ridden, that the poor were illiterate. But put yourself in their (leather!) shoes for just a moment and think; wouldn't you be bothered by constant flea bites, or by the unpleasant smell emanating from the pores on your skin? So, why do we think that our ancestors were not?

Contrary to popular belief, the Tudors were not immune to foul smells, or recognising when the meat in their butteries had begun to rot, and they were just as aware of their intellectual capabilities as we are today. The Tudors were prideful just like we are today, and were aware – sometimes painfully so – of their appearances, of their apparel, and of the way they came across to their peers. They celebrated scientific progress and lamented religious persecution, and were early champions of the rights of women and the underrepresented. We need to start perceiving the Tudors as *real* human beings, and we need to treat bygone eras like the modern day. After all, what is more greater than a history book as a mirror to the past?

Introduction

Tudor England; a country replete with sprawling landscapes, dense forests and twisting urban labyrinths. In the fourteenth century, the population of England was estimated at a little more than a million people.[1] By the time of Henry VII's accession just one hundred years later in 1485, this figure had doubled. The population of England continued to grow throughout the sixteenth century, a period marked by the rulership of one of the most notorious historical dynasties in monarchical history: The Tudors.

By the time the last Tudor monarch Queen Elizabeth I had died in 1603, the population of England had reached the dizzying heights of around four million people, ninety per cent of whom were residing in the country.[2] In London alone the population had more than trebled by the close of the sixteenth century, going from around sixty thousand residents in 1518 to two hundred thousand in 1600.[3] It has been estimated that half of all of the English population during the reign of Queen Elizabeth I had been under the age of twenty-two; nowadays, this middle mark is thirty-three.[4] Twenty-two, which in modern society is considered young, was practically middle-aged in Tudor England. The average life expectancy of a peasant-class labourer in sixteenth-century England was just thirty-five, negatively influenced by factors such as devastating plagues and high rates of infant mortality. Although these outcomes would improve by the close of the sixteenth century, rising to an average life expectancy of around sixty years old, the population of Tudor England was still a very young one compared to our own.

The exponential growth in population throughout the sixteenth century also brought about a marked class division. The gap between rich and poor widened, and by 1552 almost eleven per cent of Edwardian England was considered to be living below the poverty line. Under the rule of the boy King Edward VI, workhouses intended to cater for the poor and to provide them with accommodation in return for hard, gruelling manual labour, began cropping up across the country. In April 1553, preparations for a workhouse had even begun on the grounds of Bridewell Palace, once a residence of King Henry VIII and the place of papal proceedings in the divorce dispute between Henry and his first wife, Queen Katherine of Aragon. It was later turned into an orphanage, a prison, and a correctional house for 'wayward women', becoming the first sixteenth-century building of its kind to have its own residential doctor to care for its inhabitants. It was also the setting for one of the most impressive and popular paintings of the sixteenth century, Hans Holbein's *The Ambassadors*, its imagery celebrating the social, scientific and medical advancements of the Tudor Age.

According to social historian Simon Thurley, the average annual income for a wealthy, noble family in sixteenth-century England was around nine hundred pounds per year, equating to around £230,000 in modern sterling.[5] Compared to this however, the vast majority of the Tudor population earned just twenty pounds per year on average, a minuscule amount that barely came to £6,000 in modern money. Of course, the purchasing power of sixteenth-century currency was vastly different to our own today, but ultimately the rich got richer and the poor got poorer.

England, or at least the Crown, became vastly more wealthy in 1535 as a direct consequence of the Henrician Protestant Reformation, which occurred in the mid to late-1530s. Under the command of the Secretary of State of the time, Sir Thomas Cromwell, the Dissolution of the Catholic Monasteries in England led to a great fiscal increase in the pockets of the Crown thanks to the so-called *Valor Ecclesiasticus*, or the 'Value of the Church', a survey which recorded the wealth and possessions of every Catholic monastery and church before they were destroyed and plundered. Some of this wealth was pocketed by Cromwell's cronies; some, however, was funnelled into the domestic policy of the day, and was put toward the establishment of schools and universities, prisons and a working criminal justice system. Much of the money went into funding military pursuits, particularly during periods of war, or into the refurbishment of royal residences. The homes of the peasantry and middling classes, however, had been all but forgotten about.

Chapter 1

Building the Tudor Home

'Certainly masonry did never better flourish in
England than in his time.'
William Harrison, *A Description
of England*, 1577.[1]

When a Venetian consul visited England in the mid-1490s, he reported
back to his native court of his delight at the English countryside. It is
'all diversified by pleasant undulating hills and beautiful valleys', he
wrote, 'there being nothing to be seen but agreeable woods, extensive
meadows or lands in cultivation and the greatest plenty of water
springing everywhere'.[2]

In the sixteenth century, England was a country which was largely rural,
the majority of the nation being arable land, dense forests, and overgrown
heaths. Houses, barns and workplaces were mainly concentrated in towns
and cities that were sprayed sparsely across the landscape, the odd, tiny
rural hamlet only occasionally peppered amongst the green of the country.
Tudor England was not a place which had established motorways, of
course, and even its many roads were poorly maintained or little more than
rudimentary dirt tracks. With the exception of impressively engineered
main roads dating back from the Roman occupation of England (which
led travellers to important cities and key locations across England), the
majority of sixteenth-century English roads would have been crude,
particularly in less occupied, rural areas of the country. These tracks,
worn away by the footfall of thousands of Englishmen throughout the
Middle Ages, would have been no one person's responsibility; as such,
many paths led straight to the households of sixteenth-century Tudors,
who often found themselves shooing away trespassers, wild animals, and
harmless wanderers from their properties.

It was only in the mid-1550s that a popular new invention caught-on,
and revolutionised travel in sixteenth-century England: the horse-drawn
carriage. With more and more people relying on this mode of transport

1

to go further afield than they were ever able to before, soon, cities and towns were encouraged to construct smooth, paved roads, for better ease and comfort in travel. By 1555, every parish in England had had to abide by the law of maintaining good road conditions.[3] A horse and cart on a well-paved road would go, on average, around twelve miles per hour, according to architectural historian Simon Thurley, allowing Tudors the chance to visit neighbouring towns and markets and establish new connections and lives of their own away from their natal homes.[4] Although considerably slower than modern car journeys today (it was estimated by historian Ian Mortimer that it would take around two whole days for a Tudor to make a round trip of twenty-five miles), without the horse and cart, architectural advancements and engineering marvels would have taken much longer to develop.[5]

With the construction of improved roads (and less reliance on insubstantial dirt paths), many Tudors leapt at the opportunity to finally mark out the boundaries of their properties. Gone were the days of unwanted trespassers; now, the Tudors had begun to construct much-needed fences surrounding their homes. Traditionally, sixteenth-century fences would have been made from crudely-cut timber with planks of wood slotted amongst them, known as 'groyne fencing'. With these reinforced timber frames keeping out pests and dissuading wandering animals from trampling the herb gardens and vegetable patches of the Tudors, many sixteenth-century homes now began having entire dedicated, private outdoor areas; gardens.

The Tudors, by all accounts, were proud of their gardens and tended to them regularly; even densely populated areas of cities would have had green spaces that would have been maintained by its citizens.[6] Hyde Park in London, for example, was used as an ornamental-style garden in the sixteenth century, and was commonly the site of exciting festivals, feasts and pageants throughout the year, attended by all members of Tudor society. Many other London green spaces, including Greenwich Park and the park at St James's (along the modern-day Mall) would have been communal green areas much as they are today, with wild animals such as deer, and even pelicans, free to roam. Closer to home, the Tudors installed private 'pleasance gardens', used for leisure, most commonly being found on the grounds of the houses of the rich and wealthy. The sole purpose of pleasance gardens was the hosting of outdoor dining, picnics and merriment. So too were gardens – ornamental or otherwise – beneficial in other ways, for even small patches of greenery and even stone courtyards could provide Tudor homeowners with their own produce.

The gardens of the rich and poor of the sixteenth century alike would have been filled with fishponds, wells, ovens, sheds, flowerbeds, chicken coops and space for grazing animals like pigs and cows. In an age before electrical lawnmowers, some Tudor homeowners would employ these grazing animals such as goats and sheep to roam their gardens, chewing the long grass, and keeping the lawns neat and tidy. So too were large, two-handed shears used for the maintenance of keeping lawns trimmed and short. As Sir Thomas More wrote in 1516, the Tudors:

> set great store by their gardens […] in them they have vineyards, all manner of fruit, herbs and flowers, so pleasant, so well-furnished, and so finely kept, that I never saw thing more fruitful nor better trimmed in any place.[7]

Other contemporary commentators were not so positive about the homes of the English. In his 1531 *Chronicle of London*, the Italian visitor Mario Savorgriano wrote disapprovingly that, 'the houses are very great in number, but ugly … half the materials of wood, nor are the streets wide'.[8] Savorgriano's sentiments about the narrow, winding streets of London were echoed by even the English themselves, who complained of an increasing lack of space in the city. The chronicler William Harrison wrote:

> everyman almost is a builder and he that hath bought any small parcel of ground, be it ever so little, will not be quiet till he has pulled down the old house (if any there were standing) and set up a new after his own devising.[9]

During the reign of Elizabeth I, the population of London rose from seventy-thousand to two hundred-thousand alone.[10] Such a drastic increase in urban population meant that living spaces were simply inefficient, and thus, the Tudors needed to think of ingenious ways to accommodate all those who lived there. It was the architects of the sixteenth century that we can credit with the earliest semblances of multi-storey buildings, the modest, yet trail-blazing pre-cursor of our modern skyscrapers. In some cramped cities, it was common for buildings to be numerous storeys high, tiered upon each other with timber beam reinforcements and brick; in London, there were even accounts of buildings reaching seven-storeys high.[11] In an age before skyscrapers, these multi-storeyed houses must have looked very impressive, especially if they were located close to behemoths of buildings such as palaces, castles and cathedrals.

With this rise in population in the mid-1500s, a relocation from rural settlements and villages to urban cities and towns led to a newfound density that had never before been seen in England. Cities had always been hubs of activity – ports of trade, areas of education and the advancement in thought, hubs of social activity and commotion; but it was only now, in the latter 1500s, did cities truly begin to swell with people. Streets, according to social historian Ian Mortimer, could be anywhere between six to twenty feet wide; in areas where there were smaller, narrower streets, some buildings in the surrounding area would have had underground vaults and cellars built below Tudor townhouses for storage purposes, or even for retail purposes.[12]

It was no wonder that the sixteenth-century city has been cemented in our imaginations as claustrophobic and stifling. Tudor city and townhouses were usually jettied (overhanging) above the street below, creating a claustrophobic atmosphere, often being dark and shadowy. These jetties, synonymous with the Tudor architectural style, had exposed timber frames, dormer windows, and thatched roofs, which later became replaced with clay tiles (called 'Kent Peg Tiles') in an attempt to quell the frequency of city fires.[13] Although tall, many of the city and townhouses of merchants would have had limited space, as most of the ground floor of the building would have been dedicated to shop fronts and store rooms. As such, the houses of merchants were the first in Tudor England to be built 'up', with the living quarters of tradesmen and merchants being located above their ground-floor shops. Wooden beamed houses of merchants would often be carved and adorned to describe to those, particularly those who could not read and were illiterate, the wares of their business.

In 1580, a proclamation at Westminster was passed that limited the development of buildings to avoid overcrowding in the city.[14] We are often led to believe that the Tudor monarchs lived their lives in residences far from the hustle and bustle of cities and villages; in reality, it was very much different. In fact, royal residences and the houses of the nobility were often the nucleus that many villages and city hamlets were built around. It was not uncommon for a palace or a great house to be surrounded by houses of the rich and the poor, as well as taverns, shops, and other commercial buildings. Palaces in particular would often be flanked by eateries, shops and vendor stalls, which would offer light snacks and souvenirs to tourists, just as they do now.[15] According to social historian Ian Mortimer, there would even be markets offering refreshments to weary travellers every six miles along roads, similarly to roadside service stations today, particularly in cities.[16]

Just like in cities, the manor houses and the grand, ostentatious estates of the rich were located at the heart of a town or village, the nucleus upon which society had been built (hence why they were known as 'nucleated' settlements) and in which civil justice would have been dispensed and would have served as important civic landmarks. These houses, owned by freemen (or yeomen) and other members of the gentrified classes, would have served also as tax offices, collecting revenues from the village citizens and sending them off to the Crown. The official term for this was 'demesne', of which the owners of the manor had total control and responsibility for all those who lived within its boundaries. As well as houses, however, the demesne also maintained other communal spaces, including taverns, market squares and churches, as well as any hospitals or inns travellers could visit. As such, the attractiveness of a demesne was important, for it would bring more citizens to it, and result in increased tax profits for the lord of the manor, and then for the King. Demesnes also controlled furloughs, strips of arable land which could be rented by farmers for agricultural use. These furlough fields would be annually interchanged; so, for one year, they may be utilised for the growing of crops; the next, they would be used for the fattening of animals.[17] This would then be swapped the next year, allowing the farmer to profit from both agricultural and livestock produce.

The houses of the rich and wealthy would typically have a range of private rooms accessible within them through a long gallery. These private rooms included a chapel for personal devotion, a parlour (different to a parlour kept in a kitchen for the storage and preservation of perishables food, but rather, a room in which a seated area was located around a fireplace, principally used for conversing and entertainment), a study, and a solar, an upstairs living area named for the sunlight it got as the highest room in the house. These private rooms would typically be panelled with beautiful and intricate carved wooden panels; and were often decorated with wall hangings and tapestries, paintings and bookshelves, and even carpets, which would have been used as runners and lining for furniture and hangings. Men and women alike would make use of the solar and parlour for entertainment purposes, perhaps choosing to play musical instruments or resume their needlework in the peace and privacy of dedicated living quarters. These private rooms, also known as ante-rooms, would have been mostly used for entertainment purposes, or for light exercising, which included pacing back and forth in lengths, particularly on days where the weather was too dire and miserable to partake in exercise out of doors.

Unlike the homes of the wealthiest of Tudor England, the country houses of the vast majority of the population often lacked in these aesthetics, yet made up for it in practicality. The inclusion of household extensions such as threshing barns, granaries and slaughterhouses may not have made for a pleasant sight, especially compared to the beautifully-framed timber or stone houses of richer peers, but they served an all-important purpose, particularly for families who lived remotely and away from areas of commerce. These extensions – chicken coops, pig pens, and cattle barns – would have served the family with almost everything that they needed to survive. The building materials of these remote houses were often drawn from the proximity, and as such there was little local variant in household exteriors. Ultimately, for the vast majority of the population in sixteenth-century England (of which ninety per cent was rural and self-sufficient), their lives depended solely upon the arability of the land. However, as the century progressed and farmers and other agricultural labours began to amass more wealth, there was a noted shift in the movement toward cities and larger towns, drawing in poorer citizens who then found jobs within industrial, urban areas. In short, where the rich settled, the poor followed, and thus the village was born.

For the poorest in society who could afford housing, it was often rudimentary and little more than a basic shelter. The poor could not afford the modern advancements unlike those in more advanced, urban areas of the country. Instead, many of the houses of the poor had been standing for centuries already; thatch, stone and wattle-and-daub cottages or rudimentary wooden structures that some historians believe could have been standing and inhabited since as early as the Norman period, which began with William the Conqueror's victory at Hastings in 1066. However, this is not to say that the poorest of sixteenth-century society lived in houses akin to hovels. There is little evidence to suggest that the poorest Tudors lived in homes in which foundations were deteriorating, where walls were thin and draughty and floors were constantly muddy and wet; rather, even the poorest of Tudors would have used sheets of stone or planks of wood for the foundations of their homes, or would have spread rushes, sand, or sawdust usually perfumed with dried herbs, upon it.

Indeed, the lowest members of society, eager not to miss out on the fashionable architectural advancements their wealthier peers could afford, tried their hardest to keep up with the trends. According to architectural historian Simon Thurley, rudimentary clay, terracotta and daub infills that formed the exterior walls of the houses of the poorest in Tudor society, were often painted carefully in order to resemble stone and carved masonry.[18] Thurley also suggests that a substance known as 'leather mache' was employed in order to create faux wooden structures.[19] To create this leather mache, offcuts of leather and other supple materials were mixed with dust, dirt and 'size', a gelatinous, glutinous substance similar to glue. Size, still used today in modern construction, was often made from the concentrated gelatine that was the by-product of boiling the ligaments and joints of cattle and pigs. It was a waterproof and hydrophobic substance, and proved to be an effective and reliable waterproof glue in the construction process. This unusual, rather unpleasant mixture would have been left to set and harden to create illusions of wood, the folds in the leather creating a supposedly realistic wooden façade.[20] How convincing this technique was is debatable, though one thing is for certain; it showed the ingenuity of the poorest in sixteenth century Tudor England, and demonstrates their disapproval of being left behind.

Ultimately, the houses of the poorest of Tudor society would in some part be the most busiest. As well as serving as living quarters, the houses of rural Tudor peasants would have also included extensions of water and windmills, dovecotes, byres, malthouses, brewhouses, and bakehouses. Many of the houses of the poorest of sixteenth-century English society were built in 'tofts', expanses of land where a house had been built. A number of tofts would then make up 'crofts', similar to an acreage or an area that encompassed large residential locations. A croft is a fenced or enclosed area of land, usually small and arable, and usually, but not always, with a crofter's dwelling thereon; a crofter being one who has tenure and use of the land, typically as a tenant farmer, especially in rural areas. Longhouses, the houses of the poorest of society, and which were the most common types of houses on sixteenth-century crofts, were often split in half to accommodate living quarters for the residents, as well as the part of the house which would have occupied the 'working' half, which would include domestic items like spinning wheels, butter churns, animal care items, and general cooking and hygiene utensils like baths, pots, and tripods. A typical Tudor longhouse, which was medieval in its design, would most likely have been laid out in this manner.

Ultimately, how a sixteenth-century English home had been built was dependent wholly on the architect or the occupiers themselves. There were no dedicated residential construction companies in the sixteenth century, and certainly no uniformity; rather, the building of the home usually fell to homeowners, or whoever they could find that would have been trusted to have done a good job. Building plans, or what we now know as 'blueprints' were known as 'plats' in Tudor England, and were drawn on paper and parchment in a similar style to the method used by architects today. Although the Tudors may not have had the modern technology and advanced techniques that modern architects and builders utilise today, there is certainly evidence that they were adept at their techniques and understood such engineering feats as winches and pullies to assist in the construction process. In fact, the crane, and pullies used to hoist heavy items like construction materials were used even in the Middle Ages and earlier, and particularly inflamed the imaginations of great thinkers like Leonardo da Vinci, who took a special interest in the way they worked in the early sixteenth century.

As well as the construction technique itself, we often believe that the monuments, buildings and structures which have survived from the sixteenth century were dull, plain and devoid of any colour and pattern; rather, the opposite was the case. Household exteriors would have been an eye-catching distraction against the vast, green backdrop of Tudor England, and the ornamental facades of the ostentatious in particular would have been even more so. House facades would be painted, adorned with bright, colourful statuettes and gargoyles, or constructed from pliable materials like metal plate so that they shone and glimmered in the sunlight. Between the bright white and muted creams of plaster-walled thatched cottages, the beautiful and excessively-colourful houses of the rich and the wealthy and the criss-cross black diamond patterns (known as 'lozenge patterns') so favoured by monarchs Henry VIII and Elizabeth I and synonymous with their palaces, sixteenth-century buildings must have certainly been very eye-catching indeed. As well as this, the lush green expanses of the English countryside, the dense forests, sprawling fields of wildflowers, and golden wheatfields, must have been a truly spectacular and beautiful sight. Even the suffocating, packed city streets in which merchants sold their wares by advertising them in eye-catching window displays and shop fronts must have been overwhelmingly colourful and striking. Gone are the days of believing the sixteenth century to be a time frozen in muddy, washed-out colours; just as was written by social historian Ian Mortimer, 'we are the inheritors of a living, vibrant past'.[21]

Indeed, according to Mortimer, the architecture of sixteenth-century English cities, villages, and even tiny rural hamlets, would have been as greatly diverse in terms of aesthetics as the modern day, perhaps even more so, stating that the cities of Medieval and Early Modern England, 'show[ed] greater variety than any modern city'.[22] Indeed, on just one street alone, houses could be decorated with all kinds of geometrical shapes and patterns, which were in great fashion in Tudor England in part due to the favoured architectural styles of the Tudor monarchs themselves. 'Diapering brickwork', black bricks that had been laid to create allusions of diamonds amongst the traditional orange of black walls, and 'vitrified headers', occasional coloured bricks nestled amongst plain ones, would have been a common sight. So too would houses of all shapes, sizes and heights, all with different roofing types and foundation materials. This vitrification, the process of dipping soft, uncooked brick into sand and then firing it inside a kiln to create a black effect, was so synonymous with the Tudor era. As well as used to create ornamental diapered, diamond shapes, these vitrified bricks would have also been used in decorative friezes and in the production of 'guilloche patterns', spiral-like brick designs. Chessboard patterns, made from flint and chalk or stone tiles, became fashionable in later sixteenth-century society, and were an eye-catching, interlacing geometric pattern that many used for the floors of their houses. They were particularly common in entranceways, hallways and kitchens, as well as in pantries and under canopied porches. Batten patterns, a humorously rhyming term for a lattice-style beam ceiling, was another favourite of sixteenth-century homeowners. These patterns created the illusion of an airy ceiling, and looked sophisticated and grand. It was an affordable way for even the poor and middling classes to achieve a sense of fashionable home ownership. One such favourite pattern that decorated the houses of Tudor England, was that of guilloche, a pattern that produces tight, mechanically-produced waves. Most often these patterns would have been carved onto soft wood using hand-operated turning machines or the steady hand of a skilled craftsman. The overlapping, ribbon-like pattern was most commonly used to add an extra flair of beauty and ostentation to bedframes, table legs and coffer boxes.

The manufacturing of bricks brought about a revolution in the social housing of the sixteenth century, and, for the first time, both rich and poor alike could afford to live in properly constructed houses that would sufficiently shield them from the elements. Bricks were relatively simple to make, cheap, and required just a small workforce of men. The process was simple. Clay collected from riverbeds would have been kneaded like dough, then shaped with wooden tools – sometimes rudimentary knives, or, more sophisticated wooden boxes specifically created for the manufacture of brick.[23] Once shaped, these bricks were left to dry, most often by the air and were so left outside, or indoors and close to sources of heat. Once suitably dry and crumbly, the bricks were gathered together in a square known as a 'clamp', of which the centre would be left open for a fire to be lit. Alternatively, they would be placed in large kilns ready for firing. Because bricks were often crumbly in nature, and as such were difficult to transport, most bricks were fired as closely to their desired building sites as possible. This had an added advantage, for workmen need not have carried heavy loads of bricks upon their backs, but rather could simply build where they stood. According to Simon Thurley, the firing of bricks only occurred in the summer months, with the construction of houses taking place in the spring through to the autumn. Although Thurley is weighted in his opinion, it is implausible to suggest that no construction would have occurred at all during the winter months of the sixteenth century. For a start, this was the season in which battered houses required the most repairing; and, after all, it rained and was cold throughout the year anyway!

When bricks were not used in the construction process, wattle and daub would have been adopted. 'Wattle and daub' was a thick concoction of mud and water, and, although not as sturdy as cement, would certainly support the foundations of a home and insulate it by keeping draughts out. Another benefit would be that if any cracks began to appear, wattle and daub was easy enough to make and fill in. A 'wattle', reminiscent of the word 'waffle', was a criss-cross of thin tree branches that would be woven to create a sturdy structural foundation, that would later be smeared with clay, plaster or daub, for added waterproofing and insulation. Wattle could also be made from sour milk, horsehair, animal dung, mud and chalk, with the glue-like mortar made from animal blood. It was a fantastic manner in which to build a home, though builders would have to get their sums right to ensure that the woven mats were tight enough to withstand the forces of the elements, else they would bend with the wind, snap, or come apart entirely. The addition of the daub would therefore ensure that the wattle inside would remain upright and sturdy as was intended. Daub, simply a mixture of plaster, straw or hair, and lime, would have been painted white, considered to be a protective measure. It also served of course for aesthetic purposes, and gave rise to the black and white architectural design so fashionable with the Tudors in the sixteenth century, and so synonymous with the past today. The use of cob was also common in Tudor architecture, particularly in remote, rural areas and poorer villages of sixteenth-century England. This cob would have been made with mud instead of the more expensive plaster, and therefore would have been more affordable to the poorest of society. To distinguish between cob and daub, it is most usual that daub was most usually painted white, whereas cob was a darker, cream colour, yellow, brown, and pink. In cases where occupiers wished to simply live in bright white homes, lime-wash would have been applied to the house annually or as often as one wished, intended to keep buildings look fresh and newly constructed.

In sixteenth-century England, many houses would have been built with vaulted floors, ceilings and roofs, and there was a great dominance of timbered buildings that were supported with 'cruck frames'. Cruck frames (which were also known as 'A' frames), made from the branches of trees which had a naturally-forming bend, would have been manipulated and hammered with nails and wooden pegs to create an 'A' shape, supported by a solid wooden rafter that would ensure that they remained standing. These cruck frames were then used to support the ceilings and roofs of the houses of the everyday working man.

Even now, it is common to find cruck-framed timber beams within the attics of modern homes, the descendent of ingenious Tudor engineering. 'Box frames' were more expensive, for they simply required extra wood in order to create a square frame. For box frames, builders would have created a structure made from cruck framing, but in a cuboid shape for added structural support. These sorts of frames are typically found upon the upper half of a Tudor house, and were built upon the solid foundations of stone that were able to take the extent of its weight. Unlike cruck frames, which formed the basis of ceiling support, box frames constituted the walls for Tudor houses. As such, it was common for them to be filled with plaster or wattle and daub, but with squares and rectangles cut out to provide holes for windows and doors. These frames were, for the most part, sturdy and would insulate the home and keep its occupiers warm. However, they also had the disadvantage of getting wet and rotting, attracting mildew and pests which then resulted in their breakdowns. As such, wooden frames were often repaired or entirely replaced.

Wooden beams would have been painted with pitch or tar, not only to waterproof them, but also to ensure that they stuck together while being held in place. For some builders, however, the use of nails, pegs and pitch was not required, for simply the ingenious planning of notches cut into wooden supports that were the perfect size for additional beams, ensured that they fit snugly into place. 'Piles' made from oak planks were supports used in the construction of house foundations, and were occasionally encased with metal, or surrounded by an iron pole.[24] This would then be reinforced with elm planks, then a chalky cob mixture that worked as a cement-style infill, which was used as a glue and for insulation, and was then finally surrounded in a layer of thick, wood-fired bricks.[25] This was an early form of scaffolding, and would have been a common sight all across the building sites of sixteenth-century England. Rickety scaffolding was even installed in the preparations for the coronation of King Henry VII at Westminster Abbey. While construction was taking place, the scaffolding buckled and collapsed into the square below. Miraculously, no one was injured.[26]

The sixteenth century was a time when carpentry thrived in England. The contemporary historian, Welshman George Owen wrote that 'worse and worse is the stonemason, but better and better is the carpenter'.[27] Times were changing, and so were the fashions. Gone were the days of antiquated, draughty and cold medieval stone structures, and in were the more insulated, comfortable, and quicker to construct wood and timber-framed structures. This was none more so reflected in the wages of stonemasons compared to carpenters. Whereas a carpenter received a healthy, stable wage of around twelve pence per day by 1580 (totalling around thirty pounds in sterling today), stonemasons were paid just 8 pence, or around twenty-two pounds in sterling.[28] King Henry VIII, however, who had never been an easy boss to satisfy, manipulated his workers even further. Instead of paying his stonemasons, who were working on renovating the Royal Residences, as well as beginning the early construction of what would become Hampton Court Palace, the adequate eight pence per day in 1514, the King paid them just six pence.[29] In the late summer of 1531, almost one thousand labourers, architects and general handymen worked on the construction of Whitehall Palace.[30] A large Tudor task force was often needed for the largest and grandest houses in the country, and, renovations on the Queen's Royal Lodgings at the Tower of London took a force of around five hundred men alone in preparations for the coronation of Queen Anne Boleyn in 1533.[31]

Building the Tudor home would not have taken as long as you may believe. Unlike modern day, where the construction process requires much careful planning, the sourcing and shipping of building materials, and a large team of construction workers, many Tudor homes were prefabricated and could be erected quickly and simply.[32] Timber frames, sold in pre-fabricated sets, similar to infamous wooden kit houses popular in the American Wild West, were simple to erect, and took just a small workforce to slot the pieces together.[33] The production and filling of the infill would be a simple and quick process, as was the limewashing and aesthetic changes to household exteriors. Realistically, a Tudor home could be constructed and ready for inhabitants as quickly as a week.

Staircases could be crooked – one reason was that construction techniques were still not as sophisticated as today, and the Tudors didn't always have accurate levellers. Hence, the staircases would sometimes slope, and over time, with the natural shifting of the house, would resemble the crooked staircases we are used to seeing in old Tudor structures today. Staircases would have mainly been built out of wood, a pliable, natural material. Ladders could be used to access upper stories, particularly in the homes of the lesser well-off. Ladders were relatively quick, simple and cheap to build, and materials were common.

Additionally, ladders were not permanent – a farmer could use them to access the upper eaves of his house one day, and then use them to repair the thatch on his roof another. In a time when peasant houses were still relatively cramped, it was important and desirable to have as much living space as possible, so ladders were the ideal solution. People could also hang things from a ladder – herbs to dry, animal pelts, laundry. They were versatile!

Floorboards could also be crooked, again due to the reasons mentioned above. But also, the Tudors were lovers of expanding and building upon their houses, creating elaborate extensions and adding twists, bends and hidden corners wherever they could. If you visit an authentic sixteenth-century build, you may very well find that there are raised platforms leading to rooms, and you most definitely will find a sloped ceiling or floor somewhere. This was not intentional – the Tudors didn't like wonky floors – but over time the wood would naturally warp with the heat, moisture, or the footsteps of the house's occupants. In the times of the Tudors, these wooden floorboards would have been straight, polished, laminated – not the charming slant that is a characteristic so beloved today. Timber beams would rot, causing unstable foundations (wet rot caused by wood and brick not being able to breathe, would have caused disintegration).

Matted rushes were commonly used on the floors of the homes of the Tudors, from the lowest of society to the monarchs themselves. They would not be loose, as is typically believed, but rather they would be matted in a style similar to parquet flooring, so that it made for a solid ground on which people could easily walk without slipping or causing injury. Roofs would be tiled, chimneys would be made from wood or stone, and the actual building would be made from lath and plaster, as well as brick. Floors could be constructed from shingles, tile, wooden boards, rushes, straw and plaster. Windows, tile and glass were imported from Holland, Normandy and Venice, whereas the 'Dutchemen bring over weynskot ready wrought, as nayles, lockes, baskettes, cupboards, stools, tables, chestes'.[34] Many Tudor houses also had slanted ceilings and short door frames; not only was the height of the average Englishman shorter then, lower doorframes further added to insulation. Houses would also have archways instead of doors, meaning the house would often be flowing, which could also be problematic because of privacy and lack of insulation.

Some sixteenth-century houses would have had plumbing, but also would have used chamber pots, etc that would have been emptied into pits. Water would have been transported to a house through conduits such as water pumps, which had been dug into deep wells and water sources. This ensured that the Tudors had fresh, clean water to bathe in and drink, contrary to much popular belief. These water sources would have also been used in cases of house fires, where large barrels and basins of water would be used to distinguish flames. Fountains were popular with the wealthier members of society, and even Queen Elizabeth I paid £1,000 for the installation of a squirting fountain at Hampton Court Palace, to the delight of the courtiers who walked by and splashed bystanders.[35]

There were many advantages to the Tudor home, including the higher ceilings, which trapped heat and were less oppressive than the suffocating low ceilings of previous centuries. Additionally, the inclusion of first floors meant that people could reside principally away from kitchens, animals and areas of ease, meaning that house owners could separate their working lives from their rest and recreation. Divided rooms also allowed for additional privacy, as well as newfound spaces dedicated to serving staff away from the family. Floors would have most usually been levelled in the construction process, except perhaps for the houses of the poorest in society, who made do with simple, dirt floors. Herringbone brick floors, which were more substantial, would have been likely used in working areas, as well as in high-traffic areas like kitchens to prevent the wearing away of floorboards, rushes and rugs.

House ceilings were often high, and would be decorated with tiles, wooden panelling cut and carved into intricate patterns, or even wall paintings, reminiscent of the Middle Ages. Some houses, particularly those of the poor, sometimes had exposed timber beams, so that one could see directly into the underneath of the roof of the house. This was not always desired, for it often meant that gaps within the roof tiling or thatch could result in leakages onto the heads of the unsuspecting occupiers below. So, ceilings made of smooth plaster could be installed so to attract the eye away from the structural reinforcements of the house, to remind guests of the wealth of its inhabitants. Some entranceways to large houses would be large enough to accommodate a man on horseback! So too could doors, though wicket doors (small rectangles cut out from a larger door), were typically used by people while the main door was locked. The 'threshold' was a step that would hold rushes in place and kept them inside when a door was open, to make sure the rushes weren't blown away.

*

The chimney; a humble adage to a home that many of us are accustomed to. But it was this chimney, this simple, brick invention, which changed the course of architectural history as we know it. These chimneys revolutionised the way our forefathers lived. Gone were the days of smoke-filled ceilings, of cramped, one-room houses in which families would crowd around an open fire in its centre. The chimney ushered in an age of safety, of increased privacy, of a better standard of living that even the poorest in society could now afford. The proliferation of houses built with chimneys marked a revolution in social advancement. With the use of bricks now predominating in Tudor England, even those of the lowest standing in society could afford to heat their homes, cook their food in a dedicated kitchen area, and breathe easier. The low cost of brick production meant that people could now afford to live in more than one-storey homes. Gone were the days of one-rooms halls, not too far detached from a glorified barn. Now, people could build *upwards*, and could live in multi-tiered houses and townhouses, safe in the knowledge that their rooms – even those on the higher levels – would be warm and properly insulated. The installation of oak panels, as well as tapestries, carpets and other decorative wall hangings served two principle purposes – to keep the house finely decorated, and to keep its inhabitants warm. There were no building regulations in the Tudor times, and thus no required materials, and such things as chimneys would be made from wood, causing all sorts of life-threatening complications.

A 'louvre' was the French term for a vent in the centre of the ceiling, and was common in the houses of the vast majority in Medieval England. Its purpose was to let out the smoke and contaminated air that had gathered in living quarters, and suck it out into the fresh air outside. They had begun to die out by the time of the sixteenth century, being replaced by the more modern, safer and fashionable fireplaces and chimneys. However, they were still common features in the houses of the poorest of Tudor society, particularly in rural countryside cottages, where the smoke of occupied houses must have been a welcome sight to weary travellers. French architectural designs became popularised in sixteenth-century England, mostly in part to prior monarchs who had a particular affinity to the country. King Henry VIII too, despite his distrust of the French king Francois I, was eager to keep up with architectural trends, and as such had extensions in the French style added to his palaces throughout England. Of these French-inspired architectural motifs were friezes, decorative stone arches most often carved with beautiful figures from classical and heroic tales, or with foliage and other floral motifs.

Candles would be made from rushes, called 'rush lights', which would emit smells and smoke and would burn for only 20 minutes. Tallow candles (hemp rope that was dipped into animal fat) were a longer-lasting solution, but emitted a horrible, animal smell. However, because of this, technically it was possible to eat candles! Candles could be blown out easily, and hence shutters and curtains began being popularised in homes to avoid them blowing out. Because light was so scarce once the sun went down, neighbours could regularly use each other's candles and sit communally if work needed to be finished! Light was just so valuable. Glass was a valuable commodity found only in windows of churches before the Tudor era, but soon became popularised in houses, and kept out the cold and the weather – however, they were very expensive, and hence were very valuable in the sixteenth century. Windows would later come to be taxed in 1696, and as such, many windows of existing sixteenth-century houses would have been bricked up and entirely destroyed. During the window tax, people would even take their windows with them when they moved!

Windows would have been most likely opaque in the sixteenth century, or at least would have had impurities such as air bubbles or sediment suspended within them, for thin panes of glass were still relatively recent inventions for the houses of the poorest in society. However, by the end of the sixteenth century, the technique for manufacturing clear, transparent windows would have been more common, though the panes would have been thin and certainly not as sufficiently glazed as we know them today. Ian Mortimer even believes that many windows in the houses of the poor would have been coloured, for discarded glass panes intended for other use – such as in churches or palaces – would have been recycled to fit the panes of their own houses.[36] Proper glass windows, too, marked a social revolution in sixteenth-century England.

Glass windows became popularised in the late 1580s, when affording such a luxury was considered a social statement. Glass windows better insulated the home, and kept out the elements, something particularly important given the often wet, cold weather that the Tudors were accustomed. So too would windows allow in natural light, and they also awarded people – especially in dense areas of inhabitation – safer living.

Gone were the days of open windows, covered only with slick-oil cloths or wooden shutters. Then, thieves could easily extend a hand and reach into the houses of the Late Middle Ages, or all sorts of unwelcome vermin and live animals like birds, would wander in and cause a nuisance. Glass was safer, nicer, more hygienic. It kept out the smells, the smoke, the weather and the noise of outdoors. The commonality of glass-paned windows in sixteenth-century England was revolutionary, and the history of architecture and social housing would change as we know it. The weather could dictate areas of settlement. For example, heavier rain in Northern areas meant that people would often move away from rivers and areas of open water in order to avoid flooding. Additionally, areas that were mountainous or forest-dense meant that settlements were spread further apart than in flat, open areas typically found within the South of England.

Tudor mullioned windows were characterised by a strip of lead going through the centre of the window, separating the glass panes into smaller, fractional sections. This was in comparison to lattice windows, where a diamond effect was achieved, through strips of lead that were angled diagonally, which were more commonly used for decoration. Clerestory windows were also installed in houses across sixteenth-century England, and would have been found in the houses of the rich and poor alike. This style of window, which is centred above eye-level, was intended to let in light and air and provide an airy effect. Many houses of the Tudors, even those in rural settlements, had clerestory windows installed, and would have been particularly common in barns or multi-level houses that had interior mezzanine floors (a half-floor that would be suspended above heads like a ceiling) that would be accessed with either ladders or stairs.

Thatch roofs would be waterproofed with pitch, a thick, oil-like substance which would ensure that nothing could get in, and no heat could get out. Tudor houses that had thatched roofs were, therefore, relatively warm and comfortable. However, thatch, as a natural fibre, could break down quickly and required upkeep. From insects and small animals, vermin, birds and even humans, holes in thatch rooves could accommodate them all. Unwanted guests weren't the only issues Tudor inhabitants had, however. Thatch rooves could quickly become mouldy, smelly and mossy, and required a brushing or replacement of the reeds by the custodian balanced carefully upon a ladder, or hanging from a windowsill. Building materials would be winched and rolled on poles in order to place them.

Furniture was made from oak, and with little mass manufacturing, it meant that families would inherit the heirlooms. Over time, furniture and the quality (and mass production of it) would improve. The first prefab was built on Tower Bridge (yes, the bridge!) and was called Nonsuch House – it had been originally built in the Netherlands, and was shipped over to England. There was another prefab built from timber that was properly installed in Kingston-upon-Thames in 1510.

*

In the sixteenth century, a strange ecological phenomenon occurred that made the Tudor world around 2 degrees colder than it is today. The so-called 'Little Ice Age', which was believed to have begun in 1303 and came to an end as late as the nineteenth century.[37] It is only relatively recently that the climate has started to rise again. The Thames froze over, as did other lesser rivers and canals. This had significant impacts on the economy of sixteenth-century England, which relied on water transport for the importing and exporting that kept the country's financial system afloat. In 1597, there was a huge rise in prices and a recession occurred. Henry VIII caused the 'Debasement' of the coin, which replaced silver with lesser metals. Some took advantage of this, and paid with tokens, not money at all. This caused huge inflation in Henrician England. Because of the three types of currency systems – money, trade and tokens, inflation rose. According to a Milanese reporter, 'everything costs incomparably more in this kingdom than in any other place', rising to around five times the usual price.[38] Towns and cities in sixteenth-century England imported and exported based on the needs and requirements of their population. For London, there was a great export of wax, but a large, booming trade in the import of spices from the Middle East and other eastern countries.[39]

In Oxford, there was a great trade of parchment, no doubt for use by the students in the colleges and the scholars who practiced there. Faversham in Kent, Ware in Hertfordshire, and Henley-on-Thames in Oxford were large exporters of grain. Beverley, Lincoln, Stamford and York exported cloth and linen, Thaxted in Essex had a booming export trade in knives, and finally, Great Yarmouth in Norfolk had a popular export of freshly-caught herrings! In 1508, Newcastle exported forty-thousand tons of coal.[40] There were other mines of great coal and mineral exports in areas of Leicester, Durham, Dorset and throughout Wales, particularly in the South. There soon saw growth in cloth trade, overseas commerce, expansion and, more importantly, a stable economy.

In London, on Fleet Street alone, there were inns called: 'The Star and the Ram, the Cock and the Key, and the George'. Norwich was famous for the textile trade, Bristol for its merchant port, Stratford for its large market town, Plymouth and Portsmouth for their naval bases, The Weald, the Cotswolds and East Anglia for its booming industrial trade, London's Oxford Street and Soho as Royal hunting grounds, and Southwark for its infamous red-light district.[41] Southwark was described by Mancini as a 'suburb remarkable for its streets and buildings, which, if it were surrounded by walls, might be called a second city', and in 1504 alone, eighteen brothels in Southwark were closed.[42] The dry dock at Portsmouth was the first in England, and had been built by King Henry VII in 1494 along with a military garrison known as the Square Tower, as well as alehouses that specifically served the military and crew who worked on board the ships.[43] As well as this, there was also located in Portsmouth harbour a rest house for travellers who had crossed the sea, as well as a hospital, known as a *Domus Dei*, or 'House of God' (which was forced to close during the Dissolution of the Monasteries in 1533), and a lodging house for the poor, sick and elderly. There was also a weekly market held for the families of sailors and fishermen who lived in the surrounding area, as well as an annual fair which attracted crowds from further afield. Ultimately, however, Portsmouth's most principal trade was fishing and the manufacturing of salt. Lead was mined in Kent, Sussex, Derbyshire, Cumberland and Somerset, while coal was mined and exported from areas of Durham, Yorkshire, and Wales. Cloth too was a major export of Wales, as it was in Wiltshire, Gloucester, Yorkshire, Kent and Devon.

London in particular was a city made up of smaller, walled enclosures called precincts, which divided more affluent areas from the poorer. Cheapside, for example, was a precinct of London dedicated entirely to a shopping district, and would have been frequented by visitors hoping to purchase wares.[44] Cheapside was also relatively wealthy, despite its name, and supplied the aristocracy and the Royal Family. So too was Ludgate, a hill the Bishop of London lived upon.[45] In the surrounding, walled area were three hundred yeoman and gentry houses, and was one of the largest enclosed residential areas in London after the Royal Palaces. Sixteenth-century London must have been such an overwhelming, incredible sight, for it was even described was described by the contemporary chronicler William Dunbar, as:

> soveraign of cities, seemliest in sight, / of high renown, riches and royalties; of lordis, barons, and many a goodly knight; of most delectable lusty ladies bright; of famous prelates, in habitis clericall; of merchauntis full of substance and of myghte; Oh London, thou art the flour of cities all.[46]

*

Most noteworthy buildings in the early years of the sixteenth century were built in the Perpendicular and Gothic styles so synonymous with the Middle Ages, including the favourite home of both Cardinal Thomas Wolsey and Henry VIII, Hampton Court Palace, of which monumental arches, peaks, and turrets were distinctly Perpendicular. It is important to remember, however, that many of the palaces, castles and other residences of the Tudor monarchs that still stand today, have been added to over the centuries, and reflect whatever architectural style was in fashion at the time. As well as this, subsequent English monarchs have since left their own personal stamps on their country homes and city residences, reflecting their own personal interests and tastes. Queen Elizabeth I, for example, installed an entire covered gallery at Windsor Castle for use of exercise, building upon the extension of her father Henry VIII's 'new wharff' built in the mid-1530s, and replacing the ageing wooden beams with masonry. Long galleries like these were not uncommon in the houses of the richest of sixteenth-century England, and still exist in such places as Hever Castle in Kent and Little Morton Hall in Cheshire.

These galleries were a reflection of the riches of the wealthy, and would be used in a similar way to modern-day conservatories, a place in which the entertaining of guests, the displaying of precious furniture and works of art, and where house owners could relax in the dappling sunlight, could take place. Long galleries also served another purpose, that of exercise. For the fitness-conscious Tudors, daily walks and light exercise were encouraged no matter the weather. With the installation of fashionable long galleries, homeowners could walk miles in the safety, comfort and warmth of their own enclosed spaces while still being able to look through the long windows that ran along the walls, making it popular in times of cold, wet and stormy weather!

This period of dramatic architectural progress has also been dubbed a period of the 'chivalric architectural style', for the excessive use of heraldic motifs and decorative friezes on the ornamental decorations of the exteriors of the houses of the wealthy. These heraldic motifs often took the form of a wealthy family's coat of arms, often flanked or engraved with additional features which distinguished a family's heraldry from the next. Most often these heraldic devices included ornamental beasts or intricate foliage, and would have been painted in the colours of the family. The inclusion of heraldic devices upon exterior building works was popularised by Thomas Wriothesley, the Garter King of Arms, under whose jurisdiction families could apply for their own heraldic emblems to be envisaged and drawn up, as well as their genealogies traced. It was only with his permission could rising gentile families show their heraldry legally.

The chivalric architectural style can also be distinguished by an influx of stonework popularised by the rich and wealthy. The installation of faux battlements and turrets –which often served no purpose other than aesthetic – gave an added air of luxury to the houses of the rich. Some grand houses were even fitted with bespoke machicolations, small, jetties that were used on castles in the Middle Ages for defence purposes. Castle defenders would have poured boiling water, fat or wax through the holes of machicolations, and onto their enemies below. For the vast majority of wealthy Tudors who had installed them on their houses, however, they served only as a form of drainpipe, in which any collected water from the roofs of houses would drip through! So-called 'Wonder Houses' began popping up across Tudor England, setting a new trend and creating a shocking picture against the backdrop of a society still crawling out of the latter end of the Middle Ages. This sudden influx of wealth and ostentation quickly caught on, and even the lowliest of Tudor society grappled with attempts to keep up with the latest agricultural trends. These particular houses were intended to 'wow', and that, they certainly did. Gabled roofs, porches, mullioned windows, chimneys and fireplaces, and beautiful brickwork replaced the often rudimentary and plain stone, wood and clay structures of Medieval England. With the Tudors came a new era – the age of ostentation.

The sixteenth century was a period of vast and impressive architectural engineering and pioneering, and saw the erection and construction of awe-inspiring palaces and great houses such as Hampton Court Palace and Hardwick Hall, as well as other, more modest buildings such as Shakespeare's Globe. Some of these buildings had simply been added to in a stroke of Tudor ingenuity, with accommodations and extensions built onto pre-existing foundations that had lain for decades, sometimes even centuries before, like the Tower of London and the Royal Apartments at Windsor Castle. Yet it was the buildings of a mass scale that peppered the backdrop of sixteenth-century England that is the most fascinating; the farmhouses, cottages, and black-white timber-framed houses so synonymous with the Tudor era. It is these houses which can tell us the most about the sixteenth century, the lives of the ancestors who ate, slept, worked and lived just as we do today. This is not a story of the grand English estates once resided in by the wealthiest of Tudors, their halls now echoing with the faint remains of historical voices. No, this is the story of the houses of the commoners of sixteenth-century England, the stories of those who worked for their wages, who nursed their infants and who battled with the deadly Sweating Sickness.

The *Great Rebuilding*, which took place across England and Wales in the seventeenth century, saw a period of mass reconstruction of both commercial buildings and residential buildings in both urban and rural areas. Following devastating events such as war and plague, which decimated the sixteenth-century social landscape, houses were rebuilt often atop pre-existing olden structures, using foundations as markers in which to rebuild. Additionally, these structures would also be constructed with materials re-used from other, pre-existing structures, from wooden beams to stone and marble slabs. Note that not every house, although faithfully restored, may have a genuinely authentic façade, but rather may just be a reproduction – additions, extensions and weathering may have been added over time. You can often date a Tudor house by looking at the shifting of the house, or the uneven beams and foundations that have sloped over time. There was a distinction between genuine Tudor architecture and Tudor-style architecture. Genuine buildings can be distinguished by exposed beams, lead window panes, and an original thatched roof.

Authentic sixteenth-century houses, especially those of the lowest echelons of society are diminishing historical resources, and therefore should deserve conservation and reverence. These buildings can provide us with direct links to the past, and give us the advantage of really feeling history. Moreso than a document can, buildings teach us how to touch, breathe, and physically experience the lives of our ancestors from long-gone generations. And so, despite many no longer being occupied by families today, many surviving Tudor homes live on in the twenty-first century as monoliths of architectural pioneering and centres for learning about the not-too-distant past.

Chapter 2

Life as a Tudor

'[the English] wear very fine clothes and are extremely
polite in their language ... they are gifted with
good understanding and are very quick at
everything they apply their minds to'.
Venetian envoy to England, c. 1497.[1]

Tudor England; we are taught in history lessons and docudramas and fictional books that it was a period of provinciality, a place where everything was muddy and smelly and brown. The peasant classes all fit the same mould, skinny, unwashed, unshaven; the rich, in comparison, ruggedly handsome, seductive, ostentatious. There are no elderly people here, no homosexuals. Orphans and urchins and the infirm live only on the peripheries, and there is no such thing as racial diversity.

Or, so we are taught.

In reality, Tudor England was a country just as diverse as it is today. Young and old alike lived in the same cities and towns and villages as foreign immigrants and prostitutes, merchants rubbed shoulders with housewives who conversed with rowdy adolescents. Sixteenth-century English society was far more colourful than we are traditionally taught. Tudors could – and regularly did – live to grand old ages. Black and Asian citizens lived in pockets of cities and went about their daily lives alongside indigenous, Caucasian Tudors. A typical town in Tudor England would have been greatly diverse indeed, in everything from age, race, religion, background and social class, despite what we are typically taught to believe.

In 1538, the first official parish records that recorded all births, marriages, deaths and burials in the vicinity were established. It was these records that give us so much insight into the villages, hamlets, towns and cities of sixteenth-century England today, and of the true lives of the people who lived there. It is true that, for the most part, Tudor England still confined itself to the socially-ingrained hierarchical structures of the Middle Ages, a form of out-dated feudal system that still governed the entire population. Yet, it was during the sixteenth century that these hierarchies were becoming increasingly dismantled, the rigid social bubbles of Medieval England permeated by the lower classes who were now on the rise. The social class boundaries of the sixteenth century were beginning to fade, impacted by devastating plague and war and economic crises. The huge numbers of deaths of the rich during these periods opened up spaces for the advantageous poor to rise, and they did. In the Middle Ages, it seemed inconceivable that the son of a blacksmith could one day become England's Secretary of State, that the daughter of a low-ranking member of the gentry could one day become Queen, and that the young, rambunctious son of a lowly farmer could one day become the greatest playwright the world had ever seen. But, they did. Thomas Cromwell, Jane Seymour and William Shakespeare were all prime examples of products of dismantled social classes, and it was not only they who were on the rise.

'The common people apply themselves to trade, or to fishing, or else they practise navigation; and they are so diligent in mercantile pursuits', wrote a Venetian envoy who visited England in 1497. He was impressed; instead of conforming to rigid hierarchical rules and an unfair social strata, the envoy was surprised to see that the people residing on the lowest rung of the English social ladder were taking matters into their own hands and furthering their prospects. The sixteenth century was a period in which the peasantry was finally awarded a chance to melt into the gentrified classes. The social circles of the aristocracy and the nobility (who ranked just below the King and were often made up of his distant relatives) were slowly beginning to widen. Hardworking, ambitious labourers became wealthy merchants and performed civic duties. Even the position of the King itself was not entirely secure, as demonstrated by the usurpation of the old Yorkist King Richard III by the comparatively lowly-born Henry Tudor in 1485.

*

The gentrified classes of Tudor England, such as the nobility and wealthy landowners, collected rent from their poorer tenants, who they would permit to live on their land in return for monetary exchange or a share in their trade. These were the very wealthiest members of sixteenth-century society, and they lived in grand country estates and would have been served by droves of servants and staff. Beneath the gentry came the Yeomen, or the 'Freemen'. Despite their names, they were not 'free', insomuch as they were answerable to their superiors and relied on them for tenancy. The Yeomen were traditionally the richer merchants of society; carpenters, painters, surveyors. They were the highest rank of servant, and may have even been installed in the households of the Royal Family as cupbearers and grooms and administrators. According to the social historian Ruth Goodman, the Yeomen lived comfortable lives in houses of around six or seven rooms, and certainly had the means to provide very well for their families.[2] Servants of the Crown though they may have been, they had a degree of self-governance and autonomy, and their coin purses would have been more than adequately full.

Beneath the Yeoman came the lesser-wealthy merchants; grocers, gardeners and haberdashers. Unlike the Yeomen who typically only provided labour for their superiors, these merchants catered for the majority of sixteenth-century society and owned the vast majority of shops, taverns and market stalls. They were known as Craftsmen, and would have rented their properties from their superiors in return for a portion of the profits they made from their businesses. Although not as wealthy as the Yeomen, the Craftsmen were still a greatly wealthy cohort of Tudor society, and could afford to live in tall townhouses in cities and in large country homes.

Beneath the Craftsmen were the Husbandmen, who lived off the arable land of the Yeomen, providing their services in exchange for rent. Life as a Husbandman would have been difficult and tiring for the most part, though still relatively comfortable. Most Husbandmen had their own farms, animals and gardens, and typically lived in the three or four-roomed longhouses, cottages and thatched barns that are so synonymous with the sixteenth century. They received decent wages and were often able to raise their families and animals with relative comfort, unlike those who came beneath them on the social ladder: the Labourers.

As their name suggests, the Labourers of sixteenth-century England would carry out the most intensive agricultural work and perform gruelling manual labour, such as ploughing, sowing and construction, for their masters with often little pay and little reward. They did not often have a secure place of their own to live, but rather lodged in agreed tenancies with their superiors, perhaps renting small, two-roomed cottages on the lands of the Gentry, Yeomen and Husbandmen. In some cases, they would even reside in rented rooms within the homes of these gentrified classes. Life as a Labourer was tough; Ruth Goodman even went so far as to write that they were often just one missed wage shy of homelessness.[3]

A male Labourer could expect daily routines of ploughing, hedging and ditching, as well as milling and butchering and animal-wrangling. They often made up most of the construction task force of sixteenth-century England, and typically had physically exertive roles that required high energy and strength, including brick-making and rock-smashing. For a labouring woman, however, these roles were less physically demanding yet tiring nonetheless. Daily duties would include planting, winnowing, weeding, caring for chickens and livestock, laundry, spinning and weaving, producing medicines and organising the kitchen, as well as, of course, caring for children.

Tudor women also had the all-important job of household management, which included keeping tabs on finances, the employ of household staff, and inventorying household possessions. Many of these inventories have actually survived, and prove to be fantastic sources that can tell us not just about what the Tudors had within their homes, but where they bought them, what they looked like, how they were used, and who they belonged to. The smallest bed in the household, for example, could belong to the youngest member of the family, or perhaps was relegated for use by a servant. On the other hand, the most beautifully carved chair would be the seat of the man of the house, or of any visiting guest; the rest of the family could sit on stools or long benches. These records of furniture, financial outgoings, and receipts were kept in diligent order, and were almost obsessive in their detail. Even single items of stockings, spoons and rags were inventoried, perhaps by houseproud Tudor ladies desperate to show off their household goods, or by suspicious of thieving staff and guests. It may sound excessive to us, but the Tudors had not even half of the household possessions that we have today. What we may now discard as rubbish, the Tudors would have mended or donated – possessions were treasured much more then than they are today.

Interestingly, sixteenth-century household inventories often indicate the possessions that were most beloved by household members, with the best furniture often being explicitly mentioned or described, or passed down in wills to children and other surviving family members, and sometimes even to well-beloved servants. It was common for infant swaddling bands and pregnancy girdles to be bequeathed to young women, for example, or eating utensils and other practical household instruments left to servants and staff. Of course, items of furniture in the sixteenth century could not be bought mass-produced from a furniture store, but were each instead hand-crafted, bespoke and unique and were therefore very sentimental to a family, hence their appearances in wills. One such example of this, was the family of Walter Langrich, who was endowed with considerable inheritances upon his death; his two eldest sons received household furniture, and his two youngest sons, as well as his only daughter, received financial deposits.[4] When Walter's widow Margery died six years later, she divided the contents of her will evenly, leaving to each child personalised linen that she had embroidered with their initials. When her children died some fifteen years or so later, these monogrammed gifts were discovered in the inventories of Walter and Margery's grandchildren, indicative of the familial affection that transcended three different generations. Examples such as this shed much light on familial relationships of the sixteenth century, and, rather humorously, suggest that décor styles varied very little throughout the decades; indeed, it appears that grandchildren may have decorated their homes with the same furniture as their grandparents had, and may have even resided in the same houses.

The home truly was a woman's dominion. In the sixteenth century, women were required to be chaste, pure and homely, and the house was seen as a reflection of that. Yet, Tudor women were not solely defined by their homes, and they were more than just mothers, wives, and daughters that we are traditionally led to believe; they had hobbies and interests just as we do today, favourite dresses and foodstuffs and songs. Evidence of board games, writing desks, cosmetics and musical instruments have all been found in sixteenth-century inventories, presenting us with delightful images of individuals and families that are not too dissimilar from our own today. So too were other items commonly listed in household inventories; treasured childhood toys, waxy crayon-like writing implements, and gifts from sweethearts. Some Tudor women even proudly recorded tapestries and artworks, rich clothing and beautifully-bound illuminated manuscripts, perhaps created by their own hands, and certainly some of their most prized possessions.

Other luxurious and priceless items have been recorded in these lists, including small vessels of so-called Holy Water, dossers (ornamental screens) and mazers (drinking vessels made from pure silver). Despite the Henrician Reformation that would take place in the mid-sixteenth century, Tudor society was still one of extreme devotion, and it was not wholly uncommon for Catholics to have within their homes pieces of religious ephemera. The cult of St Thomas Becket, for example, which was still greatly popular in the early sixteenth century, was spread in some part thanks to the production of reliquaries, a sort of early form of tourist memorabilia. The Tudors, just like we are today, were partial to a gift shop, and would have purchased these small reliquaries supposedly filled with the blood of slain martyrs, tiny fragments of a saint's clothing, and even sometimes the bones and sloughed skin of their favourite patron saints, to bring religious salvation and intercession to their households. 'Pilgrim badges', small metal, wax or wooden tokens struck in the image of a saint or representing a specific motif, were also common, and a favourite possession of the early Tudors.

But it was not only furniture and oddities which can be found in sixteenth-century household inventories. Perishables too were also recorded in fine detail, homeowners proud to display fantastical, newly-imported items such as tobacco, pineapples, corn and even chocolate, which had come from the New World. These commodities are so commonplace in modern society that we often take them for granted, yet they were clearly very precious to the Tudors to warrant their descriptions in long inventory lists. Perhaps most surprisingly, however, was the importance given to tapets, an early form of bedcover, as well as blankets, mattresses and bedframes. Although not as expensive as exciting foreign foods, or as provoking as religious talismans, beds were perhaps the most precious of all items of Tudor furniture.

Sleep was important to the Tudors, and many families even reused the same bedsheets and pillows that their forefathers and mothers had once slept upon. It was little surprise that the Tudors relished sleep; tradesmen and labourers would usually rise at around five every morning, awoken by young boys who would rap on the windows of houses at the coming of the dawn. They then began work promptly at six in the morning, working until nine, before a brief break for food. The breaking of the fast (or breakfast, as we now call it) would last around fifteen minutes, and was a crucial time for the men to catch their breath, refuel, and converse with their friends over broken bread and pitchers of small ale. They would then resume work again until twelve noon, before breaking for an hour to eat dinner.

The second half of the working day would last between one in the afternoon and four o'clock, when the men would be allowed a comfort break to the pub, or alcoholic drinks would be supplied. Despite how it sounds, however, these drinks would have had very little alcoholic effect, as they were drastically watered down to prevent drunkenness on the job.[5] The men would then continue their work until six, before finishing their long and laborious day for the night. They would be paid around 7d on average per day, but 8d in the summer months where they would be expected to work longer, more gruelling shifts in the heat of the summer sun; it was a pittance for all that they had achieved that day. After work, there would be a frenzied rush as men tried to cram in as much entertainment and leisure as possible, for free time was largely limited by the setting of the sun. Once the sun had set, your light would be severely restricted, and as such many simply just turned in and went to sleep, all to prepare for another laborious day on the morrow.

*

'The nobility', wrote contemporary chronicler John Russell, 'are endowed with great honours, possessions and riches [and] can be compared to the firm ground while the lower people, who lack such endowments, can be likened to the unstable, running water'.[6] This was the sentiment felt by much of sixteenth-century society, who thought little of those who worked the hardest. The poorest of sixteenth-century England would be tempted by promises of money and security from the upper classes, especially in times of conflict; 'many', it was written, 'who had fallen into debt ... assembled together in a company and crossed over the sea to Flanders', for they felt they had little other prospects than to offer their martial skills in return for monetary gain.[7] It was a dangerous job, but the alternative was not much better. The army was not a profession – rather, it was a last resort. In times of peace, however, these men were needed elsewhere, and assumed roles tilling the land, working in construction, or entering into ecclesiastical occupations and civic law. According to the contemporary chronicler John Stow, for example, almost three thousand poor men were forced to turn to work on the ships in the docks along the River Thames, for they were little qualified for much else.[8]

Skilled workers would earn double what unskilled workers would in the sixteenth century, and thus it was important that a skilled craftsman could join a guild for it protected trade and earnings. Other occupations did not have such a luxury. Servants were paid in cash every quarter, and received bed and board as part of their wages; everyone else would usually be paid at the end of every week. By comparison, threshers earned just eight shillings on average, a minuscule amount for the hard work that they were required to do. Thresher's ploughs were crude, man-made wooden lattices that had small spokes attached to the bottom to mill the earth. They would be ploughed by men or by strong animals, either cattle or horses, and often two abreast. The horses would wear yokes around their necks and their eyes would usually be covered, and a ploughman would follow behind to ensure straight lines, keeping them in line with whips or spurs. Harvesters and sowers would follow, either picking whatever had been grown, or sowing new seeds. Seeds would be dispersed from bags with holes in them, or from crude aprons, where the sower would sprinkle them as he went. These were some of the most important jobs in the country. But so too were they the worst paid.

Considering the laborious jobs many Tudors were forced to work, it may come as a surprise to learn that, on average, sixteenth-century people were shorter and slighter. Social historian Martin Whittock has argued that, due to mineral and vitamin deficiencies, a modern ten-year-old child would probably be taller than their fully grown, adult ancestors.[9] The average height for a man in the sixteenth century was just 171 centimetres (or around five foot, six inches), compared to 175 centimetres today; for women, it was 159 centimetres (five foot, two inches), compared to the average 162 centimetres today.[10] So although Henry VIII's colossal height of over six feet may have seemed exaggerated by contemporary chroniclers, to the everyday Tudor person, he really would have cut an imposing, awe-inspiring figure.

But regardless of their height, the Tudors were proud of their appearances. 'The English are great lovers of themselves and of everything English', wrote a Venetian envoy in 1500, 'they think there are no other men worth considering and no other part of the world either'.[11] He continued; 'when a handsome foreigner walks by they say 'he looks like an Englishman'.[12] Indeed, the sixteenth-century English cut impressive figures. Clothing could be made from crude materials or luxurious fabrics, and were not available to buy pre-made. Rather, fabric would be taken to dressmakers and tailors, or to family members, resulting in bespoke and unique articles of clothing every time. This disgruntled Queen Elizabeth I, who introduced the so-called Sumptuary Laws, which limited what clothes, cuts, and colours individuals could wear, in an attempt to restrict vanity and pridefulness, as well as to ensure that no other figure outshone herself.

For the vast majority of people in sixteenth-century England however, clothing was simple. Women wore linen smocks, thin, floor-length chemise gowns worn close to the skin, that acted as a form of underwear. Lingerie was not worn in the sixteenth century, and corsets were only worn by the richer members of society. For the most part, the everyday woman simply forwent tight-fitting underwear, instead covering their chemises with gowns of simple cotton or woollen, known as kirtles. It is a common belief that most people, aside from the aristocracy, in the sixteenth century, wore muted colours of browns and beige. In reality, clothes would have been dyed with natural ingredients such as beetroot for desired red colours, citrus peels and onion skins for yellows, and leafy greens such as grass and other vegetation for greens. Black was a colour worn throughout the year, not just for mourning at funerals, and would have been achieved through the use of cochineal or wood ash and charcoal. In instances where black was required to be worn at a funeral, it was common for many everyday people to simply dye one of their pre-existing articles of clothing until it was black, rather than purchase an entirely new set. Brides would not typically wear white at their wedding ceremonies (that is an entirely nineteenth-century invention), but rather would wear their best articles of clothing; sometimes brides even got married in their everyday gowns.

Many peasant class Tudors did not wear any other additional gowns simply because they were impractical for daily use, especially for labouring. However, the women of the middling and richer classes would have then added a bodice and matching skirt to their apparel, as well as interchangeable sleeves which would be laced in to the rest of the gown at the shoulders. By the time of the sixteenth century, these bodices had become lower and more daring, cut in the French fashion and popularised by such fashionable women as Queen Anne Boleyn, who wore her neckline square and low enough to see the protrusion of the ruffled kirtle beneath, as well as, scandalously, the bust and the decolletage. Sleeves would have been loose-flowing, and often slashed, so that you could see the colours of the undersleeve which lay tight along the arm beneath. For the very wealthiest of society, a final clothing layer of furs, or other beautifully decorated fabrics such as brocade, would have added the final finishing touches to the completed dress.

Without a lady's maid, dressing in one of these elaborate gowns, complete with hood or headdress, would have been an exhausting task. Unlike the women of the lower classes, who could simply hop in and out of their gowns, the wealthier women had to be attended by a number of assistants to properly ensure that every adjoining lace or ribbon had been appropriately tied and attached, and every article of clothing folded and stored safely for use another day. Many of these garments were cumbersome to fold and air in trunks and wardrobes on account of their weight and voluminosity, and became particularly difficult to keep crease-free and neat by the close of the sixteenth century, when more elaborate, stiff accessories became fashionable.

High-necked gowns and uncomfortably stiff, wing-like collars, were popularised by Queen Elizabeth I, whose fondness for elaborate, fragile fanned ruffs around the neck and the wrists trickled down to influence the fashion styles of the rest of sixteenth-century English society. Gone were the tight, form-fitting dresses of the early sixteenth century, where low necklines and cinched waists were idealised – with the Elizabethans came high necklines, flat stomachers and voluptuous skirts, supported by layers of thin fabrics, boned hoops called farthingales, and bum rolls, a half-moon-shaped roll of padding which sat at the square of a woman's back, and created the illusion of a wider gown. In just a span of a hundred years, fashion for all calibres of society in sixteenth-century England underwent a dazzling transformation.

One added advantage of these new Elizabethan fashions was that they required very minimal laundering. As the chemise – or underwear layer – would have sat the closest to the skin, and would wick away any sweat, smells and natural bodily oils throughout the day, only they required daily changing.[13] This meant that often the same gown would be worn numerous times throughout a week, even daily, especially by the poorer members of society. Although this sounded unhygienic, it would not have much bothered the Tudors, who could accessorise their outfits in such a way with different coloured fabrics, sleeves or accessories, so that the same gown could look different every day of the week. It was only when clothing got too worn that they were repurposed as linens and rags for hygiene purposes, or were cut, dyed and resewn to make clothing for children or even their poppet dolls, as well as bedcovers, curtains and altarpieces.

By the 1600s, ruffs were all the rage in Tudor England, popularised by the monarch Elizabeth I and her courtiers. To make a ruff, it would take around six yards of lace and material, and was no cheap accessory.[14] Yet, fashion and the latest trends were influenced by European clothing overseas, and if people wished to stay on trend, they had to be able to afford it. Fashion poppets, popular in the 1500s, were little miniature dolls dressed in the latest fashions from around the fashion capitals of France, Spain and Italy. These poppets showcased to owners what was in-trend across the oceans, and were brought over by foreign travelling merchants to English customers itching to get a glimpse at the latest fashions and styles. Soon, calf-length boots known as 'buskins', coif-like caps known as 'biggins', and knee-length trousers known as 'slops' became the staple of every Tudor man, woman and child. They may not have sounded appealing, but they certainly must have looked so.

Tudor shoes very rarely had laces – rather, they were simply slip-on leather or embroidered shoes that would eventually mould to the wearer's foot shape. Shoes were akin to modern-day slippers, yet often softer, and largely waterproof. This meant that there was no such thing as hunting for the correct shoe size in Tudor England – rather, you would simply purchase a leather slipper and simply break it in.[15] This also meant that there was no such thing as shoes fitting the right, or left foot; instead, the same shoe could be worn on either. These shoes were not always the most practical, however, particularly if worn by construction workers, for they could be slippery, break apart easily, and often lacked any protection or re-enforced sole, meaning that walking across uneven terrain could be painful. They would also smell foul if they got damp, and attracted weevils who fed on the leather hide. In cases where shoes did last, however, it was common for children to inherit the shoes of their parents or older siblings, once their feet had outgrown the shoes worn in infancy. Examples of these shoes have remarkably survived, though not often in pairs, with historians and archaeologists accrediting their survival to their value and importance in daily life.[16]

*

'The world did not exist apart from England', wrote Nicholas von Poppelau in 1484.[17] It was true – undercurrents of xenophobia plagued Tudor England, particularly amongst the wealthier classes. At Threadneedle Street in London, the French lived in dedicated districts, mingling with others who had emigrated from their country, and were allowed to speak the language freely.[18] Yet, when English relations with France soured in the 1530s, attitudes towards these French Londoners shifted. On every first day of March, St David's Day, in London, effigies of Welshmen were hung from rafters and small cakes shaped like men called 'Taffies' were burned.[19] At Aldgate, Persian, Asian and African merchant residents were all forcibly deported from the country in 1601. Romanis were executed, and individuals faced a huge penalty, which could include the severing of limbs, if they associated with them. Similarly, when The Hanseatic League brought over droves of German cloth traders throughout the sixteenth century, many were killed, exported and evicted on accounts of xenophobia in 1597.[20]

But not every Tudor was so inhospitable; rather, the majority of the population in the sixteenth century was welcoming and accommodating of strangers. Having a guest, particularly a foreign one, stay in your home was exciting, albeit expensive. Not only did it mean the employment of extra staff if the guests had a large entourage, including servants, cooks, and maids, but it also meant an increase in groceries, candles, and other such perishables, including disposable and edible bread trenchers instead of plates. Additionally, provisions for horses, hunting dogs, or whatever staff the guests had brought with them, would have been provided, resulting in great expenses for the host. Even the décor of houses would be influenced; additional seating areas would be constructed, and new, fresh linens to line bathtubs or beds would be ordered. Paintings, embroideries and tapestries would have also been showcased in order to impress the visiting guests, as would intricately carved beds and the best chair at the dining table be given over by the host for use by the guest. Some houses, particularly those of the gentry, which were more likely to be visited by courtiers or by the monarch themselves, even had to be expanded to accommodate their guests. Architectural expansions could rack up extortionate sums of money, and often they would be made at short notice, resulting in substandard, and even dangerous work. For this reason, canvas tent-like structures, similar to modern-day gazebos, would be erected to house guests for they were impermanent and significantly cheaper and quicker to erect than stone or wooden structures. Even King Henry VIII spent a fortnight camping out in canvas tents in Calais in 1520, while on a visit to the French court. Ultimately, however, the more impressive the house, the more prestige it would bring a family, and as such hosts tried desperately to extend their homes and beautify them for the visiting guest. Even if you were not high up on the rungs of the social ladder, if you could demonstrate a beautifully designed and constructed house then you would be considered fashionable and your family prestigious.

Royal processions certainly gained more popularity as the Tudor era progressed. Queen Elizabeth I went on no less than twenty-four royal progressions throughout her reign, breaking-in an estimated 2,400 horses each time.[21] Those fortunate enough to host the monarch and their household would reach social acclaim, for royal progressions were exciting, momentous occasions even for the lowest in society. Any form of progress, whether it be royal, military, or religious was exciting, and provided the poor with a chance to see how the other half lived. Those living in rural villages, who perhaps had never had the chance to see a likeness of the monarch, could now see them in the flesh and in all their dazzling regalia.

During periods when masters would be away from their homes, servants would regularly strip the house of its carpets, tapestries, linens, and other soft furnishings to air. The floorboards and tiles would have been swept, the fabrics shaken, and the metals buffed and shined. During this time, household items and furniture would be kept for storage in attics or in butteries, which, despite their name, had no relation to butter, but were simply areas of storage in which butlers derived their names. Having the employ of a servant was not wholly uncommon in the sixteenth century, even for the lowest of social classes, who often paid for regular (if not daily or weekly) assistance from maids, washerwomen, or errand boys. A manservant would expect to receive around two pounds per year on average wages, whereas a female servant would make just one pound per annum.[22] An average labourer would earn around five pounds per year, a minuscule amount by modern standards, but enough to provide for provisions like food and firewood for the year round.[23] Monthly wages could come to just 4d (shillings), which would amount to just one hundred pounds in modern currency. This wage would be very insubstantial, and could afford its owners just one chicken, or two lemons at a stretch.[24]

Life as a poor member of sixteenth-century England would have been incredibly difficult. The poor had to obtain licences to beg (which would only be granted to those too ill or too old to work), or would face harsh fines and punishments, and even death if they were found to be begging without permission. Healthy beggars would be whipped and a hole burnt through their ears for pretending to suffer from malaise and for approaching employment lackadaisically. In cases of a second offence, they would be branded with an 'S' on their forehead and sent into slavery in the fields.[25] Even those hospitable enough to take in poor, homeless and unemployed people into their houses were fined one pound by the local jurisdiction.[26] This resulted in the poor being removed from homes and forced to live on the streets of Tudor cities as vagrants, and led to a great rise in displacement as people wandered to towns and villages in search of jobs.

This marked a turning point in social history – before, vagrancy had been generally accepted and beggars had been left alone to their own devices in medieval England. But, with rising pressure on local mayors to deal with the growing unemployment and homelessness crisis, English domestic policy was forced to change. The Court of Requests was established, effectively a poor man's court in which peasants could dispute landholdings, wages and revenue. It provided the poor with an opportunity to lobby their superiors and fight for better prospects; for once, it seemed like someone was listening. These prospects only further improved for the poor with the Dissolution of the Monasteries in 1533, for the great dismantling of wealthy Catholic buildings had led to an increase in charitable donations on behalf of the rich to the poor, consisting of plundered clothing, wealth and food. With the rich finally aware of the plight of the poor, a significant reform bill was passed in the highest courts of England, known as the Elizabethan Poor Laws. These laws drastically improved the lives of those living in the dark underbelly of Tudor England, and alleviated the struggles that the poor of sixteenth-century England had had to endure. Between 1550 and 1590, £100,000 a year had been set aside to assist in the cause.[27] Life for the poor was on the up.

It was not only monetary donations that the poorest of sixteenth-century England received as charity. Dedicated lodgings were also established to cater for the poor in Tudor England, providing bed, board, as well as opportunities for employment. These establishments were known as 'hospitals', and, although equipped to cure ailing patients or tend to the sick, they certainly did not resemble hospitals as we would know them today. Rather, these hospitals (also known as 'alms-houses') were more like modern-day hostels, where needy individuals could come and go in the hope of improving their prospects. These alms-houses did not ask for any charge – rather, their only wish was that individuals pay for their place at the lodgings with prayers. It was a fantastic solution for those with little or no money in the sixteenth century, who would be rewarded with free lodgings and other basic necessities for as long as they required.

Not every Tudor hospital served the poor however – the Hospital of Saint Katherine's (which was located near the Tower of London), for example, served as lodgings for the highest and noblest minds of English society; the masters, the chaplains and the scholars. Women too were admitted and accommodated within its walls, but only on the grounds that they were gentlewomen and from well-to-do backgrounds. Unlike alms-houses, which did not charge for rent or their services, the hospitals of the richer members of Tudor society often charged fees for a night's stay. This could be paid in money, or, as was often preferred, in a trade. Lodgings (and renting in general), could be paid for entirely by your craft; if you were a chandler, for example, you could settle your renting debts in candles. Cheques could also be paid, but many Tudors preferred to pay upfront in hard cash.

For this reason, many houses in Tudor England were purchased quickly, and certainly did not have the long, complicated chains that come with modern house relocation today. For the most part, people in the sixteenth century did not pay deposits for houses, but instead bought the house outright if they were able. In cases where money was limited, and a family's fiscal value was low, a landlord may accept that the family pay in other means, most often with products made by the family, such as a fraction of cheese, wool or other manufactured goods. Other new homebuyers relied on assistance from family members, or simply lived in homes inherited from deceased kin. Some even built their houses themselves from materials available to them, bypassing the need to pay for construction costs. It is for this reason that renting and purchasing houses were not the norm in sixteenth-century England; although rent, taxes and debts would certainly be collected by landowners (such as the Yeomen), many Tudor houses were cheap to build, cheap to buy, and cheap to inhabit.

*

Houses were often built wherever a family desired in sixteenth-century England, particularly if the location was prime for travel, employment and accessibility to market squares and churches. It seems inconceivable now, but houses in the sixteenth century were even built upon bridges; London Bridge, for example, was measured at sixty feet tall and thirty feet wide, and had cellars, vaults, houses and buildings alongside it.[28] Lights illuminated the bridge, like the ancestor of the modern street light.[29] It also had one hundred and thirty-eight shops along it, a church dedicated to St Thomas Becket, and even beautiful marble arches, according to the contemporary chronicler Schasek.[30] Likewise, gatehouses were also surprising locations for inhabitants, yet they were lived in nonetheless. The city gatehouse at Whitehall in London (known as the Holbein Gate), for example, was decorated with terracotta roundels of Roman emperors as well as decorative marble arches which stunned and awed locals and tourists alike.[31] Although a city fortification, it was also the home of the Duke of Lennox, and served as a storage place for papers and documents. Its other famous resident, King Henry VIII, had intended to build it to connect the eastern and western-most parts of Whitehall Palace. The King had a similar gatehouse at his private lodgings at Whitechapel, which had been carefully constructed atop a bridge overlooking an underpass below in which the hustle and bustle of the city of London could flow.[32] It is not too difficult to imagine the King keeping a watchful eye on the street below, which became known as 'King Street' for its most famous resident.

Not every bridge was so sophisticated in the sixteenth century, however. Bridewell Palace and the Dominican House of the Blackfriars in London were connected by a spindly bridge that crossed over the River Fleet and into the central city.[33] It was a precarious journey for those who had to make the journey on foot, yet often, the Tudors had little other choice. Transport was most often by foot in Tudor England, and only the very wealthy owned carts, which were around fourteen feet long and difficult to manoeuvre, especially around bends. Although they could carry fewer quantities of goods and people compared to carriages, the Tudors favoured 'cars', which were much smaller but much quicker. As transportation improved, so did the increase in immigration, travellers and foreign peddlers bringing exotic new items and selling them to the English. Imports increased, and there was, for the first time, a newfound market for exotic items rarely seen before in England. Wherries, or ferries, sailed down rivers and transported workers and tourists to destinations for just one penny per crossing, such as at Horseferry in Lambeth, which continued to be in use until 1862. Travellers would walk or ride their horses onto these ferries, which were little more than heavy, wooden floatation devices. They have come to be considered as an early form of commute transport, and certainly would have been used by those looking for a more streamlined way to travel.

In sixteenth-century London, purchasing your own cart and carriage for transport was expensive. In 1570, it cost ten pounds for a carriage alone, plus an extra eight pounds for four horses to pull it.[34] This equates to around £4,300 in today's money, yet did not include payment for a driver, provisions and upkeep of stables for the horses, or any other expenses which travelling could incur. When the average labourer could only afford one cow after saving six months of wages, it is clear that horse-drawn carriages were luxuries only available to those of wealth and standing. An average labourer, who earned around five pounds a year, would have to save for at least three years before he could even begin considering purchasing such an expensive item. As such, for those living in the countryside where travel was limited, many were born, lived and died in the same town as their fathers and their fathers before them.

By comparison, sailors and soldiers were paid very well in Tudor England. The mariners and gunners onboard the ill-fated *Mary Rose* ship were paid around five shillings a month on average, a very good pay.[35] A pack of twelve fresh herrings cost on average around one penny in Tudor England, and a new pair of good leather shoes cost just five pennies. Although it meant that a safe life on dry land in England would not always be possible, life as a sailor and soldier was a small price to pay for those men itching for wealth and gold. One solid gold angel ornament found onboard the *Mary Rose*, for example, was estimated to cost around six shillings and eight pence, or an entire day's wages for the ship's Vice Admiral, Sir William FitzWilliam in 1522.[36]

Tudor England truly was a place replete with colourful citizens who lived interesting lives, poor and rich alike. Although opportunities and prospects were certainly not the same for every individual in sixteenth-century England, on the whole, the Tudors were resilient, practical and aware, almost dismissive, of social inequality. As the Dutch humanist scholar, Desiderius Erasmus wrote fondly of the English in 1499, 'wherever you go you are received with kisses from everyone'.[37] Clearly, he had been impressed by England and its residents. He finished his report, 'I never liked anything so much before. I find the climate both pleasant and wholesome; and I have met with so much kindness and so much learning'.[38] Perhaps Tudor England wasn't so bad after all.

Chapter 3

Health and Medicine

'sodeinly there came a plague of sickenes, called the Swetyng sickenes...this malady was so cruell that it killed some within three houres, some within twoo houres, some mery at diner and dedde at supper...'

Edward Hall, Hall's Chronicle, 1518.[1]

At the end of the August of 1485, a strange malady descended upon the students of Merton College in Oxford. This 'marvellous and unprecedented sickness broke out in the University which beginning suddenly with an unexpected sweat, deprived many of their lives', wrote a university scholar.[2] The swift-spreading sickness baffled the Tudors, especially so in London, where 'three mayors died within ten days'.[3] Symptoms of the disease developed quickly, characterised by intense fevers and chills and the expulsion of excessive sweat from the body. It was called the Sweating Sickness.

The sweating sickness, or the *sudor anglicus*, was a deadly disease that gripped sixteenth-century England. This 'hateful affliction [...] which no previous age had experienced', spread quickly across the country and was indiscriminate in its victims.[4] First mentioned in 1485, it was believed to have been carried to England by Henry Tudor and his men from France. It continued to ravish the country throughout the entirety of the sixteenth century, with outbreaks (more prevalent in the summer and autumn months) occurring in almost every decade. One particular outbreak of the Sweat in 1563 resulted in 23,660 deaths in London alone, totalling to a tragic loss of around twenty per cent of the city's entire population.[5] The disease was said to particularly target those aged between twenty-five and thirty-four years old, and appears to have been more prominent in men.[6]

It was believed that contraction of the sweating sickness came about in three different ways; the first, a lack of ventilation, encouraged the

43

Tudors to throw open their windows, doors, and gates in order to allow the circulation of fresh, clean air within their homes, and drive away the lingering miasmas of the plague. Fresh air was considered all the more important in urban areas, particularly where houses were built-up and overcrowded, and the city air more polluted than in the countryside. Secondly, contrary to popular belief, the Tudors were aware that the sweating sickness was spread through a lack of cleanliness, and as such, strict cleaning regimes and instructions were encouraged to be followed in every household across the country. This cleaning regime included regularly washing the floors, replacing rushes, and stripping linens and fabrics to remove any trace of the disease. Finally, the Tudors believed that a diet excessive of salted and brined food would put you at a higher risk, and more likely to contract the sickness. As such, a diet of the freshest food available was deeply encouraged, particularly of 'cold' foods like juicy fruits and crisp vegetables, which were believed to cool the warm humours of the body and bring it back into balance. Eating heavily salted or brined foods, on the other hand, was believed to dry out the body, and therefore increase the chances of contracting this deadly plague.

There also existed the belief in sixteenth-century England that you could catch the disease through fear of it, and as such, instructions went out for people to stop excessively worrying, else they would catch it. It was probably not the most effective of controls, but the Tudors had faith in it. Across the Continent, such a frenzied panic arose that restrictions had to be set in place to limit the spread of the disease. The sick were isolated, and any travellers who entered the country's ports were sent into a compulsory quarantine so to lessen the risk of spreading the sickness. There were also restrictions enforced on travel and trade, and imports were temporarily reduced in order to quell the spread. Thomas More commented in 1517 that there was, 'less danger on the battlefield than in London' for the plague had reached such levels, and was so virulent, that it was decimating populations of Londoners.[7] It would take as little as four hours to kill a person once contracted; most people could contract the sweat in the morning, and be dead within a twelve-hour time frame. It was only those who made it to twenty-four hours that had a fighting chance of survival, but even then it was minimal and rare.

To combat the sweating sickness once contracted, the Tudors were encouraged to remain in a tepid environment so as not to exacerbate symptoms. It was believed that the warmer the room the better, and fires were ordered to be kept continuously stoked throughout the night and day, no matter the temperature outside. Additionally, instructional manuals encouraged individuals to take plenty of bed rest – not that the inflicted could do much else – with plenty of blankets and bedcovers, as well as wearing many layers of clothing to encourage the body to sweat. It was believed by some that the fresh air and consumption of cold foods and drinks were required to balance the heat of the body; however, other contemporaries believed that they would only serve to weaken the body, prolong the disease, and increase the chance of death. It was even believed that the sweat was most contractable through the parts of the body that emitted the most sweat – the soles of the feet, the neck, and the armpits. Anxiety across Tudor England reached such a point that many people began sleeping with their arms crossed and their hands beneath their armpits, genuinely believing that it would prevent contraction of the disease.

In 1578, a decree regarding the sweat was published that enforced the rule of forced quarantine for any household found with symptoms of plague for six weeks. Once those six weeks had elapsed, the household could unbolt their doors and enter back into society. But for those languishing inside the walls of their homes, painfully aware of any cough, swelling or rise in temperature, they had only two possible outcomes – a natural recovery, or an untimely death. The entire inhabitants of a household – whether it be family, or servants, would be quarantined, even those who had shown no sign of the plague. To identify individuals who had contracted the sweat, and who could be contagious, the sick carried white rods around four feet long so that they could be seen from a distance, allowing by-passers to reconsider their walking routes and avoid their neighbours. Additionally, the houses of families in which one or more individuals had contracted the plague were marked with straw bundles known as 'wisps', which would be erected upon large ten-foot poles and placed where potential visitors could see them to deter them from progressing any further. These wisps would be displayed for forty days, until either the individuals had recovered from the deadly disease, or until they had died. Either way, the forty-day isolation period marked the supposed passing of danger, and actually proved rather successful in preventing the healthy from contracting the disease from their sick neighbours. From 1521, straw wisps were replaced with more significant and hardy structures resembling the cross of St Anthony, which, unlike the bundles, could withstand harsh weather conditions, and provided the sick with the added benefit of spiritual protection.

The straw and rushes from houses infected by the sweating sickness would have been burnt in order to quell the spread of the disease to other members of the household and dogs, who were believed to be carriers of the plague, were expelled from cities or executed. However, the Tudors spared a select group of breeds – hounds, spaniels, and mastiffs – for it was inconceivable that these hunting dogs could transmit the sweat. Local law courts ordered that groups were prohibited from meeting during outbreaks of the sweat, and even established and constructed isolation hospitals, known casually as 'pest hospitals', to control the spread of the disease.

St Mary Spital in London was a hospital first founded in 1197 and established as a dedicated childbirth hospital, but later become large enough to accommodate around one hundred and eighty beds in the sixteenth century. It was believed to be one of the biggest hospitals of the Tudor world, and certainly the largest in England. At St Mary Spital, beds were often low to the floor, and were little more than rudimentary, coffin-like square frames in which a person would lie. These truckle beds would have had mattresses stuffed with straw, making the process of cleaning and removing soiled, bodily fluid-soaked hay simple and quick. Despite how they sound, however, sixteenth-century hospitals were generally clean and sanitary, and there was an awareness that bad smells and leaking bodily fluids could lead to the contagion of illnesses.

According to sixteenth-century thought, pleasant smells directly equated to good health and vitality, and as such, hospitals and other places that cared for the sick and infirm in sixteenth-century England would have been fragranced with sweet-smelling rushes that would burst with light, floral scent upon being walked upon. Pouches of dried botanicals would have also been hung in sixteenth-century hospitals, particularly herbs that had medicinal properties like chamomile and ginger. Beds and their linens would have been stripped and washed regularly, and floors and walls washed with lime often to blanche them and kill residual bacteria and viruses. Hospitals even provided bathing tubs for their patients, and, although it is hard to believe, would have served warm, often nutritious, food to their sick. For the most part, medical and germ theories were still in their grassroots in the sixteenth century, and would only be furthered with advances in anatomy and biological understanding in the Renaissance. Although we now consider the sixteenth century to be a stepping stone between the provincial Middle Ages and the glorious Renaissance, it deserves much more credit than we otherwise give; after all, the hospitals of the sixteenth century were not always pleasant, but, ultimately, there were worst places to be.

A hospital dedicated to the care of lepers in the sixteenth century was located in St James's Park in London, close to where the current Buckingham Palace stands today.[8] Then just a flat expanse of forestry and land used by King Henry VIII for hunting purposes, it was intentionally set away from the rest of the city and was walled to protect outsiders from the spread of disease. The hospital was known as the Westminster Leper Hospital, and had a host of structural extensions added to the main building, including a chapel and private lodgings for the richer of its patients. It would have been used by the wealthiest of London society; the merchants, the clergy and the clerks.[9] It was so well regarded for its sufficient medical treatment and provision of the sick, that the chapel on-site became a fashionable meeting point for even the healthiest of rich Westminster residents.

Although inconceivable to us in the twenty-first century, many Tudor hospitals served as cheap accommodation for travellers seeking a warm bed and a hot meal. For those desperate enough, the appeal of a safe place to stay far outweighed the risk of contracting a deadly disease or infection; they just had to learn to drown out the cries of patients who were in great pain and distress, and those who were at death's door. Not every hospital in the sixteenth century provided for the care of physical afflictions, however. St Bethlehem's Hospital in London (later known as 'Bedlam') temporarily and permanently housed those suffering from mental and cognitive disabilities. Although modern historians criticise the sixteenth-century treatment of the mentally unwell, for it was believed that psychological illnesses came about through the will of God, the reality was actually very much different.[10] Although provisions for the clinically mentally ill would not come about until well into the twentieth and twenty-first centuries, psychiatric hospitals in sixteenth-century England were aware of such diseases as depression (known as melancholy), anxiety disorders and other, more serious illnesses like schizophrenia, which was believed to have been caused by an amalgamation of devilish spirits. It may have been provincial, but a basic understanding of psychological disorders certainly existed in the sixteenth century, as evidenced by medical reports of both Queens Mary I and her sister, Elizabeth I, whose melancholy and tendency toward manic spiralling can still be read today.

For the most part, however, sixteenth-century medicine was greatly limited by bottlenecked knowledge passed down through shaky experience rather than medical treatises, and was largely dependent on one's literacy ability and the reliance on old wives' tales. Wrongly prescribed medicinal plants and drugs could be dangerous, and could prove fatal, and were often only prescribed because they physically resembled the ailment that they were intended to treat. Books and medical texts like John Gerard's *Book of Household* remedies contained supposed medical expertise and would have been relied upon by sixteenth-century medical practitioners, unaware that the authors themselves were often ignorant or unqualified. Some medical texts had even been written by women, particularly concerning obstetrics and reproductive health. Considering the stance that many men took toward the education and writings of women in the sixteenth century, this particularly highlights how shaky the medical profession could be in Tudor England.

However, with such monumental events as the discovery of the Americas (which was dubbed 'the New World') in the late sixteenth century by Sir Francis Drake and Walter Raleigh, interest in medicinal botanicals and healing practices rekindled. As well as food, animals, customs and clothing, English explorers returned to the country with newfound knowledge of plants and botanicals, and studies were conducted into these exciting new herbs and their healing properties. The tobacco plant was first brought over to England in 1586 by the Virginia Company, who were anxious to show their families and friends this pungent, flavourful leaf. These leaves could be chewed straight from the plant, or dried and placed at the end of special, handheld pipes for the purpose of smoking. It immediately caught on, and so the habit of smoking was born.

But even more addicting yet was the strange, long, tuber-like stalks the Americans had called 'sugar cane'. The juices of this plant would be heated and distilled, before filtered to create a crystalline white substance known as 'sugar'. The Tudors were hooked. Sugar became a regular part of the daily diet, and was included in hundreds of recipes in which the Tudors would eat in excess. The sugar, which absorbs amino acids and converts them to serotonin, quickly became equated with feelings of happiness and euphoria, and, for the Tudors, whose diets had previously been lacking in such sweet delights, it must have been overwhelming.[11] Even the Queen, Elizabeth I, was addicted, eating candied fruits and flower petals daily and implementing sugar-dusted pastries and sweetmeats into her daily diet.[12]

But newfound addictions to tobacco and sugar did not come without risk. As well as the steady decline in dental health (which, contrary to popular belief, had been very good in centuries preceding the Elizabethan era), many Tudors also developed dangerous new diseases, most notably diabetes, which became prevalent in sixteenth-century England, particularly amongst the wealthier classes who could afford the luxuries of sugar. Tobacco addiction too became an issue for many Tudors who partook in consuming it, and many smokers were beginning to notice ill effects of chesty coughs and shallower breaths. These physiological complaints were greatly undesirable, no less because many fatal respiratory diseases were circulating within England and along the Continent.

Consumption (more commonly known as tuberculosis) was a deadly epidemic in Tudor England, and had claimed many victims. It was believed to have killed Arthur, the Prince of Wales, whose untimely death ushered in the reign of his younger brother, Henry the Duke of York, who ascended to the throne of England in 1509 as King Henry VIII. Its symptoms included dramatic weight loss, breathlessness, bone and joint pain, painful lesions, and, perhaps most terrifyingly of all, the coughing up of bloody sputum. It would not kill you as quickly as the sweating sickness, but once you contracted it you were very likely to die soon after; absolutely no one survived. Consumption was a disease that principally affected the respiratory system, and was spread through the transmission of breath and bodily fluids. It impacted the lymph nodes, and was characterised by aggressive shivering and an increasingly rapid deterioration of mental state. In a similar vein to tuberculosis was malaria, a disease that was prevalent in areas of marshy landscape, most often in places like Kent, Lincolnshire, and along the English coast. This disease, which was spread through the bites of mosquitos, had symptoms very similar to tuberculosis, including great sweating and fever, and could prove just as fatal. Although medical treatments for these diseases have since come about in modern times, the Tudors were not so lucky.

Leprosy was another epidemic which plagued sixteenth-century England. The worrying symptoms of lesions, painful coughing, and sneezing was spread by skin contact, though signs would often not develop until years after initial contact. Unlike the sweating sickness and tuberculosis, leprosy was a silent killer, and many people in sixteenth-century England contracted it without realising, for it lay dormant for so long. By the time individuals were aware that they were suffering from the disease, it was often too late, and the damage had been done.

Respiratory diseases were perhaps the most common and deadly of Tudor illnesses, and anything from diphtheria, meningitis, and streptococcal throat infections could kill entire families within weeks. So too could the horrific disease of dysentery, which was characterised by excessive, bloody diarrhoea and resulted in sufferers losing much of their body mass, leading to death by dehydration. Tapeworms and whipworms were also common complaints, and frequent in many surviving sixteenth-century medical records. Small cuts could lead to big infections, and, with little knowledge of germ theory and blood poisoning in the sixteenth century, could (and regularly did) lead to death. Raw wounds (which included the womb after childbirth) were often treated with sub-par remedies that did more harm than good. Unwashed hands, dirty fingernails, and even the introduction of pests like maggots and leeches could further aggravate the wound site, and often resulted in dangerous and fatal blood infections. It was for this reason, therefore, that many Tudors died from infectious lacerations, rather than of their injuries themselves.

Blood poisoning and infections, now known as septicaemia, were especially common symptoms of the Bubonic Plague (or *yersinia pestis*) which was still in circulation in the sixteenth century, and would continue to be so until 1665. The symptoms of the Bubonic Plague were different to that of the sweating sickness epidemic, and included the swellings of the lymph nodes (known as buboes), pneumonia, and hallucinations. The swelling of the buboes was more common in the summer months, whereas it was more pneumonic in the winter and colder months, and was therefore largely dependent on the status of the weather. But regardless of symptoms, one thing was for sure; no one would survive.

The rapid spreading of the plague was in large part due to the movement of Tudors in sixteenth-century England, which had been more common as advances in transportation were made. When a wealthy family caught wind of a nearby case of plague, it was likely that they would up-sticks and travel further afield to the safety of the countryside to avoid contracting it. However, by this point, the damage had already been done, and this only furthered the spreading of the disease.

Those who died of the plague often dropped where they stood, their bodies only being removed for burial when it was convenient and deemed safe to do so. No one wanted the task of transporting contagious, infected bodies to their burial places for fear of transmission of the disease, but no one wanted to keep a festering body inside the confined spaces of their homes. It was not uncommon for unwitting by-passers to stumble across the corpses of their neighbours and friends left out in the street for collection by dedicated plague wagons that went around communities daily to collect the dead. Although in 1517, the Fraternity of Saint Katherine pledged to keep streets clean of bodies, it was an issue still unresolved even after the death of Elizabeth I in 1603. The seventeenth-century diarist Samuel Pepys, for example, wrote in the summer of 1665 that he, 'met a dead corps of the plague, in the narrow ally just bringing down a little pair of stairs'.[13] Simply put, no one wanted the responsibility of a contagious corpse.

Fear of the plague was so prevalent in the sixteenth century that many families even failed to organise funerary arrangements for their loved ones who had succumbed to it. In the case where multiple family members had died of plague, bodies would have been buried as quickly as possible, even if this meant in non-consecrated ground. Churchyards and burial sites were becoming overwhelmed with the sudden influx of bodies still contagious and who had only been breathing just hours before. As such, mass graves were dug on the outskirts of towns and villages in a desperate attempt to conceal the bodies and to bury the stench of death and decay. There were even records of some Tudors wishing for dignity in death, and who took matters into their own hands; instead of waiting for death to claim them, they would dig their own graves in their gardens and lay in them until death came. What is now just a tale for us was reality for the Tudors, who must have been beyond terrified of what awaited their fates.

*

Upon the street of Blackfriars Lane in London, which ran along the western edge of Bridewell Palace, a residence of Henry VIII, was the Apothecaries Hall. This hall, a meeting place for apothecaries, chemists and medical practitioners in the sixteenth century, produced and manufactured their own drugs and medicine until much of the building was destroyed in the Great Fire of London in 1666. It would not be too much of a stretch to imagine that the Apothecaries Hall would supply the nobility, and even the monarch, with their medicine, and certainly it appears that they were employed in the stocking of medicinal supplies for the voyage of the *Mary Rose* in 1510.

Indeed, in inventories found upon the *Mary Rose*, there is evidence to suggest that suitable provisions had been made for the treatment of diseases and illnesses onboard, including common skin complaints, influenza, and even venereal disease.[14] Cauteries, thick, metal pins that would be scorched and placed on open wounds to cauterise and seal them, were found within the records of onboard surgeons, as were saws, large butchery knives and small, hand-powered mechanical drills that would have been used in the process of limb amputation. Mallets and heavy wooden hammers were also found, but they were not used for construction purposes. Rather, these mallets would have been used as pain relief, literally to 'knock' patients out, and to avoid them waking during surgery. Razors were also found on board, both for shaving purposes, and also for the removal of small metal fragments that would lodge inside the body following explosions.

Ointments and creams too were found onboard the *Mary Rose*, including ten wooden jars containing ointment intended for the soothing of the skin, and five that held a thin, watery type of lotion. Flasks that would have held medicinal waters were recorded alongside mortar and pestles, which were used to grind ingredients to make and dispense drugs. Then came the bleeding bowls, and even smaller razors for blood-letting purposes, as well as a small selection of urethral syringes which would have filled with dangerous substances like mercury and inserted into the urethra for the treatment of venereal diseases. Dogs too were found onboard the *Mary Rose*. Although we would now consider the inclusion of dogs in medical treatments both unhygienic and rather bizarre, it was believed in the sixteenth century that animals had great healing properties. The Tudors believed in the existence of the 'animus', a ghostly figure of deceased animals like dogs, hares and deers that were believed to cure wounds and ailments, and 'temper' the humours by crossing through the mortal body of the inflicted. More practically, small lap dogs were used as a form of heat compress in the sixteenth century, with one chronicler, William Harrison, even prescribing the application of a small dog to chests and stomachs in order to alleviate stomach pains and upset, and menstrual cramping.[15]

Chronic illness such as irritable bowel syndrome was to some extent managed by these rudimentary practices, and sufferers benefited from the consumption of medicinal herbs and application of poultices. For those whose disabilities required more permanent solutions, however, solutions were also, surprisingly, available in the sixteenth century. Walking canes and even wheelchairs existed in Tudor England, and there were even rumours that the ailing, obese King Henry VIII had to rely on their services to be transported around his palatial residences in his later years. According to Tudor historian David Starkey, Henry had been forced to rely on wheeled chairs known as 'thrones on wheels' due to his decreasing mobility.[16] For the vast majority of ordinary people in sixteenth-century England, however, wheeled 'thrones' would have been known simply as trams, and would resemble a kind of high-backed armchair most likely made from a sturdy, but lightweight material like wicker, that had small wheels attached to the feet of its legs. This meant that users could be easily assisted by a helper, or were given the autonomy to do so themselves. Certainly, the disabled members of sixteenth-century England were not limited in their prospects and in their mobility; rather, they were certainly anything but.

Chapter 4

The Bathroom

'Rise, now victorious, health is now at hand,
One labour more is all I shall command,
Easy and pleasant; you must last prepare
Your bath, with rosemary and lavender'.
  Girolamo Fracastoro, *Syphilis, or a Poetical
  History of the French Disease*, 1530.[1]

There was no such concept as a bathroom for the majority of Tudor society, at least, not until the latter end of the sixteenth century. Bathrooms, as we know them today, are clean, airy spaces dedicated to one's hygiene and cleanliness; a place where sweet-smelling products and lotions and creams and pastes proliferate the shelves and cabinets. We expect our bathrooms to be installed with decent plumbing, supplying us with clean, fresh water at the twist of a handle or the push of a flush. We can expect our bathrooms to be heated with radiators, perhaps even built into the walls and floors. Our showers and baths come with waterproof tiles, scalding hot water, even perhaps luxurious attachments like power-shower heads and bubble jets. But, perhaps most importantly of all, our modern bathrooms allow us a luxury our Tudor ancestors could not afford – privacy.

For the Tudors, only the wealthiest, or luckiest of society could afford dedicated rooms in which to bathe. For the majority of sixteenth-century English society, bathrooms amalgamated with bedrooms and living spaces, and often toileting and bathing took place in the same room as one slept, worked, or even ate. Indeed, some Tudors may have even warmed their bath water by the same fire in which their family member was cooking! So, the term 'bath room' seems redundant when talking about Tudor houses. Doors did not become the norm in the houses of the lowest classes until at least the seventeenth century, and so one could expect intruders while attending to the most intimate of duties.

Neither, could a Tudor rely on the privacy of blinds or curtains – rather, they would have to hope that their thin, greased oil-cloth, or wooden shutters, would do the trick to keep out pesky onlookers.

Tudor 'bathrooms' were, effectively, portable. From baths to toilets, the Tudors could move these hygiene commodities from room to room, or even place them outside if they so wished. A Tudor would probably not have recognised a modern-day bath, sleek, probably with a glass screen or waterproof curtain, or shower attachments that rain warm water onto the bather below. For the Tudors, bathtubs were deep, low-set barrel-like objects, often wide enough to accommodate more than one body. They were most often round, and, like barrels, were slicked with waterproofing. Baths were portable, and could be carted wherever their owner wished. This meant, that in periods of cold weather especially, having a bath in front of the fireplace was an attractive and popular thing to do. Baths could also be taken outdoors, if the bather did so wish.

In the palaces of the royal family, warm water flowed from installed piping, and was heated from cisterns that were steadily and continuously heated by boilers and warmed by fires.[2] Houses in London had running water brought into the home via conduits. One conduit, built by the gentleman Bevis Bulmer in 1594 was supported by charitable donations raised by Londoners, and fed into the houses that lined West Cheap, St Pauls and Fleet Street.[3] Lady Ascue, the widow of Sir Christopher Ascue, donated £100 to the construction and maintenance of water conduits in London in 1543, as did Edward Jackman, a sheriff, in 1564.[4] Bernard Randulph, a wealthy sergeant, gave £900 to the construction of water conduits in 1583.[5] Rainwater collected in butts would also be used in the washing of hands and faces, for it was considered purer than the water collected from streams and rivers.

Soap was a commodity in Tudor England, and, contrary to popular belief, was available to purchase or simple to make yourself. Lombard Street in London was home to Italian merchants who brought over dyes and soaps. Between 1562 and 1642, there were one hundred and eighty soap-makers and traders recorded in the 'Bristol Company of Soap-makers', which specialised in the production of 'Bristol Black Soap' and 'Bristol Grey Soap', which was harder, and tougher on stubborn stains.[6] These soaps in particular were more effective than white soaps, which were typically used for the body, whereas black soap would have been used for laundry and domestic cleaning purposes. These cakes of soap would have been sold for one penny per pound. Castile soap would have also been used in the sixteenth century, though it was considered more luxurious than the rest, for it was made with olive oil from Castile in Spain, and resulted in the skin feeling silky and soft.

Fifteenth-century 'sopehouses' began popping up across England, and there was a street in Cheapside, London, dedicated to the production and manufacture of soap, known as 'Soper's Lane'. It would have been manufactured, marketed and sold on this street. White soap was a relatively safe product to use, and was made from a mixture of fern ash, unslaked lime (calcium oxide), and tallow, a form of animal fat.[7] Unslaked lime was also known as 'quicklime', which could be dangerous for human use. It often caused severe irritation and skin complaints, for it was a caustic substance, but this was only in cases where it was used in excess. For most bars of soap in the sixteenth century, only a minimal amount of unslaked lime would have been used so as not to cause a negative skin reaction. Quicklime, a substance recognised by fans of true crime and detective novels, was often used over corpses, particularly of those who had died from contagious diseases like the plague, for it would prevent the odours of putrefaction and reduce the spread of bad miasmas, which were believed to carry disease in itself.

Although quicklime is often believed to have been used to destroy skeletal remains and render the remains unrecognisable, the opposite was often the case. Quicklime actually helped to preserve bodies, rather than wear away at the natural material of the bone, and it was considered a necessary ingredient in the disposal of bodies, particularly in those who could not afford a proper burial, or who were buried in shallow and rudimentary graves. The remains of the fifth queen of Henry VIII, Catherine Howard, were believed to have been destroyed by quicklime, in an attempt to conceal the clandestine manner of her death.[8] Rather, it appears more likely that the Queen, who was accorded no coffin, was instead covered in an inestimable amount of quicklime, a chemical compound known for its hygiene purposes, simply in order to prevent the decay and the smells that came with it. But, ultimately, it is something which we shall never know for sure.

The quicklime included in sixteenth-century soap recipes was certainly not enough to cause skeletal damage, let alone skin damage, for the concentration was simply too low to cause any significant reaction. The ingredients – the ash, the lime, and the tallow, as well as any additional ingredients the manufacturer wished to include in their recipe, such as lavender, verbena, or other fragrant herbs, or even such things as ground nuts for its abrasive qualities, would have been heated and melted together, then left to thicken and cool in cakes of soap. These would then be cut, most often into bars, and sold for whatever price the vendor saw fit.[9]

Cloth rags would have been used for cleaning purposes – both domestic and bodily, on the skin and on the teeth.[10] Toothpicks would have been used in lieu of floss, as did straw, twigs or sponge. Mint leaves and other fragrant herbs may have been chewed or made into a paste to ensure freshness of breath. Salt and pumice, or even ground fish bones, could also be used as a rudimentary toothpaste, yet these were abrasive and could cause damage to the teeth and gums. Chalk dust and alabaster would have been used for teeth whitening purposes, and mouthwashes would have been created from wine, honey, vinegar or water mixed with fragrant herbs. Throughout the day, should a Tudor wish to freshen their breath, they would reach for kissing comfits, akin to modern-day gum, which would have freshened the breath.

Cloth rags known as 'wallops' would have also been used more intimately by women, who relied on them to create rudimentary absorptive pads for their menstruations. These makeshift pads were not always reliable, however, and were greatly uncomfortable. The Tudors did not wear underwear briefs as we do today, and as such there was nothing to suspend the pads and keep them close to the vagina. Some historians suggest that to combat this, rudimentary belts that would be strapped under and around the groin of a menstruating woman and used to tack the pads in place.[11] Others have suggested that the cloths would have simply been placed inside the vagina in order to soak up any blood. Wool, natural sponge, and even moss have all been suggested as rudimentary precursors to the modern-day tampon.[12] These cloths would then be washed for future use, or entirely discarded.

There is often a belief that in the sixteenth century, women simply did not experience menstruation as we do today, with the modern introduction of trustworthy and reliable contraception, paired with a longer span before reaching the age of menopause (that many historians believe that the Tudors did not often hit, since they would have died before they could reach their late middle age). Historians, like Sarah Bryson, too have suggested sixteenth-century women spent the majority of their lives pregnant or breastfeeding, naturally prolonging durations between menstrual cycles.[13] Elizabeth Woodville, the grandmother of King Henry VIII, for example, gave birth to twelve infants in a span of twenty-three years. Each of these twelve infants she had carried to term, meaning that, for at least nine months of the year, Elizabeth's menstrual cycle had ceased. Overall, this meant that Elizabeth probably experienced very few menstrual cycles compared to the modern-day woman.

Menstrual complaints were common in the sixteenth century just as they are today, and many notable figures, including Queen Mary I and her mother, Queen Katherine of Aragon, experienced great pains and irregular periods throughout their lives. Katherine's menstrual cycle, it was believed, had been affected by her regular bouts of fasting for devotional purposes, which many modern commentators have described as an eating disorder.[14] For Mary, however, her menstrual difficulties were caused by something much more serious. It was believed by modern commentators that Mary I had suffered from some kind of uterine disorder that had affected her reproductive system, and had caused the growth of cancerous cysts upon her ovaries. This resulted in horrific menstrual pains and great bleeding, now commonly known as dysmenorrhea. Her 'old disease', which had been troubling her since mid-adolescence, was believed to have been the foundation for Mary's difficulties in conceiving, as well as, more famously, the cause behind her phantom pregnancies, in which her abdomen swelled and her menstrual bleeding ceased. Mary's body was exhibiting signs of pregnancy, and the Queen was convinced of her condition, as were those around her, who witnessed the growth of her belly as well as other physiological changes such as hormonal mood imbalances. It is quite likely that Mary suffered from endometriosis, a condition only recently understood, in which the lining of the uterus grows in other parts of the endocrine system, as well as a pre-menstrual disorder, evidenced by her erratically changing mood cycles, for which she was prescribed, 'a more expensive diet and the freedom to take copious amount of exercise'.[15]

Pre-menstrual disorders did certainly appear to affect the menstruating women of the sixteenth century, whose rudimentary period care must have made an already uncomfortable time even more so. Pain relief in the form of ceramic water jugs heated on the fire did provide some comfort and pain relief to these women, as did the ingestion of herbs such as mint, tansy and lavender boiled in milk, all of which are still natural pain relief methods for menstruation today.

Superstition toward menstruating females in the sixteenth century certainly did exist, much as it still does now in many places of the undeveloped world. It was believed that the breath of a menstruating woman, for example, would cause open wounds to moulder and fester, an unfair superstitious belief that had carried over from the patriarchal Middle Ages.[16] It was also believed that a woman experienced the pains and discomfort of menstruation and pregnancy as a punishment for the sins committed by Eve in the Bible, for which every female descendent of the couple would be punished. For the most part, however, women appear to have handled their menstrual cycles with great care in the sixteenth century, and would have kept themselves clean, dry and administer pain relief if they so needed.

*

With the rise in population figures toward the latter end of the Tudor Age, the previously effective designs of multi-storey buildings within cramped cities became problematic. Although sanitation was also improving with more modern inventions and an understanding of germ theory, sewage undoubtedly rose as more and more people flooded the streets and filled the homes of already packed cities. As the number of city residents grew, so too did the need for public toilets. Contrary to popular belief, public toilets did exist in the sixteenth century, and were accessible to the everyday working man, woman and child who trawled through packed cities and bustling towns in search of a place to relieve themselves. 'Houses of Easement' were public toilets that would fit around fourteen people, and would be found around cities, particularly over rivers, streams, cesspits and enclosed sewers. Tower Bridge in London even had its own set of outhouses for use by the public, whose waste would be dropped into the River Thames below.[17]

One sewage system flowed beneath the cobbles of Fleet Street in London, and into the River Thames, a place also used by Londoners for bathing, tanning (the manufacture of animal skin), butchery, laundry, machinery and engineering, and waste disposal.[18] The sewage system was connected to a street-long communal latrine known as 'Whittington's Long House' (named after the Mayor of London, Richard

'Dick' Whittington), which was split in half and divided for use by both sexes often at the same time. Same-sex public toilets were fashionable in England until well into the eighteenth century, and it was only during the reigns of the Georgians that they were finally divided into dedicated gender cubicles. It may be considered provincial to us in the twenty-first century, yet these were the precursors of our modern-day inventions.

By the end of Queen Elizabeth I's reign, it was estimated that there were around 180,000 public toilets (not open cesspits, as is commonly accepted in traditional history) in London alone.[19] Indeed, waste disposal engineering had reached new heights in the sixteenth century; remarkably, the first flushing toilet had been invented by Sir John Harington in 1596, almost three whole centuries before Thomas Crapper patented his design in 1880.[20] Colloquially, these flushing toilets became known as 'ajax', where a circular bowl was cleverly designed to collect any bodily waste and flush it down a drain by a cistern of around eight gallons of water.

Lavatories were also known as 'close stools', and were a kind of toilet afforded only by the rich. Characterised by their silk or velvet trimmed cushioned seat, these commode-like toilets were built upon a hollow cube in which a pewter bowl would be placed inside. This pewter bowl would then be emptied after every bodily movement, sometimes by the user themselves, or, more likely, by their poor servants. Garderobes, however, were cheaper forms of toilet, and would be found in the gardens, sheds, or ditches of the vast majority of sixteenth-century homes. They were built into outhouses, small wooden shacks set outdoors that were often built over pits or plumbing networks to dispose of waste. Within these outhouses would be a wooden bench built above a draughty wooden or stone shaft. In the houses of the richer, who could afford to have their garderobes installed within the walls of their home (similar to a modern-day airing cupboard), these shafts would be installed within chutes that evacuated into open cesspits or bodies of water – such as a moat – below. The garderobes of the rich would be fitted with comfortable furnishings, like soft cushions and wall hangings to insulate them from the chilly draughts that floated up the shaft. For the vast majority of people, however, garderobes were cold, smelly, uncomfortable places, and it is probably not too much of a stretch to imagine that people were loath to use them. Spiders and other insects were common inhabitants of the garderobe, which was also used by distant family relatives and even neighbours, as outhouses typically would have been shared by whole families or, unpleasantly, by the entire street.

Tudor toilet paper was a far cry from its modern-day descendent. Now purposely designed to break down within sewage pipes to avoid clogs and overflowing, the Tudors had to make do with compostable items that would naturally decompose. It is common belief that the Tudors had to forage for their own toilet paper, turning to leaves and moss to wipe away bodily fluids. In reality, they would have used offcuts of linen and other cheap and accessible materials like wool, which would have naturally broken down in the environment over time. The use of linen came with an added bonus – it was reusable, and would have been thrown in a pot of water ready to be boiled and washed for the next use. How many people reused their toilet paper is difficult to say for certain, and it must not have been a very pleasant experience, yet the use of cotton scraps for toilet paper was still used until relatively recently, and even now there is an emerging trend in the popularity of reusable cloth products such as toilet paper, menstrual pads and baby nappies to wick away bodily fluids. That the Tudors did not wipe after using the toilet or were forced to rely on scratchy vegetation is an entirely modern concept; the reality was instead completely different.

*

Chatelaine sets, similar to a modern Swiss army knife, were small, personal items that had numerous metal instruments hanging from it, which owners used to prune themselves.[21] These would have been pocket-sized and portable, and ideal for touching up one's appearance on the go. Usually, chatelaine sets would have consisted of an ear-scoop, intended for the removal of ear wax and snot, as well as tweezers for the removal of unruly hairs. Tiny metal picks would have been used as toothpicks, to remove dirt from beneath the nail, and to smooth the edges of cuticles. Most would also be equipped with a nail file or trimmer, which would have worn away hangnails and jagged, rough nail edges as modern nail files do today. Some chatelaines even came with tiny scissors should their owner ever find themselves in need of a hair trim.

Healthy hair was a symbol of youth, vitality and beauty in sixteenth-century England, and was reflective of a balanced lifestyle. For those who could not grow their own hair, or whose hair had begun to thin in later life, wigs made from real human hair would have been weaved to specific styles and fitted to the head. However, due to the connotations of healthy hair in Tudor England, many people in the sixteenth century were loath to cutting their hair and donating their locks for the manufacture of wigs. As such, wigmakers relied instead on the hair of the dead, trimming and shaving whole handfuls of hair from the corpses of deceased Tudors before they were buried. This was such a common practice in sixteenth-century England, that it was only during periods of plague where the purchase of wigs was at an all-time low, for 'nobody will dare to buy any haire, for fear of the infection, that it had been cut off to the heads of people dead of the plague', according to the Jacobean diarist Samuel Pepys.[22] The Tudors preferred hair tones of blond, auburn and red as opposed to brunette. Indeed, light-haired Tudors were celebrated in awe by visiting foreign dignitaries and envoys, who wrote that, 'the English are, for the most part, both men and women of all ages, handsome and well-proportioned', though, when it came to hair, 'the Scots are much handsomer'.[23]

*

The Tudors, both male and female, abided by beauty regimes just as we do today. For the most part, the Tudors did not use glass mirrors, despite being invented sometime in the 1100s – rather, they would have used highly polished metal surfaces, or simply their reflections in windows and bodies of water.[24] Tiny pocket mirrors made from polished metal may have been carried by the Tudors or installed on the walls of their homes; glass, silvered mirrors as we know them today only became commonplace in domestic settings during the eighteenth century.

Commonplace too were linen towels, known as 'rubbers', for the purpose of skin and hair hygiene, where individuals would 'dry wash' their bodies by scrubbing at their skin with cloths. According to social historian Ruth Goodman, rubbers worked efficiently in creating feelings of bodily cleanliness, as well as removing unwanted oils and smells from the body.[25] Towels and bathrobes were also commonly found in the bathrooms of Tudor England, for people to both dry and warm themselves with. The Tudor home could certainly be very cold, especially in the winter months, and as such make-shift heaters would be placed in bathrooms that were made from ceramic pots filled with warm coal. These pots also doubled up as hot water bottles and as personal comforters.[26] This meant that bathrooms could be warm, without the need to light open fires that would fill the air with smoke and ash. The Tudors could bathe and dry themselves adequately, contrary to much traditionalist historical belief.

So too did the Tudors take diligent care of their teeth. Wooden, bone and feather toothpicks have all appeared in sixteenth-century household inventories, as well as linen tooth cloths, and poultices of cumin and aniseed for mouth freshening. There have even been recorded cases of white wine mixed with sulphuric acid as a form of early mouthwash – yet, unknown to the Tudors, this could be a very dangerous and life-threatening concoction. Eventually, with the introduction of sugar in the latter half of the sixteenth century, tooth care began to take a slow decline. Dental hygiene became less easy to keep up with, for the Tudors were now forced to battle with tooth rot caused by diets excess in sugar. Unaware of the health hazards of sugar, the Tudors even used it to clean their teeth, making sugar water mouth rinse, as well as toothpaste. The Tudors also turned to so-called 'kissing comfits', small, sugared fruits, herbs or flowers, that were intended to freshen the mouth and breath.[27] Of course, these methods only exacerbated tooth rot and decay, and so desperate Tudors were forced to turn to other remedies for the removal of plaque, the whitening of teeth, and the freshening of the breath. Ground coral and other seashells, as well as stones like pumice, were used in vain attempts to keep the mouth clean. But as well as causing painful damage to gums, many of these methods only sped up tooth decay and led to agonising toothaches or wobbling teeth.

When the pain got too much, the Tudors could always be rest assured of a visit to the nearest hospital. There were five hospitals in London in the 1530s, each with around 400 sick beds.[28] However, despite the generous amount of beds, these hospitals were not wholly dedicated to the sick or infirm – rather, those suffering from medical complaints often shared halls with the outcasts of society; the orphans, the poor, the elderly, travellers, unmarried mothers, women in childbirth and in active labour, beggars, the blind, and the insane. Although they did offer medical assistance, it was often a common sight for Tudor hospitals to have on-site bakeries, fisheries and other methods of food production. The majority of hospitals even had small chapels attached to their wards, as well as outhouses, studies and recreation rooms often split by gender.[29]

One particular hospital, made notorious for the patients it treated, was equipped with all of these amenities. It was called Bethlehem, and was located in London. In later years, it became notorious as a 'madhouse' and earned the name 'Bedlam', a word which came to characterise the mentally unwell, and was used by sixteenth-century Tudors to describe states of confusion, fear and panic.

The treatment of the mentally unwell was far from adequate in the sixteenth century, and many patients complained of harsh conditions, cruel treatments, great overcrowding, and poor sanitation. Conditions were so unsatisfactory, that the city of Norwich was forced to issue the Orders of the Poor in 1571, as reports of social outcasts flooded in, complaining of 'the cold [which] stuck so deep into them their flesh [which] was eaten with vermin and corrupt diseases [that] grew on them…'[30] Despite this, sanitation standards in Norwich hospitals little improved, as did they elsewhere, and patients and practitioners alike were forced to petition the King for reforms in hygiene and medicine. One such petition, sent to the Court of Appeals under King Henry VIII in 1538, complained of 'the miserable people lying in the streete, offending every clene person passing by the way with they're fylthye and nasty savors'.[31]

Indeed, Tudor London was probably full of 'nasty savors' and smells, especially in built-up, densely populated areas. In an attempt to alleviate poor sanitation, warrants were issued in 1502 and 1589 to drain and scour the Thames of waste and sediment. The operation failed on both attempts, so much so that it became 'worse cloyed and choken than ever it was before' with soilage.[32] Amongst the dregs of the Thames were found animal bones, discarded rubbish, and even human bodies. That Londoners bathed, did their laundry, and even sourced household water from the Thames, therefore, seems inconceivable. Yet, at locations like Aldwych in London, rivers, streams and even holy wells were purposely littered and allowed to build up with manure and other such waste in order to establish 'garden-plots', according to the contemporary chronicler John Stow.[33] These early forms of compost heaps eventually led to the creation of communal allotments, where Tudors could retrieve mulch to fertilise their crops. Management of a waste heap was actually a relatively lucrative job, and was given its own title of 'gong farmer'. Records of gong farmers appear throughout sixteenth-century city accounts; in a ditch near Aldgate in 1519, for example, gong farmers were paid 1 penny a day, as well as given free meat and drink for their work, plus whatever valuables they may have found amongst the waste which they could later sell for a profit.[34]

For the most part, however, gong farmers very rarely came across anything of worth within rubbish pits. It was not uncommon to spot fruit stones and vegetable stalks, discarded nut shells, bits of smashed glass and torn fabric, old straw and linens (which were often used for the absorption of bodily fluids), as well as animal bones, particularly those belonging to rodents. Human hair, discarded shoes and other articles of clothing would also regularly be found, as well as toxic bodily waste like human and animal faeces and blood. There have even been records of stillborn infants discarded in rubbish tips.[35] As such, it is not too difficult to imagine that these pits would have been the homes of many unwanted pests and parasites. Fleas, lice and ticks lived nestled amongst the heaps, and were even found upon articles of clothing and within combs centuries later by modern archaeologists excavating known sixteenth-century waste sites.[36]

But unpleasant images of dung heaps and gong farmers aside, how far is it true for us to consider the Tudors lax in their hygiene standards? To what extent did they keep their homes clean? Housework was the dedicated job of the females of the house, and keeping the Tudor home clean certainly was a challenge. The floors of most houses in the Tudor period were made either of wood or brick, but some were entirely earthen. To combat dust and damp, the Tudors would place rushes upon the floor, sweet-smelling grasses which would burst open with fragrance and perfume when one walked upon them:

> Narrow city streets and muddy country lanes, paired with the English weather, led to a 'vast amount of evil-smelling mud [to be] formed...the citizens, therefore, in order to remove mud and filth from their boots, are accustomed to spread fresh rushes on the floors of all houses.[37]

These rushes could be strewn sporadically, or were sometimes laced in a matted design, allowing for the absorption of spillages and lessening the risk of trip hazards and rogue rushes catching alight. Rushes were a fantastic, hygienic flooring option for Tudor homeowners, particularly if they had children or kept livestock, for they could absorb anything from blood, grease and urine, and could be easily removed and cheaply replaced on a regular basis, usually annually or bi-annually. Of course, not every house would have replaced their rushes with such frequency, leading to eventual smells, dampness and vermin infestations according to Ruth Goodman, but for the most part, they were particularly effective.[38] Carpets as we know them did not exist in Tudor England as floor décor – rather, rugs made from ornate and expensive material like finely-milled wool would have been used to bring warmth to the home. Given the expensive nature of rugs, they were reserved only for the most exciting of occasions, and most likely did not line the floor of a Tudor home throughout the year. Rather, it was considered much more practical to line furniture with carpet scraps, where it could be appreciated better and would attract less dirt from footfall.

Cleaning and maintaining wooden floors and scrubbing brick or clay tiles is a difficult task even today, but for the Tudors, it was even more taxing. Scrubbing brushes and broomsticks would be dipped in water (sometimes scented with fragrant botanicals or oils) and used as an abrasive to clean the floor. It was a back-breaking job, so, if a household could afford to employ a servant, the job was usually reserved for them. Housewives and servants in Tudor England would have needed considerable strength to have been able to even carry cleaning apparatus; water, which did not flow freely in the majority of houses, was sourced from pumps, streams and rivers, and would have been incredibly heavy to carry home, especially if they were a considerable distance away from the building. Tudor housewives would have made frequent trips to water sources during their daily routines, ensuring never to waste a drop, even if it meant bathing in the same water as would later be used to clean the home.

Water was the staple in cleaning the Tudor home, and little could be done without it. Sweet-smelling, naturally antibacterial and antiseptic ingredients would be added to the water to create products akin to modern-day commercial cleansers. Citrus, particularly lemon, was a favourite, as was mint, lavender, witch-hazel and other fragrant herbs that were often grown in carefully-maintained herb patches specifically for their scents and properties. Some of these herbs, like thyme and clove, were antifungal, while others like mint were antimicrobial. If a household's budget could afford it, cleaning products would have also been infused with the properties of more expensive ingredients like cinnamon, chives and garlic. Although these unusual scents would not typically be found in the cleaning caddies of modern households today, they nevertheless got the job done, their antibacterial and antimicrobial properties eliminating any risk of contamination, visible dirt, and unpleasant odours.

The cleaning of the kitchen was perhaps the biggest workload a Tudor housewife may endure within the household. Scouring was laborious, and could be quite dangerous given the abrasive nature of the ingredients. Anything from eating utensils, dairy urns and coats of armour were scoured, often with sand or with salt, in order to remove residue and grime. However, more dangerous abrasives like caustic quicklime would be used, damaging not only the surfaces to which they were applied, but also causing averse, even deadly, skin reactions for the user. Nevertheless, the Tudors certainly did wash their dishes, eating, and drinking utensils, most often with long brushes, natural sponges, or herbs like horsetail (so-called named for what it resembles), to reach difficult angles and scour away any stubborn stains.

Laundry was a task that the wealthy did not have to endure, employing washerwomen and servants to launder, iron, and fold their clothes. For the majority of Tudor England, however, laundry was a back-breaking slog. It was a chore endured as often as a household depended on the need for clean clothing; some families would have done their laundry daily, some weekly; some may have even waited longer. For the most part, though, washing baskets would fill up quickly, so it was common for laundry washing to take place almost every day. Body linen (Tudor underwear) would have been changed daily, or sometimes more often in the case of infants or those working in difficult, sweaty labouring roles. For those in society who regularly visited friends or who took particular pride in their appearance, changing one's clothes could take place numerous times a day.

Bedsheets, linen towels, menstrual rags, baby nappies, even teeth-cloths would have been thrown into the 'bucking' pot, a large barrel or bowl wide enough to accommodate the laundry. Clothes would be brushed, then placed in the wooden baths filled with gallons of boiling water, before then being agitated with a stirring-stick known as a 'beetle' or a 'washing dolly'. The use of the 'dolly', a long stick that had wooden pegs on its end, would have been laborious, heavy and difficult work. Women would often spend hours at laundry, preparing the baths, agitating the dirty items of laundry, and then hanging the heavy, waterlogged clothing on high branches or dedicated laundry drying lines. If a family had many members, or a washerwoman was employed on behalf of a lot of different customers, it could be back-breaking, thirsty work for the process would have had to be repeated, the water boiled fresh each time.

Once agitated, the water would then be added to a mixture of lye and other herbs, producing an alkaline solution that could burn hands terribly if ingredients were measured incorrectly. Solid soap known as 'black-soap' would be used, a mixture of lye and animal fat, which had been distilled at high temperatures. Washerwomen would beat at the laundry, or spin it using long rods, akin to modern-day washing machines. For stubborn stains, the use of moss or ash would have been scrubbed into the article; if the stain still did not budge, it was just tough luck – either the washerwoman would try desperately again at removing it, or they would try their best to conceal it in other ways, perhaps with dyes. Alternatively, powders known as 'sweet powders' were used as an early form of laundry detergent, and would have been made from a mixture of lye for bleaching, sweet-smelling herbs for aromatics, and manufactured black soap that was commercially marketed and sold for the sole use of stain removals. Firepans, or heated, flat slabs of iron would be used for the ironing out of creases of clothes and decorative fabrics. So too were they also used for the straightening of human hair.[39]

Doing laundry in the sixteenth century was largely dependent on the weather outdoors, which, as Englishwomen lamented, could be problematic. Unless you had an airy house large enough to dry clothing indoors, close to the fire but not too close to avoid smoke and soot getting onto the freshly-washing clothes, you were forced to rely on the scarce dry weather and hope to avoid rain spells. If the weather was poor, and rain was gathering overhead a housewife would have to wait until it was dry enough for her laundry to completely and sufficiently dry out. For the poorest in society, who often owned only a few articles of clothing, this could mean the reuse of clothing for days, unable to change and wash them due to the weather. This was particularly difficult in the winter, where the frost and general dampness of the air meant that clothing would not dry fully, and thus people were forced to wear dirty clothes, or damp ones, unless they had the luxury of large, warm, airy interior spaces or a varied wardrobe.

Clean laundry would be hung outside or in, from rafters and beams, or from tree branches. On windy days, a Tudor housewife would have been anxious to ensure that none of her clothing floated away, and hence used rudimentary pegs whittled from tree branches. Hanging laundry out to dry in the open air had additional benefits – the sunlight could bleach the materials, perfect for lessening evidence of stubborn stains, while the freshness of the air left a sweet scent. Some people did not have this option, however, and were forced to hang their clothes indoors, or above residential areas from townhouse jetties. This was not always ideal – the freshly-washed clothes would attract smells of smoke and cooking food, and could quickly get stained again. A washerwoman's lot, it seemed, was never done.

White linen was important for respectability. No one wanted to mix with people who wore stained, discoloured body linen, and thus bleaching was encouraged. To achieve this, urine would occasionally be applied to the soiled fabric, or soap applied with a feather or brush for tough spots.[40] Water in which peas had been boiled was also an effective and favoured method of stain-removal in sixteenth-century England. But, if all else failed, housewives were forced to accept that they would never erase the stubborn stains, convert their old underwear into rags for use around the home (or perhaps, to clean their teeth!), and take another trip to the seamstress in the market. Clothes would most usually be washed in cold water, which proved tricky for more expensive and denser fabrics like silk or wool, or garments that had been dyed with colour. If the coloured dyes ran in the laundry water, it would mean another trip to the herbalist or to the seamstress to re-colour the clothes in the hope of restoring them to their former appearance.

Although Tudor standards of hygiene and sanitation may not have been as sufficient, effective or as safe as they are today, there was no doubt that the Tudors tried their best to keep clean. For the most part, the Tudors were houseproud and made sure to 'clene [their houses] from tyme to tyme and as oftyn as nede shall require', as well as maintain hygiene and beauty routines that formed much of the precedent of our own regimes today.[41]

Chapter 5

The Kitchen

There hath been much more time spent in eating and drinking than commonly is in these days … we had breakfast in the forenoon, beverages of nunchions after dinner, and thereto rear suppers generally when it was time to go to rest'.

William Harrison on Food and Drink, *The Description of Elizabethan England,* 1577.[1]

The kitchen was truly the heart of the Tudor home. Centuries of innovation had culminated in the creation of an entire space dedicated to food and eating, and the dining room eventually became an all-important extension to the rest of the home, vital in escaping the smells of cooking, and the noise of the kitchen. Those who could afford dedicated dining rooms could also probably afford kitchen staff, and hence kitchens became considered 'servile' spaces well up into the twentieth century.

Most sixteenth-century homes, particularly those of the rich, would have dedicated compartments in their kitchens intended to store different types of food. Spiceries, which, as they sounded, were small stores of spices that were common in dry nooks of the kitchen. Although it seems unusual to us today, spiceries in sixteenth-century kitchens were perhaps one of the most important aspects of the dining areas, for they held the prized possessions of seasonings and spices which were expensive luxuries in the sixteenth century. Cinnamon, for example, which was brought over from the New World, would cost a month's wages.[2] The majority of fragrant herbs and spices would be bundled and dried from ceilings, not only acting as a way to preserve them, but also as a way to freshen the room. In an age where even salt and pepper were valuable commodities, dedicated storage for such things as cinnamon, ginger and clove was of great importance to the Tudors. Most of the poorer population of sixteenth-century England had never even tasted seasonings and spices such as saffron or sugar, let alone owned some for themselves. As such, those whose houses had dedicated spiceries must have been very impressive indeed.

The Tudors loved flavour, and spices were used to bring much-needed taste to otherwise largely bland dishes. Spiced bread loaves, ginger biscuits and even aromatic milk flavoured with cinnamon would have been treats for the sweet-toothed Tudors. As well as spiceries, many wealthier Tudors had dedicated areas of their kitchens called sauceries, which, as the name suggested, were spaces where sauces, soups and pottages (a sort of thick, porridge-like stew most often made with meat, vegetables and grains) were cooked up and stored. Larders, cold, dark rooms or nooks that were found in the majority of sixteenth-century houses, were traditionally used to store dairy products like cheese, cream and eggs and other quick-to-perish foodstuffs. Larders were also used to store freshly butchered meat and fish, and were kept as cool as possible in order to prevent its decomposition. In an age before refrigeration, it was the pantry that was perhaps one of the most vital and important rooms in the entire Tudor home.

Keeping a kitchen cool was of utmost importance to the Tudors. Kitchens, writes architectural historian Simon Thurley, would have most often been located on the colder end of a house, the side which received less sunlight.[3] His reasoning for this suggestion was that the kitchen, a room in which would naturally get hot throughout the course of the day, would create its own heat, while other rooms intended for living quarters remained cold and draughty. For these rooms to get the natural heat of the sun, therefore, would be a benefit, while simultaneously keeping kitchens and their foodstuffs cold and fresh.

Perishables did only mean edible foodstuffs in the sixteenth century, however. We now, having the luxury of electricity, need not worry about the preservation of certain types of items around our homes, but for the Tudors, whose reliance on cold larders could only take them so far, finding ways to preserve perishables of all kinds was key. Perishables included such things as herbs, aromatic flowers, spices and flour, which were often preyed upon by intrusive weevils who rendered the ingredients unusable. So too was such items as charcoal and candles considered perishable, for they were used regularly, usually daily, and were made of natural ingredients that would eventually wear down. Candles (which would often be made from animal or vegetable fat) would often exude smells of fat and drippings. They could be, if you were brave or hungry enough, potentially edible, though probably not very tasty. Sixteenth-century candles would often melt and moulder if left for a long time, and coal, which emitted a sulphurous smell if left for a long time in the open air, would often crack and crumble, rendering it useless. Even clothing was considered perishable in the sixteenth century, and it was common for linen and leather clothing in particular to fall prey to moths and weevils. Leather, particularly if sodden, would eventually break down and grow mould, and as such, the Tudors aimed to keep their precious clothing stored away in beautifully carved clothing chests and wardrobes, and often scented with small bags of lavender, or other pest-repellent scents.

Unlike larders, which were kept as cold as possible, pantries were encouraged to stay dry for they would be used to store products like grains and salted, dehydrated foods. Salt was a surprising way in which the Tudors could keep their food fresh and preserved, and as such, it was bought in large quantities for use in the salting of meats and fish. Once salted, these meats were usually smoked, the salt forming a crust that added extra flavouring. Meat, fish and poultry would also be cooked through a process known as 'scalding', similar to blanching today, where the meat would be plucked, gutted, de-scaled and boiled. The best cuts of meat in the sixteenth century could be very expensive, and as such most poorer citizens had to rely on offcuts or offal, the viscera of the animal. Despite how it sounded, the Tudors relished offal, and invented creative ways to implement it into their diets. Pies and even blood pudding (now known as black pudding) were favourite dishes of the Tudors, who used every bit of the meat and let nothing go to waste; broth made from boiled animal bones, for example, was another favourite of the Tudors, and would have especially been enjoyed by weaning, teething children.[4]

The Tudor consumption of certain types of meat would surprise us today. As well as poultry, beef, pork and lamb, the Tudors also favoured goose, rabbit, pheasant and swan.[5] Other meats, like pigeon and even beaver were enjoyed, perhaps even too much, for beavers were later hunted into extinction in England in the sixteenth century. Fish too was a massive part of the sixteenth-century diet, with salmon, mussels, shrimps and plaice perhaps the most common. Lampreys and eels were traditionally eaten particularly those who lived close to rivers like the Thames in London. Herrings were a cheap and regularly dish in the sixteenth century, with twelve herrings costing just 1 penny in the early 1500s.[6] So too were bigger aquatic life, including turtle, seal and even dolphin, which would be imported into towns and cities from the coastal areas of England.[7]

For the most part, however, the majority of animals that were owned by the Tudors were kept only for their by-products, rather than for their meat, and only farmers would breed livestock for the purpose of their meat. Keeping an animal could be very lucrative, and many families at least owned one or two chickens, who would provide them daily with fresh eggs. Cows were also commonly found grazing in the gardens of the Tudors, particularly those of the lowest classes, who relied on its milk for the production of dairy products. These products would then either be consumed by the family or would be sold for a profit – in the year 1598 for example, three pints of milk cost ½ a penny.[8] If a family milked their cows daily, or turned this milk into other products, they could easily supplement their household income with minimal effort.

The Tudors were certainly inventive. Without the convenience of supermarkets, most Tudors relied on producing their own foodstuffs, visiting weekly markets or even generous neighbours with whom they would trade items of food. Foraging also was another favoured way to source food, yet it was strictly controlled by the Crown in the sixteenth century. People were banned from hunting large animals or game like deer, and had to appeal to the monarch for express permission. The Crown even introduced bounties for those who hunted restricted animals, particularly if they had been poached for their fur and pelts, and one Act of Parliament in 1496 even outlawed the thievery of swans and their eggs; anyone found to have committed the crime would be sent to prison for a sentence of exactly one year and one day.[9] Pests, however, were encouraged to be hunted, especially if they caused damage to nearby properties; pigs, for example, who were often left to roam around wooded areas of the country, became such pests that they were literally free game to anyone who could hunt them, providing landowners been given a proportion of foraged and hunted food as rent payment. The majority of birds were considered as pests, for they would feed upon the seeds that peasants and farmers had attempted to sow. Tudors tried desperately in vain to hunt these birds, yet they very rarely succeeded. In their frustration, the Tudors turned to erecting large, humanoid figures to keep watch over their crops, and so began the life of the scarecrow.

Foraging became especially popular during times of bad harvests, when the prices of foodstuffs like flour, meat, poultry and dairy products exponentially rose. Throughout the sixteenth century, bad harvests repetitively hit the Tudors, resulting in much desperation for food, particularly amongst the lowest social classes. The period of 1500 to 1503 was particularly difficult, and was marked by a great famine which resulted in many English markets relying on foreign imports. Even firewood was in short supply and taxed, with laws passed that prevented the Tudors from taking it directly from the forest floor. Instead, they were forced to use leafy green branches, which ultimately gave less of a burn and produced more smoke.

Yet, this desperate reliance on foreign imports in the sixteenth century was not all bad, and actually resulted in a taste revolution in Tudor England. Following the bad harvests in England, imports of grain, garlic, dates, onions, olive oil, prunes and even certain types of apples from countries, most notably from Denmark, Germany, the Baltic States, Holland and Brittany massively allowed the economy to continue to thrive, and resulted in the Tudors growing more adventurous in their tastes. Succade, a type of sugared, candied citrus peel became a favourite amongst the Tudors, as did treacle and fruits like limes and lemons, which became an instant hit. One such favourite dessert with the Elizabethans was whole slices of lemon drizzled in sugared syrup and dusted with the so-called 'white gold'. Citrus became such a phenomenon that even the lowest classes were desperate to try it, coining a word that, until 1540 had not even existed in the English vocabulary: orange.[10]

Potatoes and tomatoes brought over from the New World were also exotic luxuries that many could little afford. These social status symbols reflected the wealth of a family who would be able to afford them, as well as presented its owners as fashionable and wonderfully chic. Yet, it was only the richest of these few who could actually afford to consume these delicacies. With the prices of potatoes so high, they were used as décor or occasionally shared once the novelty had worn off, but rarely as everyday foodstuffs. It may not have been uncommon for an Elizabethan gentleman to exhibit a loaf of sugar or a plump peach upon his dinner table, but to eat them would be reserved only for the most special of treats. Voyages to Holland in 1596 brought over cabbages and onions to England. Voyages to the Netherlands just a few years prior in 1593 brought over root vegetables like parsnips, turnips and orange carrots. The Virginia Company brought over a variety of exciting imports to England, including pepper (both white and black), currants, raisins, oil, salt, spices, silks, cotton, glass, dye, sugar and tobacco. Truly, advancements in travel had greatly impacted food in England for the better. In fact, without the Tudors' love for these exciting new delicacies, we would not have much of the food we are used to today. Francis Drake, for example, took with him a large barrel of a type of dried, glutenous foodstuff on his voyage to the West Indies. It was boiled and served with additional ingredients like spices and cheese, and it became an instant hit with his sailors, and it was one of the first mentions of pasta in the early modern world.[11]

Wine was a commodity in Tudor England and was drank daily, though it would not have been as strong as we are used to today. In fact, in the 1530s alone almost 12,000 tons of wine were imported to England, most notably from areas of France, Spain, Italy and Cyprus. The English love for wine was so great, that one Venetian envoy to the country in 1497 wrote:

> three or four persons drink out of the same cup. Few people
> keep wine in their own houses, but buy it, for the most part,
> at a tavern; and when they mean to drink a great deal, they
> go to the tavern.[12]

The English fondness for sugar and sweets was well-known across the Continent, and an influx in imports of such fruits as peaches, grapes, figs, pomegranates and pears were quickly turned into cakes, jams and preserves, and marmalade (called citronade), which was available to buy to all members of sixteenth-century English society, though was often made at home. The cost of strawberries rose to around 3s and 4d, exploiting demand. In comparison, a loaf of bread or a tankard of ale cost around just 2d in the poorer areas of sixteenth-century England.[13] Sugared confits, early Tudor confectionary, most often took the form of berries and fragrant flower petals dusted with sugar, or would be made into a paste that could be moulded to recreate the allusion of other foodstuffs, sometimes even dyed to be further convincing. Food dye was created from such things as cochineal, which would create a red colour, or parsley, which would create green. These would be dried, crushed and ground into a powder, then simmered in water to create a coloured liquid. The liquid was then strained to remove any impurities, and then was added to water food required the dye. Even Queen Elizabeth I was said to be fond of these elaborately decorated sugar decorations, and supposedly had a particular obsession with sugared violet petals.[14]

Sweetmeats, despite how it sounds, were not a form of meat, but rather a sweet dessert such as a cake or flaky pastry, and was enjoyed just as much by the Tudors as they are today. Most often, sweetmeats would be made from a mix of sugar, nuts, fruit and pastry, and were eaten with the fingers. They were also known as sweetbreads, which, as the name suggests, were small, finger-sized portions of sweetened breads similar to a biscuit or a dense cake. These were then flavoured with the ingredients of choice; rose water, honey, citrus, or just a simple mixture of egg white and powdered sugar. They were particularly popular with travellers or visitors to local markets, and would be sold in bags similar to modern-day baked treats and sweets, a delightfully sweet snack that satiated the cravings of the Tudors. Sweetmeats could also be deep-fried in oil and dusted with sugar, resembling what we would now know as a modern-day doughnut!

Sweet desserts like pie, liquorice, barley sugars and sweet milk puddings would have most likely been a staple in the homes of almost every Tudor in the sixteenth century. It was not surprising, considering they were relatively simple and cheap to make, and would last for a relatively long time if stored correctly. Below is a sixteenth-century recipe for marchpane, the predecessor of our modern marzipan, a beloved confectionary by every class in the sixteenth century. It was a sweet, dough-like treat that was dried and moulded into shapes, often to create decorative embellishments like flower petals and animals, similar to our modern-day cake decorating fondant.

A Tudor Recipe for Marchpane (**serves 5**)[15]
200g of ground almonds
100g of caster sugar
A pinch of icing sugar
1 tablespoon of rose water
Decorative fruits and flowers (optional)

1. In a bowl, mix together the ground almonds and sugar, slowly adding the rosewater until the mixture forms a

paste. Ensure that the mixture is not too wet by adding more of the dried ingredients, but also make sure that to prevent the mixture cracking you add sufficient water.

2. Once the mixture forms a stiff ball, roll out the dough into a thick sheet. To prevent sticking, lightly dust your surface with flour or icing sugar.

3. Cut out your designs; perhaps a crown or a Tudor rose?

4. Place the marchpane in a cool oven, on gas mark 2 (150 degrees Celsius), and leave for 15 minutes. Check on it routinely, until the mixture has turned a light golden colour. Once stiff and golden, remove from the oven.

5. Glaze the marchpane with a mixture of rosewater and icing sugar, then return to the now-cooling oven for 5 minutes until glossy and set.

6. Remove your marchpane and serve. Why not serve it on a decorative plate, or with edible flowers, fruits or even gold leaf?

*

Of course, excessive consumption of sugar and other sweet treats did not come without risk in the sixteenth century, when the true extent of its dangers on teeth and other parts of the body was still yet unknown. Indeed, numerous diseases (sometimes referred to as man-made epidemics) came about through an addiction to certain foodstuffs and a lack of nutrition, including such things as anaemia (caused by a lack of iron in the blood), rickets (due to an unbalanced diet, little adequate sunlight, and essential vitamin deficiency), and teeth abscesses.[16] The carbohydrate-rich diet that was standard for the poorest of the sixteenth century, brought about tooth decay and disease, as well as diabetes from refined sugars. Although excavations of skeletons dating from the sixteenth century have shown that the teeth appear to be in good condition for the most part, they were also often worn down, particularly the molars, from a lifetime of grinding gritty bread and fatty meats.[17] These osteological excavations can also prove valuable in allowing archaeologists insight as to when sugar became a common part of sixteenth-century diets, for teeth of skeletons go from well-formed and generally healthy, to built up with plaque deposits, or have been entirely rotted away.

So, what was the Tudor diet really like, and was it considered healthy? It is commonly known that in later life, King Henry VIII had developed what we would now scientifically consider morbid obesity, his love of food eaten in excess reflected on his physiology. But so too were other Tudors at the whim of their food addictions – as previously stated, Elizabeth I's obsession with sugar did little for the Queen's health, and resulted in many of her teeth rotting away and blackening. Katherine of Aragon, too, supposedly suffered from an eating disorder brought about by religious devotion, where she would severely restrict her calorie intake, resulting in hormonal imbalances and even the occasional cessation of her menses.[18]

Katherine's daughter Mary, the future Queen Mary I, also suffered from a form of eating disorder which greatly limited her diet. In a note written by Mary's physicians in 1538, it was stated that:

> she was much desirous to have her meat immediately after
> she was ready in the morning or else she would be in danger
> of returning to her infirmity.[19]

Dietary requirements, tricky to manage even in modern day, were even more difficult to navigate in the sixteenth century. Mary's 'infirmity', commonly believed to be a disorder affecting her reproductive and endocrine systems, seems to have been only alleviated with meat. This strange problem baffled sixteenth-century physicians, who were forced to prescribe a rich diet of a variety of meats immediately upon Mary's waking so as not to worsen her painful symptoms.[20] Indeed, dietary restrictions are not modern inventions, and such things as lactose intolerance and gluten and nut allergies did exist in Tudor England, though arguably not on as large a scale as they do today. Why this was the case still perplexes historians and scientists today, although it is traditionally accepted that it was largely due to the introduction of lactose-stimulating enzymes in our diets in the nineteenth and twentieth centuries, through such things as baby formula and additives. In the sixteenth century, the vast majority of infants would have been weaned from the milk of their mothers or wetnurses, or would have been fed a mixture of animal milk and fruit juices, causing a tolerance to build up of the lactase enzyme within the human body. Some dieticians have gone so far as to suggest that the vast majority of our ancestors *did* have some form of lactose intolerance, going so far as to place this estimate at around eighty per cent of the population, and that it was by far the norm in historic societies.

In the 1400s, it was estimated that people would eat around five times their recommended daily calorie allowance compared to today.[21] Although this appears shocking, it is important to remember that sixteenth-century people were largely more active and less sedentary than in modern day, and therefore very little suffered the consequences of obesity and related illnesses. Additionally, it was often the poorest in society who had the best diet, on account of the vegetables that the rich shunned, plus a diet of less sugar and fat which they could simply not afford. They were, however, hit more greatly in the cases of poor harvests. The indication of horizontal 'Harris Lines' in osteo-archaeology suggest that there were great instances of stunted growth and hindered physical development due to malnutrition through diet.[22] Just prior to the reign of King Henry VII in 1424, archaeology in Norfolk indicated that on average, a person would consume one pound of meat, six pints of ale, and around two pounds of bread on a daily basis, according to social historian Martin Whittock.[23]

Yet, that does not go to say that the Tudors had totally unhealthy diets. With the introduction of such things as cabbages, cauliflowers and broccoli in the mid-sixteenth century, salads and other vegetable dishes became favourite meals of the Tudors. Salads, although a seemingly modern invention, were popular dishes in the sixteenth century, particularly when the weather was hot. The Tudors mostly made theirs with whatever homegrown vegetables they could grow themselves, from lettuces and cucumbers, to onions and even plant and flower seeds. Cheese and meat would also be mixed into salads, especially smoked and salted varieties. Even salad dressing was popular in the sixteenth century, and would have been made from oil and whatever tasteful, fragrant herbs one could forage.

Although veganism had not quite caught on across sixteenth-century Tudor England, there are records which lead us to believe that some individuals across the country were certainly practicing vegetarianism. Although the diets of the Tudors made it difficult to practice vegetarianism for ethical reasons, since diet could vary vastly daily depending on what ingredients were available to patrons, there were days in which the Tudors were encouraged to eat vegetation only.

The Catholic Church dictated a harsh and strict regimen when it came to food in the sixteenth century, which limited the diets of many Tudor individuals. Meat, in all forms aside from fish, was forbidden to be consumed on Wednesdays, Fridays and Saturdays. Fasting days, also known as 'ember days' fell around periods of Lent and Advent, and meant that the majority of people had to eat their meals after the sun had set, an awful predicament in the summertime when sunset did not often fall until nine o clock or even later.[24] Fridays, in particular, were especially strict, with only one meal allowed, according to the Catholic faith. This meal, often a large, extravagant meal similar to a Sunday roast, was expected to keep a Tudor family sufficiently satiated until the next day. In the sixteenth century, there was no such thing as chemical insecticides, and as such everything was organic and fresh. Additionally, air and light pollution of the nineteenth and twentieth centuries would be a long way off for the Tudors, and as such, we can assume that the lifestyles of the Tudors would have been much 'cleaner' than even perhaps we live today.

Many Tudors grew their own fruits and vegetables in dedicated patches within their gardens. The father of sixteenth-century chronicler John Stow had a summerhouse at the bottom of his garden, located where the present Stock Exchange is in London, where he was fond of growing crops and other vegetation.[25] In fact, the Tudors took great pride in their gardens. Thomas More, writing in 1516, spoke proudly of his fellow Englishmen, who:

> set great store by their gardens. In them they have vineyards, all manner of fruit, herbs and flowers, so pleasant, so well-furnished, and so finely kept, that I never saw thing more fruitful nor better trimmed in any place.[26]

Gardens also had the added advantage of being communal, and many neighbours would have traded certain crops with others. Bread too could be baked in communal, local bakehouses used by numerous different families. These brick ovens would allow for consistent, even bakes that could occur all throughout the day. Indeed, oven fires were very rarely put out, and rather were allowed to continuously burn, or simply be dampened down until they were ready to be stoked again the next day. Ovens would be lit with faggots and pimps, bundles of wood and twigs

1. *Gathering Twigs*. Simon Bening [Illuminated Book of Hours]. (Bruges, c. 1550), MS. 5093., MS.19v. Image courtesy of The J. Paul Getty Museum, Los Angeles.

2. *Cosmeston Medieval Village, Vale of Glamorgan*. Unknown photographer. Image courtesy of Vale of Glamorgan Council.

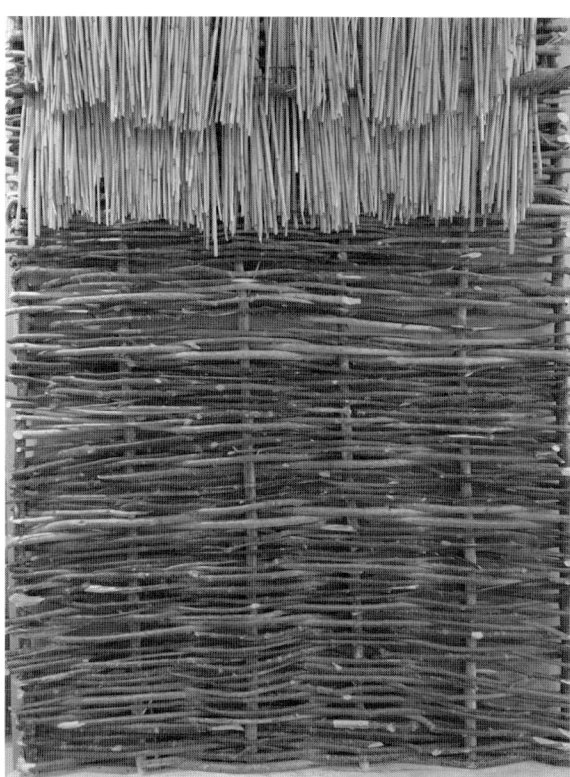

3. *Wattle Fencing*. Item held at The Museum of London, Barbican. Author's photograph.

4. *Wattle and Daub*. Item held at The Museum of London, Barbican. Author's photograph.

5. *Tudor Farmhouse*, Jonathan Heggie (Pembrokeshire, c. 1400s). Image obtained with kind permission of Mr Heggie.

6. *Sopwell Priory*, Eleanor Grana (Hertfordshire, c. 1500s). Image obtained with kind permission of Miss Grana.

Above: 7. *Close-up of Sopwell Priory*, Eleanor Grana (Hertfordshire, c. 1500s). Image obtained with kind permission of Miss Grana.

Left: 8. *January*. Simon Bening [Illuminated Book of Hours]. (Bruges, c. 1540), MS 24098, f. 18v. Image courtesy of The British Library, London.

9. *Door and Doorway,* A.25:1, 2-1913. Unknown (England, ca. 1500 – 1530). Image courtesy of the Victoria and Albert Museum, South Kensington.

10. *Tudor Merchant's House*, Unknown (Pembrokeshire, c. 1500). Image courtesy of St Fagans National Museum of History, Cardiff.

11. *Mary Arden's Farm*. Robert Arden (Warwickshire, 1514). Image courtesy of Tudor History.org https://tudorhistory.org/

12. *Cutlery Set*, M.602 to C-1910.
Unknown (France, c. 1550 –
1600). Image courtesy of the
Victoria and Albert Museum,
South Kensington.

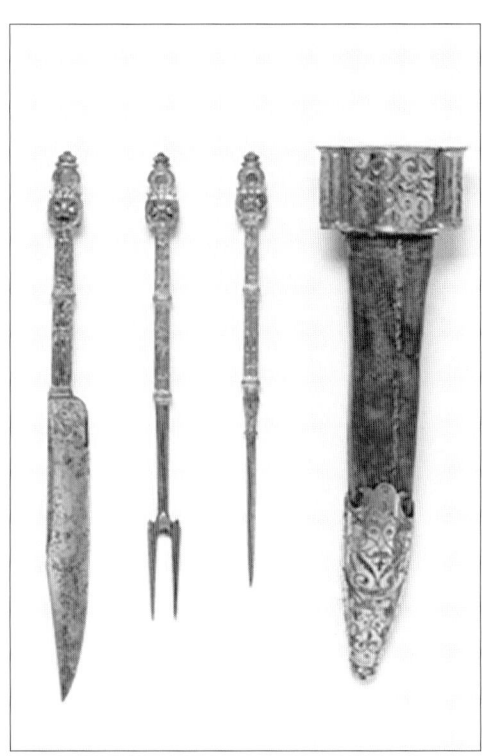

13. *Armchair*, W.21-1965.
Unknown (Salisbury,
c. 1600 – 1620). Item held at the
Victoria and Albert Museum,
South Kensington. Author's
photograph.

14. *Copperplate of Bridewell Palace* (c. 1553). London, England. Image in Saunders, A., and Schofield, J., *Tudor London: A Map and a View.* (London: London Topographical Society, 2001).

15. *Sir Paul Pindar's House*, 846 to M-1890. Unknown (London, 1600). Image courtesy of the Victoria and Albert Museum, South Kensington.

16. *A set of Miniature Whistle Pendants*, LOAN:MET ANON.1-1984. Unknown (England, c. 1525 – 1530). Items held at the Victoria and Albert Museum, South Kensington. Author's photograph.

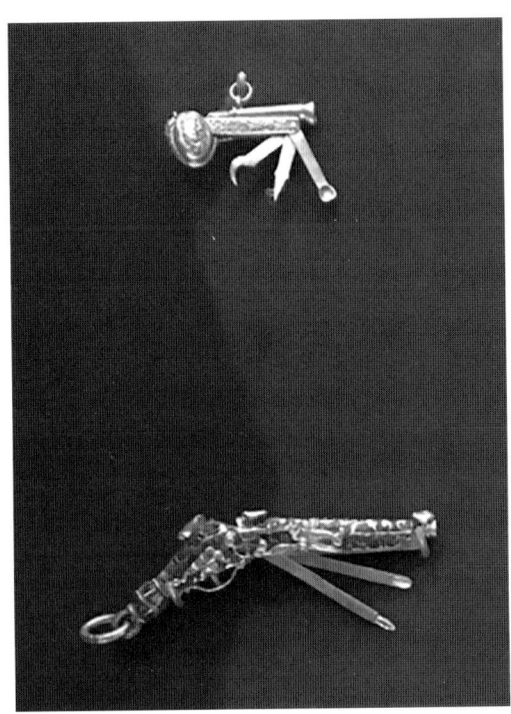

17. *Portrait of Elizabeth Vernon, Countess of Southampton*. Unknown [Oil on panel] (England, c. 1600). Courtesy of the Private Collection of the Duke of Buccleuch and Queensbury.

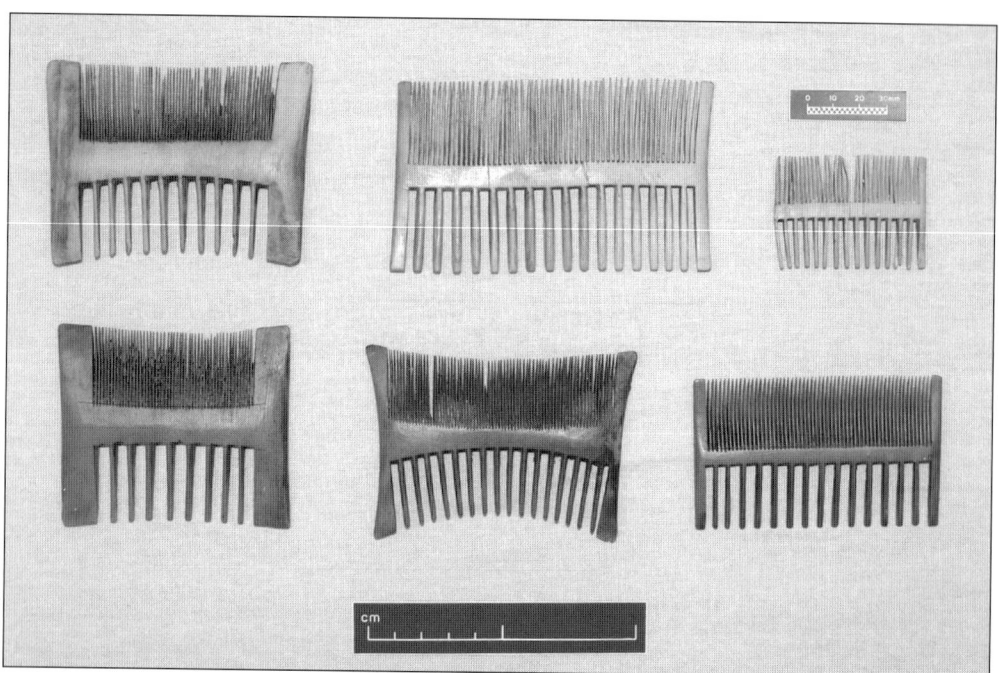

Above: 18. *Nit combs*. Unknown (England, c. 1545). Image obtained with kind permission of the Mary Rose Trust.

Left: 19. *Carpet*, T.348-1920. Unknown (Turkey, c. 1500 – 1600). Image courtesy of the Victoria and Albert Museum, South Kensington.

20. *Cushion Cover*, T.21-1923. Unknown (London, ca. 1600). Item held at the Victoria and Albert Museum, South Kensington. Author's photograph.

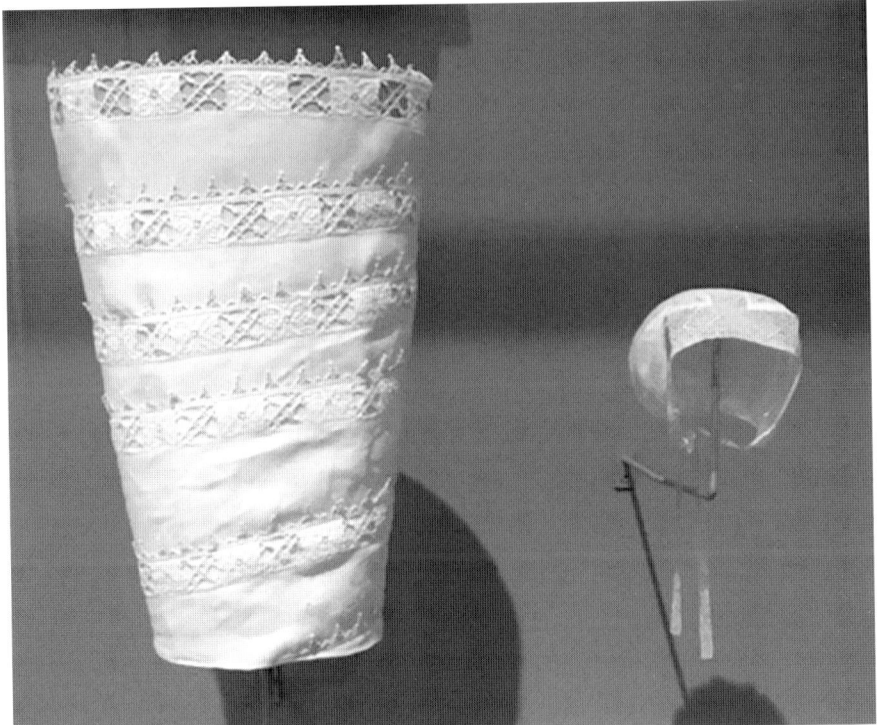

Above left: 21. *Swaddling Band*, B.878-1993. Unknown (Italy, c. 1590 – 1600). Item held at the Victoria and Albert Museum, South Kensington. Author's photograph.

Above right: 22. *Baby's Coif*, 7523-1861. Unknown (Flanders, c. 1550 – 1600). Item held at the Victoria and Albert Museum, South Kensington. Author's photograph.

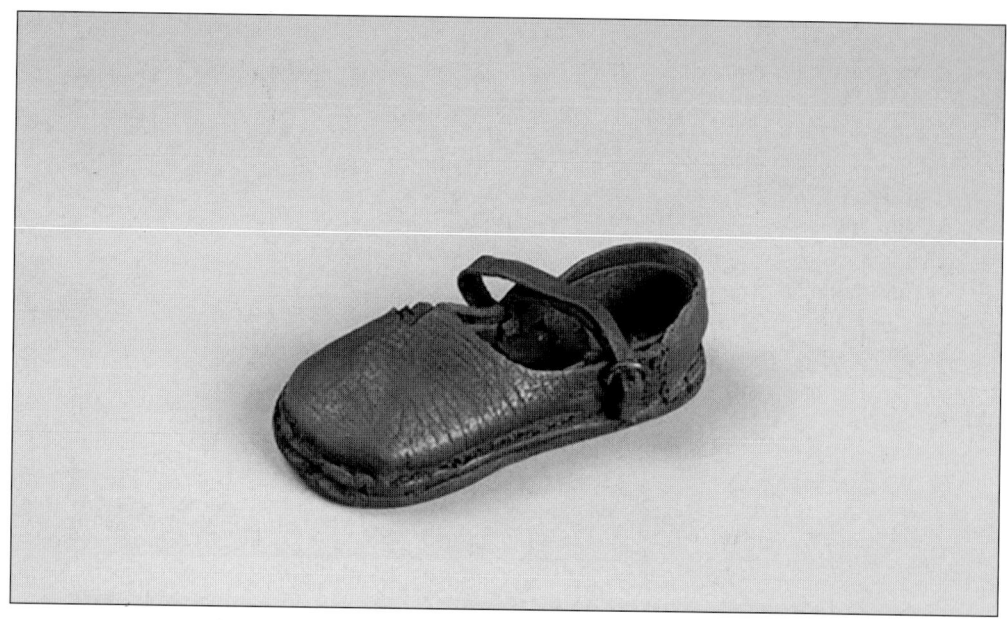

23. *Shoe*, T.602-1913. Unknown (London, c. 1450 – 1550). Image courtesy of the Victoria and Albert Museum, South Kensington.

24. *Kinderspiele*. Pieter Bruegel the Elder [Oil on panel] (Belgium, 1560). Image courtesy of The Kunsthistorischen Museums Wien, Vienna.

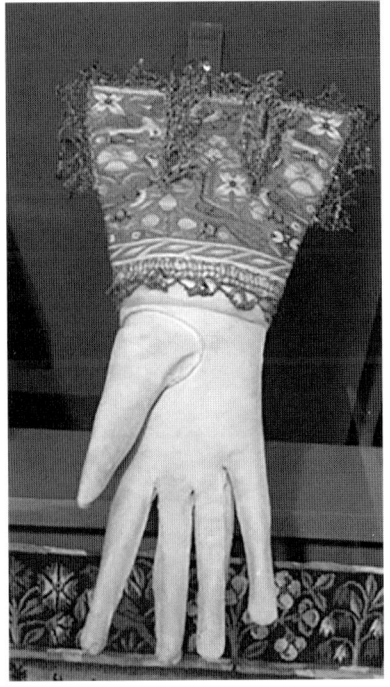

Above: 25. *Cap*, 1562&A-1901. Unknown (England, c. 1500). Image courtesy of the Victoria and Albert Museum, South Kensington.

Right: 26. *Pair of Gloves*, T.145&A-1931. Sheldon Tapestry Workshops (Warwickshire, c. 1590 – 1610). Items held at the Victoria and Albert Museum, South Kensington. Author's photograph.

27. *The Earl of Southampton*. John de Critz [Oil on canvas] (England, c. 1603). Image courtesy of the Private Collection of the Duke of Buccleuch and Queensbury.

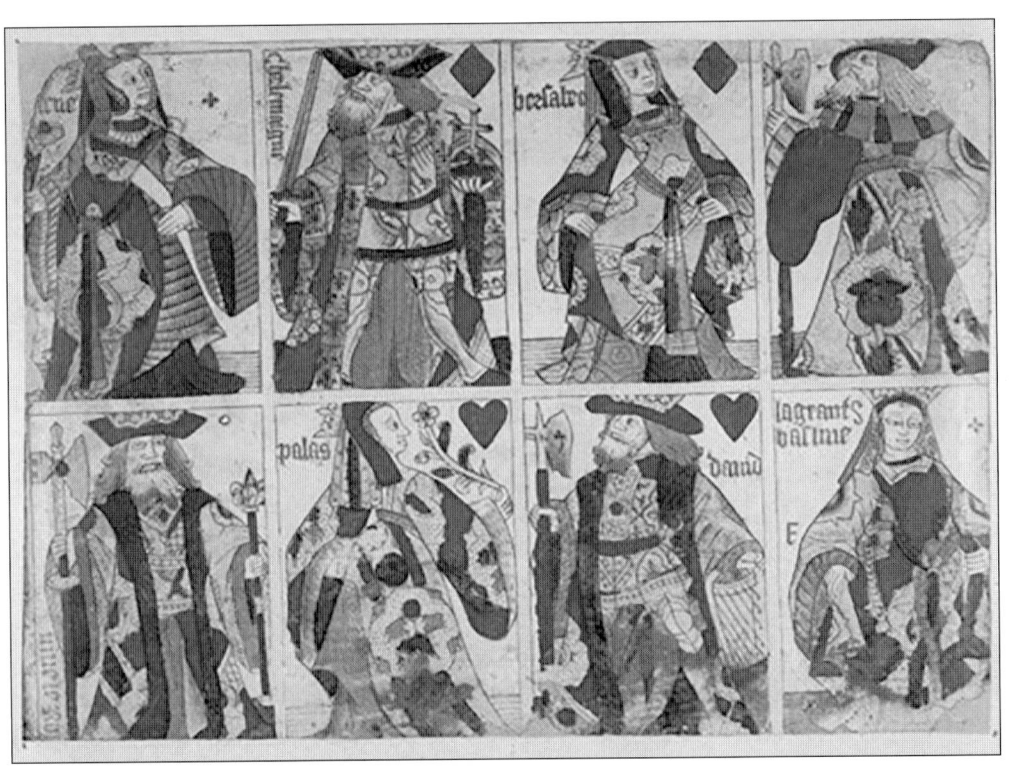

28. *Playing Card*, E.1256-1916. F. Durand (France, c. 1500). Image courtesy of the Victoria and Albert Museum, South Kensington.

Above: 29. *The Cadaver Tomb of John Baret*. Unknown (Suffolk, 1463). Image courtesy of the Churches Conservation Trust.

Left: 30. *Monumental Brass*, M.125-1922. Unknown (England, 1518). Image courtesy of the Victoria and Albert Museum, South Kensington.

that were intended to burn quickly and fiercely. These pimps and faggots were especially used in hearthstones and beneath spit-roasts and trivets, a tripod-like instrument which allowed for pots to hang above fires without the need to manually hold them up. Although these were very basic, they were greatly effective, and always resulted in an even cook. Indeed, these trivets often took less time to set up and burn than the larger fires of the wealthier classes, who had to wait until their hearths had reached the desired height before they could cook upon them. These large, wide chimneys and fireplaces were known as inglenook fireplaces, and would have been deep-set into their own alcoves in kitchens, complete with chimney flues that would carry away excess smoke and avoid it from entering the room. The fires of the poorest of sixteenth-century England society would be lit by 'tinderbox men', who would travel from house to house with a lit taper to set alight the kindling of those otherwise too poor to afford firewood.[27]

The baking of bread was perhaps one of the most important aspects of a sixteenth-century diet. There were two principal forms of bread in the sixteenth century.[28] One, known as 'manchet' bread, was finely milled and white, its impurities completely sifted out. For this reason, manchet bread was expensive, and was often afforded only by the richest in society, who could afford to spend such luxuries on perishable items. For the rest of Tudor society, 'cheat' bread was available, which was coarser and often included grains and seeds. Despite this, it was the healthier of the two options! Bread was, ultimately, a simple foodstuff to make, and was often baked at home rather than purchased. Housewives would travel to the market and purchase milled grain, oats and flour, which was sometimes made from seeds and nuts, and would mix it in a recipe with salt and water. It was simple, cheap and quick to produce, and so it was a dish – quite literally! – eaten regularly and with many accompanying foodstuffs.

Even plates could be made from bread in the sixteenth century. Trenchers were the precursor of plates, and were often made from a soft-carved wood with a shallow, hollowed-out middle that would hold food and also serve as a bowl. These would be washed and eventually replaced, though some Tudors, particularly those who baked daily and had an abundance of fresh bread, also made their trenchers from crusty bread. The crusty cob loaf was usually purposely stale, and would be filled with soup and other liquid-like foods. The bread would absorb the juices, and allowed eaters to consume the bread at the end of their meal, meaning that no part of the meal would go to waste. Oftentimes, the trencher bowls of the rich would be saved up and sent to the animals, or to the poor who gathered at the doors of the house, desperate for a bite of food. Although we as a modern society are now used to eating from plates and bowls with eating utensils, trenchers are still around today. Children's meals are often served in trencher-style platters, and there is a recent resurgence in 'bread bowls', in which soup is served in thick, hollowed bread. Trenchers were usually left to harden for around four days in order to reach the desired staleness.

Not all kitchen utensils in the sixteenth were so rudimentary, however. Among inventories of Tudor kitchens were mentions of wicker drinking flasks, wooden and pewter spoons, cauldrons, rulers, rolling pins, and even ceramic dishes used for baking, similar to a modern metal baking tray today. The Tudors even had recipe books, aimed entirely at women, and were named such things as the *Good Huswifes Treasurie*. These books were often small and portable, so that they could be carried around the kitchen or to markets to remind its owner of ingredients to purchase for the creation of certain dishes. These recipe books were small and lightweight, and barely larger than three-by-five inches, perfect for transporting to and from marketplaces, butcher shops, bakeries, and the stalls of foreign food traders.

Markets in the sixteenth century would be open at least one day per week, but were not open every day, meaning that housewives living in rural locations would have to carefully plan and arrange to pick up food on their weekly trip to the market, or else they would have problems in sourcing their ingredients. Those lucky enough to reside closer to shops and other retail areas found it easier to travel to pick up their groceries, but, alternatively, grocers stores could arrange for food parcels to be delivered to the residences of their customers.[29] In fact, much food was often purchased pre-made and ready-cooked from market stalls, taverns and other eateries, similar to our fast food outlets today. Hot and cold pretzels, baked animal ribs, buttered corn (after Columbus's voyage to the Americas in the early sixteenth century), and meat pies were all favourite types of fast food in Tudor England, as were pancakes, meatballs, sweet and savoury jellies and dowcet, an early form of sweet custard.

Fast food stalls were indeed erected in city marketplaces and areas of high foot traffic in sixteenth-century England, for passers-by to grab food while on the go. Convenience stores of hot pasties, meat skewers, fruit, drinks and even oysters, were popular and commonplace sights in cities and large towns, especially near tourist attractions, alongside roads, and by waterways for travel.[30] Depending on the location, the food sold in these convenience stores would differ. Nearer rivers, stalls would sell fresh-water fish for example, whereas nearer areas of high import traffic like docks and shipyards, exotic items like potatoes and tomatoes would be sold for a delightful and exciting snack. Streets around Cheapside in London, which was a bustling market area in the sixteenth century, were named such things Honey Lane, Bread Street and Milk Street for the products that merchants and shopkeepers sold.[31] There was even a street named Friday Street, where a fish market would be held every Friday, and would have been inhabited by fishermen and fishwives. One street located close to the churchyard of St Mary Woolchurch Haw in London had no less than twenty-five fishmongers and eighteen butchers living within it.[32] Although unusual in today's society, it was typical for many sixteenth-century cities to be built up around guilds, and as such, whole areas dedicated to one type of product would have been a common sight.

Streets were also named for the products that they were most famous for selling, and as such there are many examples of such places with names as Cornhulle (where corn was traded), New Fish Street, and even Candelwrickstrete in London, which specialised in the production and trade of candles.[33] One London street was even known simply as 'Poultry': it took no guessing as to what they sold there.

*

For many in the sixteenth century, eating regular, delicious meals was one of the only luxuries they could afford. Although breakfast was typically just bread and ale and was consumed upon rising, lunch, which was known as dinner, and was the Tudors' main meal, could be much more inventive. Dinner was served at ten in the morning, and would have consisted of anything from soups, stews, salads and roast meats, and would have often consisted of more than one dish, even for the poorest in society. Sweets and other desserts would have been served at dinner, and as such many Tudors greatly looked forward to it.

One delightful poem from the sixteenth century even conveys a sense of the love Tudors had for their food:

> Then cheese with fruit on the table set,
> With biscuits or caraways, as you may get.
> Wine to them fill, else ale or beer
> But wine is meetest, if any there were.[34]

Finally, after a hard day's work of manual labour, household chores or academic study, the Tudors could settle down to supper at around four or five in the evening.[35] Unlike at breakfast and dinner, supper required a form of etiquette that diners were required to follow, particularly if guests had joined them. The Tudors would have first dipped their fingers into sweetened water that had been fragranced with herbs, flowers and other such aromatics; after all, the fingers were the main form of eating implements in the sixteenth century. Knives tended only to be used for the spearing of meats or fruits, and were required to always be kept sharp, as this poem instructs:

> Thy knife see be sharp to cut fair thy meat,
> Thy mouth not too full when thou dost eat;
> Not smacking thy lips, as commonly do hogs,
> Nor gnawing the bones as it were dogs.[36]

But rules and etiquette aside, the Tudors greatly enjoyed their diverse, delicious diets, and popularised dishes and ingredients that we now enjoy and love today. Without the Tudors, such things as sugar and spice would probably not make up such a large part of our modern diets, and for that, we only have them to thank.

Chapter 6

The Bedroom

'When moderate sleep thy head hath possessed,
And given thy body his natural rest,
Shake sluggishness off, bethink thee of things,
That for thy soul's health sweet melody brings'
Richard Weste, *How Thou Oughtest
to Prepare Thyself, When Thou Risest
in the Morning,* 1619.[1]

Before the sixteenth century, the concept of a dedicated bedroom was virtually non-existent in Medieval England. Until the 1500s, most poor families slept together in the hall of the home, which was often the only room in the house and doubled up as a kitchen, a parlour, a dining room, and even a washroom. But as well as sleeping in the same room, many poorer families also shared the same bed; it was common for siblings to sleep in the same beds as their parents, and there were even recorded instances of servants sharing their master's beds.[2] With entire households sleeping in the same room, the want for privacy reached an all-time high; and thus, the Tudor bedroom was born.

Perhaps the most important piece of furniture a Tudor could own was the bed. Central to the home and its everyday goings-on, the bed saw rest, toil, passion and pain. It was the retreat of the sick, the welcome comfort to the weary worker. Lives were brought into the world upon it, and lives were taken out. Beds were so important to the Tudors that they were commonly left in wills to grateful benefactors. William Shakespeare, for example, left his second-best bed to his wife, Anne. Although the offering of the second-best bed connotes a snub, the opposite was actually the case. The 'first' bed – the best, most expensive, and most luxurious, was often just a 'show' bed intended to impress guests; most people tended to sleep on simple truckle beds known as 'box beds', which were low to the ground and would often have high edges to keep mattresses tucked in snugly, and ensured that sleepers did not topple out during the night.[3] Many Tudors, particularly the rich and the wealthy, slept in 'tester beds', items of furniture that closely resemble our own beds today.[4] Tester beds would often be canopied with heavy curtains suspended from high posts (hence why they were also more commonly known as 'four post beds'), which afforded occupiers longed-for privacy away from prying eyes, as well as keeping in the heat and keeping out draughts and the bad smells of the household, including cooking smoke and even the scent of wandering livestock and pets.

Indeed, beds in modern day have changed very little from the sixteenth century. Most beds were made up of the frame itself, as well as a mattress, pillows, linen sheets and woollen blankets. Tudor mattresses were known as 'ticks', so-called for they were specially manufactured in order to prevent common household pests like fleas, ticks and lice from nesting within. This was achieved through the soaking of insect-repellent essential oils and other fragrant herbs and botanicals in the mattress, which would have been made from absorbent materials like straw, rushes, wool or featherdown.[5] So, as well as providing medicinal benefits, many sixteenth-century mattresses presumably smelled very pleasant due to their perfumed stuffing. Wardrobes and large, deep chests would be used for the storage of bedlinen and fabrics, which would be regularly fumigated in order to remove vermin. Bedsheets would have also been washed, aired and dried just as in modern day, the regular laundering considered vital to health.

But just as the composition of beds mattered to the health of the Tudors, so did rest and sleep itself. The Tudors did not have 'set bedtimes' as we may have them today; rather, they would have slept with the ceasing of natural daylight, going to bed as soon as the sun went down (in the early evening in the winter, for example). This was due to the lack of natural light – with only thin flickers of candlelight, many Tudors were limited in their abilities once the sun had set. Unless a household had large fireplaces, which whole families would gather around to continue their work or recreation, there was often very little else for the Tudors to do in the dark, without running the risk of injury to themselves or to others. However, that did not mean that the Tudors immediately slept once the sun had set; in fact, the Tudors would often wake in the night to carry out duties like prayer, or even eating, before resuming a 'second sleep' which would last until dawn. Then, the Tudors would awake properly with the rising of the sun the next morning, it acting as a natural alarm clock that awoke individuals with its gentle rays of light.

The Tudor workday started at sunrise, regardless of the actual time of day. The coming of dawn signalled the day. A working day in the sixteenth century was never actually streamlined – rather, it could last the whole day in the summer, or just a handful of hours in the winter months. One foreign ambassador to England in the early sixteenth century complained of the country's lack of sunlight:

> I observed the length of the daylight with great attention, and there were never less than seven hours together, in which one could see to read and write.[6]

Structuring a working day around the duration of sunlight was always problematic, and undoubtedly disrupted the daily routines of many occupations, including most notably agriculture and husbandry, which depended largely on labour being performed while the sun was setting in the sky. It was further problematic for servants, who would sleep only when their masters had also gone to sleep, meaning that they were expected to be awake before their masters had awoken, and go to sleep after their masters had gone to bed.[7] This often meant that the working days of sixteenth-century servants could last a full twenty-four hours, only amplifying how exhausting that particular occupation could be.

The ringing of curfew bells around sixteenth-century English villages would alert residents when the working day had officially come to a close. The word curfew comes from the French to 'cover the fire', and indeed Tudor families would have extinguished the flames within their homesteads in preparation for their daily night-time routines.[8] According to the social historian Ruth Goodman, curfew men would be randomly handpicked from village communities, and tasked with prowling the hamlet to ensure that its citizens were abiding by the curfew rules.[9] But it is unfair to imagine that life in sixteenth-century England ceased with the setting of the sun; rather, the night-time could be a very busy period of the day, with revellers in search of entertainment, or alehouse frequenters goers heading toward their usual haunts. Beggars too would most often be found at night, for they were often working on odd jobs during the day, and needed the additional funds to supplement their incomes; as such, it was common to find the poorest members of society working throughout the night in jobs only suitably performed under the cover of darkness, such as undertakers and gong-farmers, to spare the more gentile of Tudor society the sights (and smells) of these unsavoury jobs.

The Tudors did not wear pyjamas, according to social historian Ian Mortimer.[10] Rather, it was common for many people of both sexes to wear thin, linen shifts (similar to full-length dresses), which doubled as underwear. Slippers however were worn, but were typically used as daily shoes, particularly around the house. The slipper became especially popular during the reign of King Henry VIII, where it became fashionable for men, in particular, to wear them around the court.

Naps were common in the sixteenth century, and not just for children. Rather, many Tudors took daily naps after their dinner, which was served at midday, especially on Sundays. However, the Tudors were encouraged not to take much sleep, for 'much sleep engendereth diseases and pain [...] It dulls the wit and hurteth the brain', wrote an educational treatise targeted at children in 1577, known as *How to Order Thyself When Thou Risest and In Apparelling Thy Body.*[11]

*

Sleeping was not the only thing that occurred within a Tudor bed. On a visit to England in 1497, one Venetian envoy wrote:

> I have never noticed anyone, either at court or among the lower orders, to be in love; whence one must necessarily conclude either that the English are the most discreet lovers in the world, or that they are incapable of love. I say this of the men...it is quite the contrary with the women, who are very violent in their passions.[12]

There is often a misconception that in the sixteenth century genuine love matches did not exist, and that marriages were little more than calculated, economic transactions. Certainly, many aspects of Tudor marital traditions differ greatly from our own understanding of marriage today; but to what extent is it fair to consider the sixteenth century as a period where romantic love was wanting, and marriages were binding between two miserable parties?

The Fourth Lateran Council of 1215 (convened by Pope Innocent III) revised and outlined marital traditions across Europe; marriage was declared to be a sacrament, meaning that divorce, sex outside of marriage, and sex before marriage were all considered to be heinous acts of sinful lust. The Council also outlined marital prohibitions, including marrying too close within a family's affinity (too close in blood relations), as well as spiritual affinity, meaning that an individual could not marry their godparents, or the children of their godparents, as they were considered spiritual relations in the eyes of the Catholic Church.

Despite being referred to as 'prohibitions', the rules outlined by the Fourth Lateran Council actually improved marital conditions in Medieval England. Not only did it encourage monogamy, but it also directly resulted in reduced instances of incestuous relationships, which had been more likely to occur in the early-Middle Ages between close kin. The ruling about sex before marriage also mattered little; after all, the minimum age a child could marry was around twelve for girls (the typical age of menstruation, and thus the signifier of womanhood), and fourteen for boys (the traditionally-accepted age of majority where boys were expected to receive martial training and education). Although horrific by modern standards, the true extent that child marriages occurred in the Late Middle Ages and Early Modern period was presumably minimal; most Medieval and Tudor couples married in their mid-twenties, allowing them time to establish good incomes, connections and networks, as well as cleave an independent life for themselves.[13] Marriages occurring between early adolescents were uncommon in the sixteenth century, and only really tended to occur amongst the uppermost social classes; even then, these marriages would occur by proxy, meaning that many couples were married only in name. They would not have typically lived together, let alone have even met, until they had reached an acceptable age (often in their late teens or early twenties), unless they had received parental consent and the blessing of practitioners of Church Common Law.[14]

A marriage could not occur in the sixteenth century without a pre-contract, a ceremony akin to a modern-day engagement. The pre-contract between a couple would be made before a priest and was effectively considered a legally-binding entrance to marriage in the eyes of the Church. After this pre-contract would follow a more formal arrangement, which would often occur in the family home of the bride in the presence of the families of the couple, who would bless the union. The third and final step in the marriage ritual was the exchanging of the vows at a church, which was formally known as the 'solemnisation'. This often occurred outside the church door, on the steps, and not actually within its walls.[15] This would be the point when a couple would be officially considered to be married. Then followed the wedding breakfast, a meal which was often served in the morning, followed by the all-important wedding night, in which the union would be consummated and the couple known officially as man and wife.

The consummation of a marriage was perhaps the most important aspect of the wedding ceremony. Sex and sexuality were important to the Tudors – it was considered a sacred act between a monogamous couple, and was necessary for procreation. Sexual satisfaction, however, was not, as the Church believed, a necessary aspect of marital life. As such, marital sex was regulated; sexual acts would be allowed within marriage but only if a couple could prove that it had led to conception. As such, Tudor couples were restricted in expressing themselves sexually; only one sexual position was encouraged by the church, with oral acts, masturbation and same-sex intercourse expressly banned. Even nudity was considered prideful, and sleeping together naked was akin to intercourse in the eyes of the church.[16] So too bathing naked, according to Ian Mortimer, so much so that it was discouraged amongst the members of the clergy, for it was believed to spark flames of desire and carnal lust within individuals.[17] As such, many historians have argued that marriage in the sixteenth century was considered little more than a repressor of sexual appetites, intended to extinguish the flames of sexual desire and cause Tudor couples to consider sex as a tedious chore.[18] It is no wonder, therefore, that historians continue to assert that the frequenting of brothels in sixteenth-century England was a way in which men could explore avenues of sexuality and sexual expression.[19] Wives were required to play a submissive role in the bedroom, taught by the church; yet there was little doctrine about prostitutes. As such, it would not be too far of a stretch to imagine that the sexually-repressed men of sixteenth-century England would frequent brothels and stew-houses in order to explore their sexualities, as well as to challenge traditionally accepted views on masculinity. Anxieties of pregnancy, the contraction of venereal diseases, and reputational ruin aside, Tudor men would have experienced in brothels refreshing new attitudes toward sex; women were permitted to assume more dominant roles, more scandalous sexual positions would have been favoured, and even illegal acts of oral sex and sodomy would have been performed.

Sex on Sundays, Thursdays and Fridays was not permitted, as they were considered holy days and were days in which preparation for communion was intended.[20] Abstinence also occurred during Lent, Christmas and around the Pentecost, each of which could last around twenty days at the minimum. Oral sex, sodomy, masturbation, incest (within the closest degrees) and bestiality were all banned by the Church in Penitentials (a sort of Christian instructional guidebook) that wrote about the rules of sex and sexuality. Punishment for fornication, dressing as an effeminate man, or masturbation could include fasting over a period of twenty days, or flagellation.[21] Only the missionary position was allowed, for it equalled less pleasure, as well as exaggerated the passiveness of woman, with the dominant role of the man.[22]

Despite the Church's staunch teachings about monogamy in marriage, these rulings appear only to have been intended for wives and women. For men, regular sexual intercourse was considered part of a healthy lifestyle, and the frequent emission of semen was considered to balance the four bodily humours; blood, phlegm, black bile and yellow bile. The build-up of too much semen in the body was believed to be bad for the heart and could lead to death, and it was believed that abstinence and celibacy were also considered life-threatening, for they could cause weight loss, fatigue, headaches, and anxiety.[23] As such, sixteenth-century English men were encouraged to have as much regular sex – whether it be with their wives, or with prostitutes – as possible. One contemporary chronicler even wrote, 'in the morning they are as devout as angels, but after dinner they are like devils'.[24]

Although Tudor England was not too dissimilar from its predecessor, the Middle Ages, in that it was rigid and reticent about female sexuality, it was far more tolerant of the sexual practices of men, even surprisingly allowing for the pimping out of prostitutes. The motivation for this was simple; sex sold, and paid-for prostitution brought about revenue for brothel owners. It also had a more surprising advantage; by giving Tudor men dedicated avenues for sex, brothels ensured that there were lower instances of rape and forced sexual interactions in the sixteenth century. An old profession, perhaps one of the oldest in the world, prostitution was deemed a 'necessary evil' that allowed men to prove their masculinity. Brothels also provided unmarried or sexually-repressed homosexual men to explore their sexualities in a safe environment; indeed, gay sex certainly, did occur in the sixteenth century despite the best efforts of the Church to stamp it out.

Evidence that prostitution was openly tolerated in sixteenth-century England is perhaps most oblique in the numerous municipal funds that went into the construction and maintenance of brothels in city areas and large towns.[25] Brothels were strategically built away from places of devotion, away from nunneries, and away from residential areas, cautious to avoid unwanted penalties and ecclesiastical reprimand.[26] Instead, brothels were typically located near dockyards, inns, and universities, all places in which a constantly-changing tide of men would frequent. These particular brothels became treated favourably amongst the highest of sixteenth-century society, for their proximity to houses of learning and law made them appear considerably high-brow. For those who did not want to mingle with public prostitutes who performed for large quantities of customers, or for those who wished not to explore the dark underbellies of Tudor England in search of an affordable night with a prostitute, many wealthy men even turned to hiring personal escorts who would satisfy them at their own homes.

Prostitution was a lucrative occupation, and resulted in daily pay. In fact, sex work was perhaps one of the highest-paying methods of employment for women in sixteenth-century England, and certainly provided women with lodging and food. Additionally, these brothels would serve as safe havens for women who had fled their marital homes or who had been living as vagrants, and were often places in which a sense of sisterhood was born. Prostitution, despite its modern connotations, was not considered wholly unsavoury in the sixteenth century; rather, it was an occupation that many self-respecting and ambitious women turned to in the hopes of carving out independent lifestyles of their own, on their own terms. In sixteenth-century France there were four types of prostitution, each considered more favourably depending on rank; controlled prostitution within municipal areas, which was regulated by the state and was regarded as the highest and most respectable level of prostitution; bath houses (or stew-houses) where prostitutes could provide services for their customers in safe, and even hygienic, conditions; private brothels; and self-employment. Even the way that they dressed allowed prostitutes a sense of identity and individuality. Prostitutes would typically wear their hair loose or covered with a coloured silk scarf, coif or headdress. In Bristol, in particular, women would wear striped hoods to signify that they were prostitutes; across the ocean in Milan, prostitutes wore white, and in Spain, they typically wore gowns of bright yellow.

Adolescent boys, it was believed, were most likely to take advantage of prostitution in the sixteenth century, allowing for virginal young men to experience their first sexual encounters without the need for marriage, and without any strings attached. Barbara Hanawalt, a historian of childhood and adolescence, wrote that it was only the females of the wealthier classes who could escape early life with their purity in check – while boys were dallying in brothels, young, poor females were forced to marry early, and thus be exposed to sex at a young age, in order to protect the interests of their families and bring added revenue to their households.[27] Whether this is to be believed is up for debate, but for the most part, children in the sixteenth century were presumably more accustomed to sex, childbirth and pregnancy than perhaps they are today – after all, in many houses across sixteenth-century England, the walls were thin, and many beds were located in the same area; some children even had to share with their parents.

Many retired prostitutes, whose beauty and youth had long since deserted them, either went on to establish brothels of their own or retired to convents. It was not uncommon for ex-prostitutes to have turned to the Church, seeking repentance for their sins and providing motherly and sisterly roles to fellow nuns just as they had within the brothels. Additionally, it is quite likely that these places were one of the only institutions within early sixteenth century English society that would accept such former social outcasts within their walls, allowing retired or reformed prostitutes a second chance at life. Unless these women married, or managed to wrangle respectable positions in later life, such as matrons of dormitories or as business owners, their futures lay in the charity of those willing to accept them. Although prostitution in itself was permitted, prostitutes were often marginalised and prejudiced against in sixteenth-century England, particularly by men. This was none more so evident than in the wages a Tudor prostitute would earn; payment for a sexual service was extremely cheap, argues Barbara Hanawalt, who estimated that, on average, it would cost just 4d per appointment, which was the equivalent of 'a sheaf of wheat'.[28]

Prostitutes and sexually-informed women were often considered to be temptresses by patriarchal sixteenth-century minds, who dabbled in black magic and witchcraft in order to seduce lovers and to entrap them into bonds of marriage or children – Queen Anne Boleyn herself was considered by her enemies as being a seductress who achieved her goal of attaining the King through witchcraft. Yet, attitudes toward casual sex in the wider sphere of the Tudor World were nuanced; although English stereotypes maintained that those who kept mistresses, particularly the French, were decadent, vulgar, immoral and promiscuous. Of course, King Henry VIII, ever anxious to prove his virtue to the other monarchs of Europe, conveniently failed to comment upon the fact that he too took openly took many mistresses, even siring an illegitimate heir by one. Indeed, almost incredulously, King Henry had even *shared* a mistress with the French King Francois I. Lady Mary Boleyn, the sister of Henry's future second wife Anne, was allegedly called, 'a very great whore, the most infamous of them all', by the French king Francois I, who personally recommended Mary's services to Henry.[29] King Henry must not have been so bothered by the immorality of extra-marital sex after all.

As the sixteenth century progressed, prostitution slowly became more tolerated in English society. As well as the King setting the outlier for casual sexual relationships outside of marriage, the expansion of the Catholic Church also led to a bizarre marked increase in large monetary donations on behalf of English brothels. Indeed, toward the latter end of the sixteenth century, prostitution became so commonplace that it almost became desirable, a sentiment which would last well into the following century, and see an onslaught of young women vying to attract the attentions of high-ranking figureheads in seventeenth-century society. Prostitutes (in London at least) were known as Winchester Geese, a legacy dating from 1374, where it was estimated that around eighteen bathhouses owned by the Bishop of Winchester had been rented for the use of promiscuity and prostitution, all of which were located on the aptly named 'Cock Lane'.[30]

It is interesting to note that many of the Church Penitentials that discouraged extra-marital sexual intercourse were written by sexually-repressed members of the Church, including monks and Church fathers, and thus, cannot be taken as a true and accurate reflection of the sexual lives of the English in the sixteenth century. Rather, many of these ideas and rules were already considered antiquated and old-fashioned even during the Middle Ages, and were certainly not abided by with as much rigour as the Church intended. In fact, during the reign of Henry VII, it was believed that out of eighty priests in the dioceses of Bangor and St David's, every one of them kept mistresses.[31] This is evidenced by the sheer amount of illegitimate children being born in the Tudor period, clear that extra-marital sex was commonplace; even Cardinal Wolsey and at least four sixteenth century Popes (Julius II, Paul III, Pius IV, and Gregory XIII) fathered children despite belonging to religious orders.

With a society so accustomed to sex and sexuality, it is no wonder that the effects of polygamous sex wreaked havoc on sixteenth-century English society. The spread of venereal diseases was a true problem for the Tudors who didn't have sufficient medical treatments to deal with the ferocious sexually-transmitted infections. Amongst the worst of these diseases was syphilis, a painful condition that resulted in the eruption of scabs upon the face and even the deterioration of the cartilage in the nose. King Francois I of France was a sufferer, and even the English King Henry VIII was suspected of suffering from its horrific symptoms, which included:

> paines or aches, ulcers, nodes and foule scabbers, with corruption of the bones [...] venomous pustules, scabbes upon the head, browes, face and beard, and in other partes of the bodie, about the secret partes, or in the corners of the lippes'. It was described by the contemporary medical practitioner William Close as a 'pestilent infection of filthie lust.[32]

To cure syphilis, the Tudors believed that the injection of pure mercury (an extremely toxic metal) into the penis or the vagina would bring about the cessation of symptoms and allow sufferers to resume a normal sexual life. As would be expected, the application of mercury did little to cure the infection, and only served to worsen it. As such, men and women alike were instructed to cease sexual relations with immediate effect; how many followed this advice, however, will never truly be known for certain.

Informed medical knowledge had its grassroots in the sixteenth century and Early Modern period in part thanks to the Renaissance that began in England in the 1600s. However, little was still understood about the sexual organs of the human body in particular, proving a considerable problem for medical practitioners who were tasked with treating venereal diseases and uncomfortable genital problems. In the sixteenth century, it was believed that regular crying, sweating and urinating, as well as daily consumption of cold food, iced water, salted fish and watery vegetables, thickened a man's semen, resulting in stronger and more virile sperm and better chances of conception. Women, it was believed, were also capable of producing their own kind of semen which would join with the emission of a male's during intercourse, and result in conception. It was believed however that women only produced this discharge after sufficient satisfaction in the marital bed, with conception serving as proof that the female had enjoyed intercourse. This was greatly problematic for women who had conceived during instances of rape; as it was believed that they had enjoyed the intercourse enough to conceive, their rapists would get away free of charge.

Unlike men, whose lack of sufficient semen emission was believed to cause hot-headedness, anger and frustration, if a woman was unable to emit semen of her own it was believed to bring about fainting and a lack of breath, the idea being that excess seminal fluids caused a build-up in the uterus which then in turn affected the heart, lungs, and the rest of the respiratory system. For this reason, women were encouraged just as strongly as men to have regular intercourse with their husbands in order to maintain a healthy and active lifestyle and purge themselves of damaging seminal excess. In this case, masturbation *was* allowed, as were vaginal suppositories of sponges soaked in vinegar, of which aromas it was believed would find their way to the opening of the cervix and penetrate the uterus.

But as well as the belief that this sort of vaginal suppository would increase a woman's chance of conceiving, dangerous methods such as this also had the complete opposite effect on women's gynaecological health. Emmenagogues, natural medicines intended for the onset of vaginal bleeding, would have been inserted into the vagina or consumed by women seeking to stimulate their menstrual cycles; they were also used as abortifacients in the sixteenth century.[33] Emmenagogues would most often take the form of consumable medicinal drinks, where often toxic herbs such as rue and pennyroyal, as well as chamomile and wormwood would have been boiled and drank in a disgustingly bitter – and wholly dangerous – concoction.[34] As well as causing intense stomach pains and vaginal bleeding upon consumption, these herbs were particularly dangerous to the nervous system, and could often cause seizures and even death if consumed in large amounts.

If a woman chose not to orally consume these emmenagogues, herbs would also be inserted into the vaginal canal in small pouches as pessaries, which, although achieving the desired effects, would have also caused considerable damage to the kidneys, reproductive organs, and the delicate mucous membranes of the vagina. They were, therefore, taken only in the most desperate of cases. Most commonly, if a Tudor woman wished to abort her foetus, she would often turn to other greatly-dangerous methods including inserting sticks and other sharp implements into the vaginal canal in the hope of puncturing the womb. Of course, these practices were wholly unsafe and unsanitary, and many women died from infections that would rapidly develop. In my own study of abortion and pregnancy in the early sixteenth century, I discovered that many women who had fallen pregnant out of wedlock would simply carry the unwanted foetus to full term, before leaving their newborn babies on rubbish heaps, in forests, at orphanages, with strangers, or drowned in rivers. Either way, prospects for unmarried women who fell pregnant outside of wedlock were bleak, and they often turned to whatever choices they had, even, tragically, going so far as to commit infanticide so as not to cause considerable damage to their own bodies by bringing about an abortion. In the words of Sir Walter Raleigh, which reflected the attitudes of illegitimate children in the sixteenth century, it was 'better were it to be unborn than ill-bred'.

For those women who carried their babies to term, a considerable lacking of sophisticated pain relief medication, adequate sanitation, and knowledge of obstetrics must have been a terrifying prospect. These obstetrical issues would not be truly understood until well into the late eighteenth century, and still arguably had a long way to go until well into the twenty-first century. Labouring Tudor mothers had to make do without the use of epidurals, ultrasound scans, and regular check-ups from midwives and gynaecologists, and as such had little knowledge of the health and wellbeing of the baby that was growing inside them. In an age where caesareans could kill you just as much as the unwashed hand that pulled a mewling infant from the body, pregnancy and childbirth was a terrifying time. From the moment a woman fell pregnant, to the moment that that child had been safely delivered, it must have been an incredibly anxious time for any couple.

*

In the sixteenth century, it was believed that those women who wore cosmetics and perfume were seductresses, and as such the use of makeup was discouraged. Despite this, hundreds of sixteenth-century cosmetic recipes have survived, and as such, it is wholly plausible to imagine that a considerable portion of both Tudor men and women applied creams, lotions, powders and stains for the appearance of clearer, more youthful complexions.

To begin, many Tudors washed their face with fragrant waters, most often scented with rosewater, lavender, wine, citrus or even urine. Once the face had been washed; it was idealised for a Tudor to have the palest of complexions, and as such many applied toxic mixtures of white lead, mercury, carbolic acid and chloride, as well as a base of finely-milled flour to make a thick, white foundation. Face powders would then have been applied to set the tacky foundation, and would have been applied with a cloth or with the fingers. Some Tudors even went to lengths to draw thin, blue lines upon their temples and beneath their eyes to offer the illusion of thin, glass-like skin and a clear complexion.

Ground charcoal or soot would have been used as a rudimentary eyeliner, or mixed with water as a mascara, which would have been applied to the lashes with the fingertips or a small bristled brush akin to a modern-day toothbrush. The bright juices of beetroots and other vibrantly red and pink fruits would have been used for the staining of cheeks and lips, a surprisingly effective, subtle and safe method of makeup application. To remove makeup, the Tudors simply washed their faces with water. When applied correctly using natural products, sixteenth-century makeup could look surprisingly fresh and youthful, albeit with numerous hazardous implications. However, for the upper classes, thick, unsightly makeup became the norm in the latter part of Elizabethan England, and even the Queen herself, Elizabeth I, became infamous for her exaggerated mask-like white face.

Unlike what is traditionally accepted, hair powders (akin to a modern-day dry shampoo) would not attract vermin, as the typical ingredients included cloves and citrus, which were natural flea and lice repellents.

The hair and skin were also perfumed with a multitude of scents available to the Tudors, who had their own personal preferences; ambergris (the fat from a whale's stomach) was a favourite, as were concentrated liquid forms of citrus, sage, mint, jasmine, camomile and fennel. Surprisingly, many of these scents are still firm favourites in today's modern society.

Honey or egg whites would be used to set the hair as a rudimentary hairspray and gel, but could produce sticky and crunchy results. Hair would be combed, often with combs made from wood, shell or bone. Hair could be dyed and lightened with citrus juice and sunlight, or it could be darkened with soot and charcoal powder. Hair pomade could be made from fat, and would have been used by both men and women. Beards in particular may have been shaped with pomade. Hair for women was encouraged to be as long as possible, and many females went their whole lives without a haircut. Hair would have been set and styled usually only once a week – when going to church. Although the Tudors did not use hairbrushes, strands of Tudor hair would have been surprisingly healthy, as regular combing with wide-tooth combed would have allowed for natural oils to be dispersed throughout the head, so dandruff and scalp build-up would have been relatively uncommon.

On the other hand, fine-tooth combs would have been used by those suffering from the dreaded headlice. Rudimentary lice-shampoos would have been made from salt water, lye and oil, or quicksilver and pungent-smelling herbs. Animal grease may have been applied to the hair in order to trap lice, or it may have been cut short. Combs soaked in a parsley or mustard seed solution also would have been used to repel headlice. Grease and animal fats would have also made for a rudimentary hair wax, and would have presumably produced an unpleasant smell, as well as resulted in a sticky, greasy feeling that would have undoubtedly attracted insects, pests and other wildlife! In this case, perhaps the wearing of cats and coifs were preferred!

In the sixteenth century, beauty ideals for women were often difficult to achieve. Women were encouraged to have blanched, pure skin, devoid of any blemishes like scars, freckles, spots or redness. Blonde or golden hair was the ideal, and most women were expected to wear their hair long, many often never having their hair cut in their entire lifetimes. High foreheads were fashionable, as were large, glassy eyes of a green or blue colour. Women were encouraged to stay lithe, but curvaceous, and to achieve a flushed complexion without the assistance of makeup.

Small, straight, white teeth were also favoured. However, achieving these ideals were difficult for the vast majority of women in sixteenth-century England, even those who had been born with light hair, eyes and skin. Acne, not just a modern skin complaint, bothered the Tudors just as it bothers us today. Remarkably, many late medieval and Tudor remedies for acne are similar to modern-day advice, which included eating well, washing the face with fresh water, and getting plenty of sunlight. The application of astringent herbs, particularly fresh witch hazel and mint, directly to the skin, proved particularly effective in the sixteenth century, and is still a natural remedy relied on today. Of course, more serious complaints of acne, such as that of cystic acne, where spots erupt in painful swellings, were just as common in the sixteenth century. Cystic acne regularly causes facial scarring, and was as much of a problem to the Tudors as it is for us. The Tudors also had to deal with other skin scarring, from sunburn, and, more commonly, from smallpox.

Queen Elizabeth I was so plagued with facial scarring from her bout of smallpox in 1562, that she took to concealing the pits the disease had left in her skin with thick layers of leaden makeup for the rest of her life. Elizabeth's insecurity was not uncommon, and soon the trend of covering the faces of both men and women in makeup for the use of covering scars became commonplace at court, which then, in turn, trickled down to the masses, who sought to create expensive cosmetics from ingredients they could make or forage at home.

To achieve the desired golden hair so famed by women at the court of Queen Elizabeth I, many men and women alike turned to temporary dyes. Surprisingly, Tudor hair dyes were made up of much of the same ingredients as modern box dyes, and were often better for the body. Henna, an ingredient still used today, was accessible to the Tudors, and was a luxury product brought over to England on overseas voyages. It was a temporary solution, and so was favoured by some, though many wanted something stronger. For those who could not afford to purchase henna, a golden, blonde look could be achieved through the creation of a paste made from saffron and cumin, which would be crushed, mixed with oil, and then combed through the hair. Lemon juice was also applied directly to the hair root, with the user then encouraged to sit directly in the sun for it to bleach. All of these methods are still in use today across the globe. Alternatively, waxes and animal grease could be applied to the hair from root to tip, and would be dusted and set in place with a powder – sometimes made from simple flour – to create the illusion of brighter hair. Ultimately, these techniques worked only temporarily. For those who wished for long-lasting, bleached hair, they often turned to the same thing which stripped houses of its colour, and paintings of its pigment; lye.

Lye, in small quantities, was added to the hair and left to sit until bleached. It certainly was a solution that worked. But no sooner had the bleaching occurred, so too would skin irritation and the breakage of the hair follicles. Soon enough, entire handfuls of hair could fall out in clumps. It was much safer to therefore stick to a harmless, natural, semipermanent recipe, therefore. Hair for unmarried women and girls would be left loose, and would have often reached long lengths, since haircuts for females were not common in the sixteenth century. The only women who had regular haircuts were nuns, whose monastic orders required the maintenance of closely-cropped hair. Once a woman had married, her hair was then required to be covered with a headdress denoting her position. Coifs – close fitting, linen caps, were common amongst the peasant classes, and could be washed and interchanged so that a fresh item was worn every day. Hair nets were also favoured, but more often by the women of the wealthier classes. Either way, the majority of women in sixteenth-century England wore their hair most often parted in the centre and braided in one single braid along their back, or wrapped in elaborate, beautiful buns kept in place with hair pins.

For the wealthiest women in society, particularly those who made regular appearances at court, hoods were worn to conceal their hair. In the early sixteenth century, the gable hood, a pentagonal, angular-shaped headdress was made fashionable thanks to high-status women wearing them, most notably Queens Katherine of Aragon and Jane Seymour, both of whom favoured the English tradition. But even before then, the first Tudor Queen, Elizabeth of York, had cemented the Gable Hood as a fashion must in Tudor England, with decorative, velveteen lappets to conceal the ears, as well as a baggy receptacle to hold any excess hair.

At the turn of the 1510s, another style of hood became fashionable amongst the wealthier classes of women. Although typically believed to have been brought over to England by Anne Boleyn, the French Hood, a semi-circular, stiff board covered with velvet, silk and decorative beads, was actually introduced to England by Mary Tudor, the fashionable younger sister of Henry VIII who had served a brief stint as Queen of France in 1514. Either way, the French Hood became an instant hit amongst wealthy, upper-class women in sixteenth-century England, and became a status symbol. Even smaller versions of the French hood were made for use of wear by children, and it remained a firm favourite in fashion until well into the reign of Queen Elizabeth I. A long, draping black silk would hang down from the French hood, intended to fully conceal the hair and back of the necks of women. For the poorer classes who could not afford this luxurious headpiece, however, they turned to other, less expensive forms of head coverings.

Lettice caps did not resemble lettuce, but rather was an angular cap closely resembling the English Gable hood that was worn snugly to the head. Lettice caps were traditionally made from a thick material, often wool or felt, and as such were popular amongst all classes particularly during the winter months. Lettice caps were relatively simple to construct, and, as such, were popular amongst all classes of sixteenth-century England. So too were Biggins, a type of linen cap more sophisticated than the coif, that was popularised amongst the lowest classes in the Elizabethan Age. The plain but practical Biggins caps, which had been popular in the Middle Ages, had made a resurgence at the latter end of the sixteenth century, and would have been worn by men, women and children alike. By the turn of the seventeenth century, they were a staple item in the wardrobes of almost every peasant across the country. They served to keep hair and sweat away from the face, and would be perfumed with fragrance or changed daily in order to keep them fresh.

Hairstyles for men were much simpler. In most cases, men were required to wear caps if they were above the age of six, or risk heavy fines. They would have kept their hair short and cropped, though longer styles that fell around the ears were favoured also, so long as they were neatly trimmed and combed. Facial hair was considered a sign of a man's virility, for it was believed that its appearance in puberty was directly linked to the heat of a man's body, which presented itself on the exterior through the excessive production of bodily hair. For most men, then, beards were a symbol of sexual prowess and unbridled masculinity, and as such beards kept in square cuts were fashionable, at least in the mid-century. By the Elizabethan Age, however, the pointed beard came into fashion, no doubt in large part due to its favour with the likes of high-flying courtiers like Sir Walter Raleigh, and even goatees, made fashionable by court favourites like Robert Dudley, the Earl of Leicester. This trend of pointed facial hair even continued past the sixteenth century, and well into the reign of the first Stuart King of England, James I. Although it is often disputed whether Henry VIII had introduced strict bans on facial hair – in particular, of moustaches – in 1535, there is no evidence to suggest that the King actually intended to go through with the taxation of those of his subjects who wore their beards long. After all, the King had kept his own beard long throughout most of his adult life, and had even quipped to his first wife, Queen Katherine of Aragon, who apparently detested his beard, that he would please his queen by resolving 'to wear his beard till the said meeting (of Francis I), and said surely he would never put it off till he had seen him'. Katherine must not have been very impressed.[35]

Shaving was popular with men in the sixteenth century, and neatly-trimmed beards in angular, square shapes or smoothly-shaved faces were the aesthetic preferences. The shaving of bodily hair was much less common, however, and the embracing of natural body hair was the norm for both men and women in the sixteenth century. That does not mean that everyone was a fan of this trend, however, and certainly many men and women alike took up a razor to remove any unwanted, unruly hair. Recipes for hair removal creams were also in circulation in Tudor society, but these were dangerous and caused harmful effects to the skin, even resulting in irreversible and life-threatening effects. One such recipe came from Turkey in 1532:

1. Create a rhusma (paste) from a mixture of one pint of boiled arsenic and one eighth of a pint of boiled quicklime.
2. Sit in a hot bath and smear the mixture directly onto bare skin.

You would know when the mixture had begun to take effect when you could feel a stinging, burning sensation. Then, you would be required to wash it away from your skin as immediately as possible with fresh cold water. It was true that this recipe was efficient in the removal of bodily hair; but it was also efficient in the removal of skin, too.[36]

The term 'barber' comes from the Latin *barba*, meaning beard, and was a well-paid and popular occupation in the sixteenth century. Barber shops, now principally trading in the removal and styling of bodily and facial hair, would have had a plethora of other jobs which they would carry out, including dentistry, amputation, and other rudimentary surgery. The thought of a barber performing surgery upon a patient seems horrifying, although they were perhaps the most qualified members of sixteenth-century society to carry out the gruesome duty, and would have not only had great knowledge of the human body, but would have also been equipped with the sufficient surgical tools. Barber shops in sixteenth-century England would have been furnished with chairs, as well as trestle tables that could quickly be constructed in the case of an emergency. Patients requiring surgery would lie upon these tables, often with pewter bowls at their feet which were intended for the capture of blood, bone, limbs and any other bodily matter that the barber-surgeon was tasked with removing from the body.

Barber-surgeons would have had a whole host of instruments within their cabinets in the sixteenth century, not only razors or shears used for the trimming of hair. Rather, it was common sight for barber-surgeons to have jars of leeches that would assist in the letting of the blood, as well as maggots, that would be placed within open wounds to remove any necrotic, festering bodily matter by eating away at it. Barber-surgeons also would have used forceps, scalpels and needles, as well as hammers and even bone saws to cut away at bodily parts. Even Henry VIII had his own dedicated barber who regularly attended to the King's facial hair, as well as styling and trimming his royal head; his name, given for his profession, was Piers Barbour.

Wardrobes came at a later date for poorer families who owned more than a few sets of clothes – until then, families who did own numerous articles of clothing used 'perches', or clothes hooks. Uniforms were worn by a select few of Tudor society, including those required to wear liveries while serving members of the richest of society, as well as in the army. Found within the inventories of the *Mary Rose* were uniforms costing four shillings each, of a white surcoat lined with beautiful green braiding. This uniform would have been worn only by the soldiers on board, of which there were around three hundred. Everyone else made do with a simple uniform of brown tunics and breeches, costing around two shillings each. Skull caps too would have been worn by sixteenth-century men, particularly soldiers, sailors and fishermen. These caps were often made from a thin, breathable and lightweight material such as linen, and were closely cropped to the head to absorb sweat, and even keep lice at bay. Indeed, amongst the personal items recovered from the shipwrecked *Mary Rose* in the Solent were a multitude of lice combs, as well as silk embroidered pouches, pocket sundials (the predecessor of the modern wristwatch) thimbles for sewing, rings (especially signet rings that had the personal signifiers and family heraldry of the individuals upon them), rosaries, whistles and personal wax seals and stamps for use of closing letters.[37]

Ultimately, the bedroom was a concept still foreign to many Tudors at the opening of the sixteenth century, and would have been used for all sorts of recreational activities aside from sleeping, including the enjoyment of hobbies and entertainment, as well as the exploration of intimate relationships and sexual intercourse.

Chapter 7

The Nursery

'...then the whining schoolboy, with his satchel and shining
morning face, creeping like a snail unwillingly to school.'
William Shakespeare, *As You Like It*:
Act 2, Scene 7., 1599.[1]

The life of a child was precarious in Tudor England. A woman could
give birth numerous times in her lifetime, though only half of her infants
would survive to their first birthdays, and only a quarter would reach
adolescence. Almost half of all children in sixteenth-century England
died before the age of ten, and the loss of offspring was a heartbreaking,
but expected, part of any parent's life.

The nuclear family of sixteenth-century England consisted of a
father, mother, and two children, much like it is today. We often expect
the numbers of Tudor families to be much larger, given the inefficiency
of contraception resulting in repetitive births and numerous pregnancies
throughout a sixteenth-century woman's lifecycle. Yet, death,
indiscriminate in who it targeted, came for both old and young alike,
and as such many sixteenth-century parents prepared for the worst.

If they were lucky to survive infancy, a child may grow up surrounded
by siblings in their natal homes. For the vast majority of children,
however, the loss of siblings would have been just another part of life.
Suddenly, their playfellows were gone. It is often asserted by modern
historians that children felt little at the loss of their siblings. In reality,
however, there is much evidence to suggest that the bonds formed
between siblings in early life were some of the most vital to kinship
networks when they reached adulthood.[2] This was particularly true in
cases where a set of siblings had lost their parents, causing a reliance
on each other where older siblings typically assumed pastoral roles over
the younger.[3] Almost all children in sixteenth-century England could
expect to see at least one – if not both – of their parents die before they

had reached adulthood, particularly during periods of social devastation, such as wars or plague. Mothers could, and regularly did, die in childbed, leaving surviving children orphaned or lacking in maternal influence. Even King Henry VIII and his two sisters, the Princesses Margaret and Mary, had been devastated by the loss of their mother, Queen Elizabeth, when she succumbed to puerperal fever giving birth to their youngest sister Katherine at the Tower of London in 1503.[4]

The loss of children shattered local communities in sixteenth-century England. In Stratford-upon-Avon in the year 1560, sixty-three infants were recorded in the parish records as being baptised.[5] Yet tragically, not even half of these infants would survive to reach their first birthdays, and of the sixty-three baptised, forty-three were buried later that year. A community once thriving with new life had been forced to face an horrific reality; only twenty infants had survived in the entirety of Stratford that year, and many more would be expected to die before adolescence.

It is often traditionally asserted by popularist historians that parents cared little for their children in the sixteenth century, with many evidencing their arguments with the Tudor custom of sending their children away to live in the homes of others.[6] Even foreign contemporaries visiting England were baffled by this custom. One Venetian envoy wrote:

> everyone, however rich he may be, sends away his children into the houses of others, while he, in return, receives those of strangers into his own.[7]

The same envoy later wrote, scathingly, that:

> The want of affection in the English is strongly manifested toward their children; for after having kept them at home till they arrive at the age of seven or nine years at the most, they put them out, both males and females, to hard service in the houses of other people.[8]

Clearly, this English custom had not caught on across the Continent, with many contemporaries and modern commentators alike considering it akin to 'wilful neglect' and evidence of a lack of parental devotion to their children.[9] But for the Tudors, this custom was entirely normal, and many sixteenth-century adolescents expected to be sent away to the homes of family members and friends in order to receive a good education, form social connections of their own, and find their all-important independence away from their families. In fact, there are numerous records which suggest that many adolescents left home of their own accord to pursue education and apprenticeships, similarly to teenagers in today's modern society.[10]

Adolescents from all corners of sixteenth-century society would be sent away to begin to lay the foundations of their own adult lives. Even princes and princesses could expect to leave their natal homes while still in the midst of childhood. Both Arthur Tudor, the son of King Henry VII, and Mary, the future Queen Mary I, were sent away from their parents to live in households of their own in the countryside. Anne Boleyn had even been sent to the French court to pursue her education. It must have been jarring for some adolescents to move away from the family home, particularly if they came from the city and had since found themselves residing in the countryside. However, once a year or so had elapsed, their studies proven sufficient, and their apprenticeships come to a close, many adolescents returned to their families to assist in their parents' businesses, applying the skills which they had acquired during their times away. Many remained in the area, eventually raising families of their own, and relying again on the strong familial bonds formed between siblings in childhood, who would eventually come to house their own nieces and nephews and assist in their educations.

Sending an adolescent away for education in the sixteenth century was akin to sending a modern child away to boarding school today. Ultimately, Tudor England was much more sparsely inhabited than it is today, and as such, many families had little other option but to send away their children in the hopes that they attain the education and etiquette desired to set them in good stead for later life. Catherine Howard, the fifth Queen of King Henry VIII, had herself been sent away to a sort of Tudor-style boarding school entirely for females of a similar age and social rank, in Horsham in Sussex.[11] Catherine's adolescent life at Chesworth House would have been dictated by strict, daily regimes of learning and courtly etiquette, music lessons, needlework, and hours of idle gossip. The girls at Chesworth would have been custom to a monotonous daily routine of eating and sleeping only at the manor, where they were imposed with strict instructions not to drink beer, or to swear, or to fraternise with any males. They were also banned from gambling, sleeping too late or laying in too long, and were required to be on their best behaviours at all times. Of course, this was not the reality. Teenagers in the sixteenth century were just as teenagers are now, and it quickly became common knowledge that the teenage girls residing at Chesworth were lavishing in drink, gambling, and sex, which directly led to Catherine's downfall and to her execution in 1542.

The behaviour of children and adolescents in the sixteenth century was highly regulated by manuals aimed at both youths and their parents, and dictated everything from table manners, to diet.[12] Children were told not to talk in Church, nor to laugh too loud, else they would face reprimand. They had to doff their caps to their social superiors, greet others courteously, and were taught not to imitate others behind their backs. They were instructed not to throw sticks and stones at animals or people, to fight, swear, or to wear dirty clothes. They were allowed to play without adult supervision, but had to be sensible around open bodies of water and fences.[13] The fact that so many rules had had to be written suggests that sixteenth-century children got up to all sorts of trouble; they certainly were not as well-behaved as we are often led to believe. There is a school of thought within historiography that suggests that the majority of children in the sixteenth century had little fun, or little imagination, and that they were little more than 'miniature adults' with no semblance of childhood.[14] Certainly, the strict rules that they were to observe do support the idea that the lives of children were greatly regimented. But the true extent to which these rules had been enforced will never be known for certain.

It is certainly true that children in the sixteenth century would have been privy to such things as sexual intercourse, marriage and death at an earlier age than children of today's society. By the time a boy had reached the age of majority of fourteen in the sixteenth century, he may have already witnessed the deaths of his siblings or of a parent, and may have been employed for a number of years. Many boys in their early to mid-adolescence may have also been conscripted into the Royal Army, particularly during periods of turbulence and war. Sixteenth-century girls, by comparison, may have been married and even have produced children of their own while still in their own adolescence. As soon as a girl had begun to menstruate, it symbolised her biological ability to procreate and to have children, and as such, younger brides, often barely out of their teens, were encouraged to enter into contracts with often much older husbands. Margaret Beaufort, the mother of King Henry VII, for example, had married and fallen pregnant when she herself was just thirteen years old. The birth had been traumatic for Margaret, whose body simply had not yet matured fully enough for childbearing, thus resulting in a difficult labour and lasting physiological and psychological scars. Margaret never fell pregnant or gave birth again, with many modern historians since accrediting her reproductive inability in later life to the trauma she had endured during the birth of her son.

*

There was a traditionally accepted belief in the sixteenth century that the uterus was split into many chambers, and was not one 'hollow' organ as we now know today. It was also considered to be an inversion of the male reproductive organ, the penis. It was believed that, if sperm reached the left chamber, it would result in the birth of a baby girl, but if it entered the right side it would result in a boy. There was also the belief that girls were conceived from defective sperm, whereas males were created from strong, more potent semen. Old wives' tales predominate in the medical manuals of the sixteenth century, particularly when it came to pregnancy and childbearing. The belief that mothers could determine the sex of their baby from the size of their breasts was another common belief that many Tudor mothers and medical practitioners alike believed. It is easy to laugh, but in reality, mothers had few other signifiers of their pregnancy and of the health of their growing babies; it was only in the recent twenty-first century that obstetric advances have led to such things as ultrasounds and pregnancy tests, allowing expectant mothers to determine the length of their pregnancies and the sex of their babies.

Old wives' tales did not just concern mothers and their babies. It was typically accepted in late medieval and early modern England that the duration of one's sleep could greatly impact their physical health. Seven hours of sleep was encouraged for children, but no more, for it was written that 'seven hours for a child is temperate and good, if more, it offendeth and hurteth the blood'.[15] Children were expected to wake at six every morning 'at the farthest', and laying in any later was strictly prohibited.[16] However, it is quite difficult to imagine many older children and adolescents in particular abiding by this rule, and it is more plausible that youths would have lounged in bed in the mornings just as many modern teenagers do today. Additionally, rulings instructing that child sleep a maximum of seven hours suggests that Tudor parents allowed children to remain awake until late at night, not turning to bed until ten or eleven in the evening. Again, the extent that this rule was followed by Tudor parents is unclear, but, considering adults were encouraged to get almost ten hours of sleep in the sixteenth century, it was most likely that many parents simply put their children to bed early out of want of privacy and peace.

Immediately upon waking, a child was encouraged to say prayers for his or her family, and then dress themselves (or with the help of maids if their families could afford their services) in clothes that they themselves had brushed and folded.[17] Like adults, most children in sixteenth-century England had only a few pairs of clothing, so the selection would not have been that great. However, Tudor clothing was still notoriously fiddly, and the rulings of Sumptuary Laws meant that even young children had to be conscious of what they wore. Boys older than six, for example, were required to wear a flat felted cap daily; if they failed to do so, they would face a harsh penalty fine. Upon dressing, children were then required to wash their faces and their hands, and to brush their teeth, nails and hair. It was only then, when these miraculously self-disciplined children had completed their morning routines, were they then permitted to head into the kitchen and break their fasts, as well as greet their parents for the first time that day.

Children would be allowed occasional cups of alcohol throughout the day in the sixteenth century, though certainly not in as large quantities as is traditionally believed. Watered-down wine or ale, known as small ale, was often given to children if no other suitable drink, such as milk or water, was available. It is quite unlikely, however, that the children of the sixteenth century would have found these alcoholic drinks appealing, for they were notoriously bitter and too weak to have any significant alcoholic effect. Quite simply, the alcohol given to children in the sixteenth century was little more than a malt drink, and would have only been given in very small quantities of two cups a day so as not to run the risk of drunkenness.

Table manners were important to the Tudors, and even children were taught to abide by rules outlined in behavioural manuals.[18] They were told not to slurp their drinks, or to blow bubbles, and had to sit at designated spots at the dinner table.[19] They were discouraged from scratching their noses, spitting out food or eating noisily, and were expressly instructed not to bring pets to the table. Dinner time was meant to be a communal, family affair, and children were encouraged to share their food and drink with the person sitting beside them. They were even taught not to pilfer food from the kitchen, not to steal fruit from bushes and trees, and were not allowed to help themselves to crops without the permission of those who were growing them.

Dinner table etiquette was simpler for babies. Just like today, infants and young children were fed a different diet than older children and adults, and were encouraged to take a diet of milk and other, soft foods such as pulped fruits and tender meats. Teething infants were allowed to suck on fruits, vegetables and other soft foods, such as bread and meat, in the hopes that it would soothe swollen, broken gums. To wean very young infants on meat and other such solids today is often considered dangerous, but for parents in the sixteenth century, it was the norm. Baby formula had, of course, not been invented by the sixteenth century, and would not be until well into the 1800s. Most babies were therefore fed on the milk of their mothers, or, for those who could not breastfeed, turned to other helpful female relatives, friends, and even community members to feed their babies.

Wet nurses were women who had recently had babies of their own, and whose milk was still in such good supply that it was used to feed the babies of others. Wet nurses were often chosen for their qualities, their appearance and their family standing, for it was believed that the qualities of the woman passed through to the child through her breastmilk. Wet-nursing could be a lucrative business for some women, particularly those who had been head-hunted by rich, noble families to nurse their newborn infants. Wet nurses could also have more than one charge, resulting not only in increased wages, but also, charmingly, allowed for the formation of close affinities between nurse and child.[20] There are numerous delightful accounts of children honouring their wetnurses in later life, particularly in sixteenth-century wills and inventories, as well as in letters.[21] Even the teenage King Henry VIII remembered his wet nurse, Anne Oxenbridge, with great fondness, so much so that he personally wrote to her inviting her to his coronation. Additionally, the wet nurse of one little Robert Apslon had been recorded as 'treating the child as [if he were] her own'.[22]

Because of their pastoral roles and close relationships to their charges, wet nurses often became surrogate mothers to their children and were regularly known as milk-mothers in Tudor society.[23] This idea dated well back to the Middle Ages; Richard the Lionheart himself referred to another child who was fed by his wet nurse, Alexander Neckham, as his 'milk-brother'.[24]

Indeed, there is plenty of evidence to suggest that children were loved and cared for by all members of sixteenth-century society, not just their own kin. Employees, for example, have been known to leave great sums of money and other generous bequeaths to their adolescent apprentices in wills; one even left the ownership of his wife.[25] Another apprentice had been buried within the same grave as his master.[26] Certainly, apprenticeships were fantastic ways for youths to enter into the world of work and to seek employment and independence of their own in sixteenth-century England. The employ of apprentices, however, had to abide by strict regulations as outlined in an injunction written in 1510.[27] In this, it was written that apprentices had to be at least sixteen years old to carry out their duties, had to be tall, lithe, and 'not disfigured' or disabled in limb. Male apprentices were also required to have a basic knowledge of reading and writing, and had to be of English parentage and origin. The sons and daughters of villeins were dissuaded from apprenticeships, and any youth considered disobedient, uncomely in the liveries (or uniforms) of their masters, were rejected. It could be a cruel world for already image-conscious Tudor adolescents.

For those who were successful in attaining apprenticeships, their lives would have greatly mimicked those of the adults around them. Girls stayed within the home, and learned the trade of homecraft with their mothers or employers. They were taught the arts of cleaning, cooking, and tending to children, a sort of multifaceted housemaid. Although by the sixteenth-century education for girls was being encouraged, no doubt in large part to the influence of the most learned woman in the country Queen Elizabeth I, it was still far from widespread and commonplace in Tudor England. Girls of all classes would have learnt to read or to spell at the very least their names if nothing else. However far their education continued after that was entirely dependent on the wishes of their families. For the most part however, sixteenth-century girls did have some decent understanding of counting, animal rearing, and household management, as well as softer skills like weaving and spinning. Those who did not pursue education instead remained at home with their families and were employed in the family business; young girls are especially prevalent in records of fish, ale and cloth trade.

Ultimately, females were discouraged from pursuing any sort of employment that would take them too far from home, and they were denied all academic, medical, and religious occupations. Girls could not go to university, or train as lawyers. They very rarely owned businesses in their own right, and only inherited them from their fathers or husbands if no other heirs were available. Employment prospects for girls were limited; they could turn to midwifery, enter into religious service (at least, in the first half of the sixteenth century) or assist in apothecary shops, but, for the vast majority of females, they had to content themselves with futures as homemakers, servants, nurses, or mothers. As was written in the poetic medieval manual *How the Goode Wife Taught Hyr Daughter*, 'dwell at home, daughter, and love thy work much'.[28] There was little else to do.

For boys, however, prospects were brighter. Many young boys could expect to learn their rhetoric and writing, their numbers and sums, and the *Trivium* and *Quadrivium,* modules that included the study of music, grammar and even astronomy. The sons of wealthier members of sixteenth-century society were given opportunities to end their educations once they had reached the age of majority to pursue careers or apprenticeships, or they could continue to university, and training in law, religion and other civic roles. Sixteenth-century educators took great pride in their students, whose intellectual capabilities were encouraged; 'sweet children, for love of whom I write, I beseech you, with very loving heart, that you set your delight upon knowing this book'.[29] Boys and adolescent young men were encouraged to leave behind martial pursuits in favour of education, and were taught to walk with their heads held high and their eyes straight, and to be proud of their prospects.[30] Whereas girls would while away their days playing with poppets, small, cloth or wooden dolls that prepared them for motherhood, young Tudor boys were gifted feathered quills sharpened to a point, charcoal and waxy-crayon-like implements, and tablets with which to practice their writing. Boys would read such books as the *Anglorum Praelia* (1327 – 1558) and the *Elizabetha: De Pacatissimo Angliae Statu imperante Elizabetha* to gain knowledge of the world around them and prepare them for adult life.[31] Male illiteracy had indeed significantly lessened by the close of the sixteenth century, thanks to the acknowledgement of the importance of education, which had influenced much of the domestic policy of the time. Gone were the days of illiteracy and learning by doing; now, the youngest generation of sixteenth-century England was disseminating their knowledge through pen and paper. It appears that this 1579 Tudor proverb rang true; 'youth and white paper do take any impression'.[32]

Chapter 8

Fun, Games and Entertainment

'We shall have a madding time in our youth.'
Henry Howard, Earl of Surrey,
Private Letter, 1543.[1]

The Tudors were great lovers of entertainment, and often spent lavishly on games, sports, and other leisurely activities to relax and indulge in. Many houses of the richest members of sixteenth-century England were fortunate enough to have dedicated ante-chambers for entertaining purposes, as well as dedicated watching chambers that were suspended above halls by wooden hoists, purposely balconied so that onlookers could watch and cheer on festivities that occurred below. They also served as hidden niches in which musicians could sit to provide music to those galivanting below. Some houses would have also been built with extensions of libraries, studies, solars (private sittings rooms), ballrooms and even home apothecaries, where housewives, servants and the scientifically-minded of Tudor society could practice the cultivation of medicinal herbs and dispense their own drugs without needing to take a trip to the nearby village.

Perhaps one of the most popular forms of entertainment in the sixteenth century was the playing of musical instruments. Instruments of all forms were played across the country by all walks of life, rich and poor, educated or otherwise. Favourite Tudor instruments included drums, fiddles, oboes, tabors (a medieval amalgamation of a lightweight hand-held drum and a bagpipe), pipes and flutes. Sackbuts, a rather humorous name for an early form of trombone, were also played in the sixteenth century, as were virginals, a type of keyboard-like harpsichord, as well as the lute, the ancestor of the modern-day guitar.[2]

Musical instruments were especially played alongside the telling of stories, providing a soundtrack to Tudor plays and theatre. Indeed, the theatre proved an instant success in sixteenth-century English society, no doubt popularised by medieval predecessors and famous playwrights like William Shakespeare and poets like John Skelton. The social historian Ian Mortimer estimated that around one-third of all middle-class Londoners attended theatre shows and watched performances every month in late Elizabethan England, a testament to its popularity.[3] Both Tudor men and women alike enjoyed frequent visits to the theatre, and even performing on stage. Men began taking the roles of women in plays from the 1450s onwards, and were performing regularly as women by the time of Shakespeare's occupation of the Globe in the late sixteenth century. In a time before newspapers and television broadcasts, stage plays were often the first avenue for Tudors to hear important news and gossip, including both local and communal affairs, as well as news from further afield.

Writing for pleasure too was a pastime that many Tudors enjoyed. From poems, to short stories, diary extracts and nursery rhymes, many Tudors used notebooks or leaves of bound paper to record their thoughts. King Henry VII himself apparently kept a private journal in which he would record his most private of thoughts.[4] It later transpired in a 'merry tale', wrote Francis Bacon, that when the king's pet monkey had gotten a hold of the journal and tore it to pieces, 'the court, which liked not those pensive accounts, was almost tickled with sport'.[5] Henry, presumably, did not find it so humorous.

Writing allowed for those who were literate to express themselves, as well as provide a commentary on the world around them. Indeed, many plays, poems and even nursery rhymes were written as a reflection of the society in which they were inspired. The popular nursery rhyme *Little Jack Horner*, for example, was believed to have been an allegory of the pillaging of ecclesiastical buildings during the Dissolution of the Monasteries:

> Little Jack Horner
> Sat in the corner,
> Eating a Christmas pie;
> He put in his thumb,
> And pulled out a plum,
> And said, What a good boy am I!.[6]

Jack Horner, depicted as a greedy child, is believed to represent either Thomas Cromwell, the executor of the Dissolution, or the King,

Henry VIII himself. Jack's lust for the prize of the plum has been understood by historians as reminiscent of the valuables pillaged from destroyed monastic buildings. And, as Jack Horner proudly states, 'what a good boy am I!', it is not too difficult to imagine the same sentiments being expressed by the King, lavishing in his new-found wealth and drunk with tyrannical power.

Although paper was not produced in England in the early sixteenth century, books were often imported to England from William Caxton's press in Bruges. Wynkyn de Worde, Caxton's most trusted partner, took over the charge of the press and moved it to Fleet Street in London in 1500, where books were printed on an increasingly mass-scale to hungry audiences. According to household historian Simon Thurley, the Tudors did not store and display their books vertically upon shelves as we would today.[7] Rather, he asserts that sixteenth-century bookcases would have been stacked horizontally, with one book atop another. Ultimately, it probably came down to individual preference and aesthetics, but we can probably be assured that, like many of us today, the bookshelves of many Tudor households were probably overflowing with these special new goods.

The introduction of affordable reading materials in the sixteenth century delighted the Tudors, who frequented booksellers and shops for the latest releases. Crowds went wild for printed versions of Geoffrey Chaucer's titillating *The Canterbury Tales*, as well as Arthurian legends and poems like William Langland's *Piers Plowman*. The introduction of the printing press to sixteenth-century England also allowed for the mass manufacture of such things as playing cards and tiny, pocket-sized copies of the monarch's image, which were favourite souvenirs to those who visited the city. Indeed, shops were frequented not only for necessities, but also for retail therapy, with London being the largest hub of shopping and trade throughout the whole of sixteenth-century England. Despite its name, Cheapside in London was a very wealthy area with streets full of shops, stalls and travelling merchants that sold anything from gold, silver, and other precious metals, as well as dyed cloth, carpet, tapestries and 'much other exotic merchandise' according to the contemporary chronicler Mancini.[8] London was a city diverse in people and tastes; German citizens frequented stores of linen and precious stones and metals, whereas those who had come from the Low Countries favoured pottery and crockery, as well as playing cards and board games.[9]

The playing of board games was a popular pastime in Tudor England, and would have been enjoyed by the rich and poor alike. Favourite board games included chess, backgammon, draughts, dice, and 'nine-mens morris', a game that would test one's strategical abilities in a one-on-one competition.[10] As well as these, the Tudors were also fond of playing shuffleboard, and 'quoits', a game in which players would stand in a circle and throw rubber rings onto a hook in the middle, hoping that their hooks would latch.[11] Bowling, which more closely resembled modern-day lawn bowls than ten-pin bowling, was a game which attracted men and women alike. Thick wooden discs – not too dissimilar to a wheel of cheese! – were used as balls, with the aim of the game to hit a 'jack', a sedentary marker that sat at the far end of a bowling alley. Whoever got their disc closest to the jack won the game. It was a simple, cheap and entertaining game that could be played practically anywhere, from flat lawns to dedicated alleys sloped for additional difficulty.

Ball games truly had their footing in the sixteenth century, and quickly became established as one of England's most favourite forms of entertainment. The game of football has been recorded in annals as early as the twelfth century in England, and certainly, there are recorded instances of organised matches occurring between entire teams in the sixteenth century.[12] In 1170, William FitzStephen, a chronicler of the life of Saint Thomas Becket, wrote of a game favoured by youths that was played in the fields with a ball. FitzStephen continued, writing that:

> the elders, the fathers, and the men of wealth come on horseback to view the contests of their juniors, and in their fashion sort with the young men…there seems to be aroused in these elders a stirring of natural heat by viewing so much activity and by participation in the joys of unrestrained youth.[13]

Clearly, football hooliganism was not a modern invention. In fact, many medieval monarchs had hoped to quell the football craze by enacting laws against it during their reign, and King Henry VII even outlawed the playing of the game entirely a year after ascending to the throne in 1496. Subsequent pleas and petitions were made to the king after illicit football matches between youths had been discovered to have taken place, causing much disruption. In the 1583 book, *Anatomy of Abuses*, Philip

Stubbs even wrote that 'football playing and other devilish pastimes withdraweth us from godliness'.[14] But not everyone was convinced. In 1576, records of a mass game of football, played between around one hundred young men, were written, and numerous matches, organised by male youths, were broken up and fined after they had been discovered to have been played within church cemetery grounds.[15] King Henry VII's attempt to ban the game was entirely in vain, for even his son, the future Henry VIII was a fan, and even purchased his own pair of bespoke football boots in 1526, studs and all.[16]

Although we may consider sportswear to be a modern invention, even the Tudors were known for sporting a fashionable tracksuit. King Henry VIII was known to play tennis in specially made slippers to stop his feet from slipping on the surface of the court.[17] He also owned an overcoat made from black velvet, which he wore with coordinated shorts.[18] The King was indeed a keen tennis player, whose famous passion for tennis sparked a wave of enthusiastic players taking up the racket across sixteenth-century England. Henry had had courts installed in many of his palaces, including at Windsor, Richmond, and even the Palace of Westminster; those who lived in the proximity of palaces like Hampton Court in London could even rent one of the many tennis courts for personal use, for a princely sum of 2s 6d per day, or around forty pounds in modern currency.[19] When you consider the average annual wage of a labour worker was around £11 in the sixteenth century (or just £3,000 in modern sterling), the divide between rich and poor seemed ever wider.[20]

Tudor Tennis courts were largely similar to their modern-day counterparts, except that they were most often located indoors (known as 'close' tennis) rather than out (known as 'open' tennis). This meant that, no matter the weather, the game was accessible and allowed players to forgo the risk of slipping and injury. Alongside Tudor tennis courts ran covered galleries for spectators to stand and watch, protected by a net of interlacing wire which would bounce any wry tennis balls back toward the opponents.[21] The game became known as 'Royal Tennis', or 'Real Tennis', and was most often played with a large racket, tightly interwoven with string for a satisfying bounce. These rackets, which would have been slightly more oversized than their modern-day descendants, were more oval-shaped than circular, and resembled paddles. They would have been made from lightweight wood, and bound together with leather straps wrapped around the handle, which stopped the player's hands from chafing. The balls would be made from animal hide wrapped around human or animal hair, and would have been closely related to modern-day cricket balls than tennis balls.[22]

*

Cock fighting – now condemned for its unethical practices, was a favourite form of entertainment in sixteenth-century England, and dedicated wooden marquees known as 'pits' were erected to house the obsession.[23] In these pits, spectators sat in a round circle on raised seats, overlooking an octagonal piece of ground below. Beneath the seats of the spectators would be the coops in which the chickens were kept, kept trapped inside by tiny wooden gates to stop them from escaping. At the sound of a shout, the gates were flung open and the cocks were forced into the octagonal pit, a vicious game of chase occurring. The roosters would also be fitted with sharp, armour-like implements upon their backs and their feet, and were specifically chosen and selected for their strength and viciousness. Whichever cock drew blood, or even killed its opponent, was considered the victor. The loser was often discarded upon rubbish heaps, or, even sometimes kept and eaten for meat. Roosters, noisy even at the best of times, create such a noise when they are angry, that it often disturbed villages that lived close to communal cockpits. Even Queen Anne Boleyn was known to detest the sport, and in 1533 ordered the destruction of the cockpit at Greenwich Palace, for it was located too close to her bedroom window, and kept her awake in the morning with their high-pitched shrills.[24] Clearly, not everyone was a fan.

Popular pets of the time included dogs, particularly breeds like mastiffs, beagles and spaniels, as well as birds or cats. Small monkeys and marmosets too were popular pets amongst the upper echelons of society, and reflected the wealth and status of the owners. Only the wealthiest in society owned more exotic, wild animals, with leopards mentioned in records of King Henry VIII. Elizabeth of York, the wife of King Henry VII and the mother of Henry VIII, owned her own lion. Dogs make a special mention in many contemporary sixteenth-century chronicles, including the *Description of England* (1587) by William Harrison, in which dogs received their own chapter, dedicated, 'Of Our English Dogs and Their Qualities'.[25] Another book about dogs – specifically those popularised in England – was published in 1576, and was called, *Of English Dogs*, by Arthur Fleming. Dogs were not so much regarded by their breed, as we would distinguish them today; rather, they were known casually for their functions, the roles that they played in society. Dogs had jobs just as men and women did – from hunting hounds, to sheepdogs, to smaller lap-dogs, who were more companionate in nature. There was also a category of dogs known as 'toyish curs', those who were bred for entertainment purposes, and who were taught tricks and to dance.[26] They sometimes even assisted in household chores, from carrying items from one room to another, to turning the spit roast of the kitchens (called 'turnspit' dogs). Then there were the 'warner' dogs, named for their barks and high-pitched squeals, which were believed to protect their owners from household intruders. Then there were the 'comforter spaniels', who were primarily used as a form of hot-water bottle, intended to keep their mistresses safe and warm up on their laps and in bed.[27] They were even marketed as footwarmers! They were also considered to be 'confidants', little friends in which women could confide with gossip and the most private of personal matters. Some Tudors doted on their dogs, and it is common to see in contemporary artwork dogs depicted with golden, jewelled collars, or leather, silk and velvet. There were even records of some dogs, like the Great Dane, wearing miniature suits of armour, some even adorned with togs or spikes, intended as battle dogs to create an imposing presence. Clearly, love for dogs ran deep in sixteenth-century England, and the Tudors were certainly affectionate of their animals; it was even considered 'wholesome for a weak stomach to bear such a dog'.[28] Dogs were even given biscuit-like treats known as 'chippings' alongside whatever meat scraps its owners had left over from their own dinner tables, a diet that often even the poorest of Tudor society could only hope to afford.[29]

However, there were also strict rules regarding the ownership of dogs surrounding the Tudor court. Any dogs residing near a forest must be below a certain size so as not to hunt the King's game. In order to test the size of the dog, it was made to jump through a small hoop – if it could, it would be allowed to roam the forest without penalty.[30] Anything larger was barred. Large dogs were also discouraged from court, with the exception of the Royal Family's own dogs. This was in order to regulate the household, to keep it 'sweet, wholesome, clean and well furnished'.[31] However, dogs certainly were allowed within the households of the Tudor monarchs – both Henry VIII and his daughter Elizabeth were fond of dogs, particularly of spaniels, and even Anne Boleyn had her own lapdog, possibly also a spaniel, named Purkoy (deriving from the French quip, 'pourquoi?'), who she was recorded to love dearly. Purkoy was beloved by Anne, and when he died in an accident after falling from a window just months after she had received him as a gift, she was devastated:

> the Queen's Grace setteth much store by a pretty dog, and her Grace delighted so much in little Purkoy that after he was dead of a fall there durst nobody tell her Grace of it, till it pleased the King's Highness to tell her Grace of it.[32]

Anne was heartbroken, and had to be told of little Purkoy's death by her husband, the King. Anne Boleyn was known to despise ornamental birds like peacocks, for the noises that they made kept her awake at night as they wandered the grounds of the palaces beneath her window, as well as monkeys, which she could not abide, perhaps possibly due in part for her rival, Katherine of Aragon's love of them.

Dogs could wreak havoc at court. Anne Boleyn also had a greyhound typically believed to have been named Urian after the brother of one of her favourite courtiers William Brereton, who was executed alongside the Queen in 1536. On the 25th of September 1530, Henry VIII was forced to pay ten shillings in reparations to a poor farmer, whose cow had been mauled to death by Anne's dog, 'Itm the same daye paied for A Cowe that Uryren a Breretons greyhounde and my ladye Annes killed'.[33] Clearly, both Henry VIII and Anne Boleyn had instilled in their daughter a shared love for dogs. Elizabeth was reported to love Maltese dogs in particular. Her sister, Mary I, also had a group of spaniels that would accompany her, particularly when she went out hunting or walking. Henry VIII was said to be fond of beagles, while Edward VI was known to sleep with his pet Spaniel, who, legend has it, warned the sleeping boy King of an intrusion from his murderous uncle Thomas Seymour in 1549. Henry VIII named his two beloved pet dogs Cut and Ball, and paid a substantial sum of money (around sixteen shillings, or around two hundred and fifty pounds in today's money) for their safe return after they had escaped from the palace and ran into the forestry around. Henry even installed the Royal Kennels which housed his dogs in his numerous palaces across England.[34] The treatment of these pets, ultimately, was often a lot better than the treatment of the poorest in sixteenth-century society.

Mary, Queen of Scots also was renowned for her love of dogs. She owned a Highland terrier, who famously smuggled itself beneath her skirts at her execution. As the story goes, the little dog had nestled beneath the skirts of the ill-fated Queen while her execution was taking place. It then got covered in its mistress's blood as it ran out from beneath the skirts as her severed head fell below. Katherine Howard received two lapdogs from her husband King Henry VIII on New Year's Day in 1541, though it does not appear that she was a great dog lover, for she later gifted them to the fourth of Henry's wives, Anne of Cleves, who was then living at the childhood home of Anne Boleyn.[35]

Henry VIII was a lover of animals, and, as well as his dogs, he also owned 'two musk cats, two little monkeys and a marmoset'. These musk cats, however, were not felines. Rather, it referred to a sixteenth-century name for an animal such as a musk deer, that secreted smells of musk and roamed around in the acres of the rich. Henry VIII also kept songbirds, his favourites apparently being nightingales, that would sing from their ornamental brass cages which sat upon the windowsills of his palace residences. Ferrets too were also a common choice for a pet in the sixteenth century, and their fur was particularly considered luxurious for it was so soft. Dogs were regularly brushed with so-called 'hair cloths', similar to the body clothes humans would use to cleanse and exfoliate their skin. When Henry VIII died in 1547, almost seventy dog collars, leashes, hair cloths and other canine accessories were found in the king's personal inventory.[36]

Henry VIII was a great lover of horses, and it is estimated that he owned around 200 of the Barbary breed. Henry's great love of horses resulted in the popularisation of horseracing in the sixteenth century, as well as an increase in betting and gambling on horse winnings. But unlike the King, who could own as many horses as he liked, there were separate rules for other members of society. Dukes and archbishops were each allowed to own twenty-four horses, but no more, whereas chaplains were allowed to have only three horses in their possession. For those living in the lower rungs of the social ladder, permittance to own horses was even less, with most families owning just one horse to share between them, unlike the wealthy who could afford a horse for each member of their household. Horse-breeders, carriage drivers, and farmers too were allowed around four horses each for the maintenance of their trade, but otherwise only the richest of society could afford to pay for the animals and their upkeep.

Larger dogs, like mastiffs, greyhounds and whippets would have been trained to hunt and to protect, more so than smaller dogs which were bred for companionate purposes. Larger, purebred dogs would have been kept by the richest and noblest of Tudor society, whereas mixed breeds would have been kept by the marginal classes. It was believed that three mastiff dogs could easily overtake a bear in a fight, while four could easily combat a lion. The French King, Charles IX, was even believed to have his own English mastiff kill a bear, a lion, and a wild cat in a single arena, serving as entertainment for the king and his courtiers. Lap dogs were considered:

> little and pretty, proper and fine, and sought out far and near to satisfy the nice delicacy of dainty dames and wanton women's wills, instruments of folly to play and dally withal…[they are] playfellows for mincing mistresses to bear to their bosoms, to keep company withal in their chambers, to succor with sleep in bed and nourish with meat at board, to lie in their laps and lick their lips as they lie in their wagons and coaches.[37]

Cats did not fare so well in Tudor England. Although Cardinal Thomas Wolsey had had his own pet cat, they were not common domestic animals and were certainly not considered in the same favourable way as dogs. Wolsey insisted on taking his pet cat to court with him, and by all accounts allowed it to sleep on a cushioned chair while working on court matters and attending his court duties.[38] In 1484, a papal bull issued by Pope Innocent VIII declared that cats were the 'companions' of witches, and that their spirits were vessels in which Satan would affect individuals. Black cats in particular were considered the most dangerous of all felines, leading to the popularisation of witches – the wives of Satan – commonly depicted with black cats, and contributing to superstitions even maintained by some today. Although the cat became a more popular domestic animal during the Middle Ages, particularly during periods of plague where they were used principally to catch rats and prevent the spread of disease, this would dissipate by the time the Tudors came to the throne. According to a contemporary report of the coronation of Queen Elizabeth I in January of 1559, a group of cats were rounded up and placed inside a hollow, wicker basket made to resemble the Pope. This effigy was then burned atop a bonfire, a symbol of the casting away of Roman Catholicism, and the embracing of Protestantism that Elizabeth I intended to usher in during her reign.[39]

Cat lovers certainly did exist in Tudor England, however. The father of the Henrician poet Thomas Wyatt, Henry, was imprisoned in the Tower of London, his only companion a stray cat who supposedly kept him alive by bringing Wyatt a dead pigeon regularly, so that he didn't starve. In a later chronicle of the Wyatt family, it was written that 'a cat came into the dungeon with him...he was glad of her, laid her in his bosom to warm him, and by making much of her, won her love... [Henry Wyatt] would ever make much of cats, as other men will their spaniels or hounds'.[40] Another cat lover was Henry Wriothesley, the third Earl of Southampton, whose portrait in 1603 shows him depicted with his beloved cat Trixie. Similarly to Wyatt, Wriothesley's cat had smuggled its way into his cell at the Tower of London, who had been imprisoned for rebelling against Queen Elizabeth I.[41] The cat had, by all accounts, crawled into the chimney of the cell and had made itself at home, but the myth was only further alighted by rumours that Wriothesley's wife Elizabeth had smuggled in the cat to her husband's cell upon a visit to her sick husband in October of 1602, intending it to be a companion and a confidante to her incarcerated love.[42]

The indigenous peoples of the New World brought over unseen animals and other circus delights to England in the mid-sixteenth century, including Harry Hunks, a black bear, who lived at the Tower of London and performed acts, becoming a celebrity in his own right.[43] There had lived a polar bear in the Thames during the Middle Ages, who was chained to a wall near the Tower of London in order to prevent it from swimming too far out; it is quite likely that other bears replaced it in subsequent years. Lions, elephants, bears, leopards, wolves and monkeys were also kept at the menagerie at the Tower of London, and were a tourist attraction that even the poorest of Tudor society could hope to see for their own eyes. Ornamental birds like ostriches, and birds of prey, particularly eagles from the Americas were also kept there, and in 1598, the Elizabethan historian John Stow, on his own visit to the

Tower, recorded that there were three lionesses, a lynx, a wolf, an eagle, a porcupine and a male lion at the Royal Menagerie.[44] The animals were not moved from the Tower of London until 1826, so, until then, it would have been common for Londoners in the proximity to hear the howls of the wolves, and the roars of the lions. It was written, somewhat incongruously, that King Henry VII had an avid dislike of falcons, for they were said to have been capable of killing eagles, birds which were considered to be 'kings of the air'. Henry VII even supposedly went so far as to issue out hanging warrants for falcons all across the country![45]

Tourists were common in any major Tudor city just as they are today. Many of the London landmarks that modern tourists and sightseers visit today, like Shakespeare's Globe, Charing Cross, and Westminster Abbey open for visitors to wander and muse. The Tower of London offered tours of its grounds and of its armoury, where tickets could be purchased in exchange for twelve weeks of an average working man's wages.[46] These tickets certainly were not cheap, and only those who had money to spare could enjoy such exciting, albeit expensive days out.

*

In 1509, there were around one hundred and nine parish churches along the route of the Thames in London, alone.[47] These churches would have been frequented not just on Sundays, but throughout the week by the pious, and by the poor. Churches were safe-havens, and protected their congregation from the vastly unfair prejudices of the time. In an age where the gap between rich and poor was wide, it was also nominally narrow, and as such Parish Churches, such as the ones in the Thames Valley, would have provided shelters, hubs of education, and givers of food and medicine. Although the popularity of pilgrimage lessened by the time of the sixteenth century, many pilgrimage sites across England had since turned into tourist attractions. Many of the monumental, colossal sites that we visit today, such as Westminster Abbey and York Minster would have been attractive sites to any Tudor who found themselves journeying to the area, desperate to get a glimpse of rare magnificence and opulence that they could only hope to ever afford. At Candlewick Street in London was the 'London Stone', a stone supposedly donated by the Trojan King Lud, who supposedly gave London its name; it was reportedly a huge tourist attraction, where vendors would sell souvenirs to passers-by, as well as fast food and informative tours.[48] Tourists would also go to see the tombs of prominent figures, including the infamous diarist Samuel Pepys, who went to see the corpse of Queen Catherine of Valois, which had been on public display and handled (quite literally) by visitors since her death in 1437.[49] Pepys, never the one to shy from uncomfortable situations, embraced the decaying corpse of the long-dead Queen, who had been dead for almost three centuries, and even placed a kiss upon her lips.[50] Pepys later remarked, proudly, in his diary that:

> I had the upper part of her body in my hands and I did kiss her mouth, reflecting upon it that I did kiss a Queen and that this was my birthday, thirty-six years old, that I did first kiss a Queen.[51]

*

To have a faith in Tudor England was important, and most people fell into one Christian denomination, or another. As well as Catholicism and Protestantism, Puritanism, Lutheranism and a whole host of other religious off-shoots were beginning to gain traction in the late sixteenth century, though you would be forgiven for believing that the Tudors were tolerant of a diverse nation. Rather, it was dangerous to openly acknowledge your religion, for you never knew who was listening. While Protestantism had been hailed as the 'true religion' in the reign of the boy-king Edward VI, his half-sister Mary I superseded its beliefs, and instead encouraged the restoration and practice of Roman Catholicism with a fiery fist. This led to a blanket enforcement of Catholic practices in sixteenth-century England, with the vast majority of the English acknowledging Catholicism as the only true form of religion. However many of these Catholics were true believers, however, this is difficult to measure, for faux-believers did their best job to obey the law and follow whatever religion was in fashion, cautious not to rock the already-unsteady boat of religious doctrine and upset the monarch. But, should the news of your true faith catch the ears of your enemies, it could prove fatal. Spies sent to stalk alehouses, brothels, schools and markets, watched with a cautious eye. Those accused of following an unacceptable faith would be sent for punishment, which ranged from anything from a brief telling-off, to imprisonment, whipping, branding, the slitting of noses, or the cutting off of hands, feet, ears and noses.

An injunction against the practice of Catholicism was passed in 1547 under the reign of Edward VI, who banned numerous Catholic practices, including Mass, which was now intended to be known as 'High Communion'. The wooden tables of a Catholic church were replaced with a consecrated altar or communion tables, and pulpits were installed where scholars could recite Protestant doctrine. Images, icons, paintings and relics were banned, covered, painted over, or destroyed entirely, and there was even a blanket restriction on the use of candles and processions in the performance of ceremonies. Organs were dismantled, and religious hymns and chants popularised by the Catholics were replaced with 'reformed' versions more suitable to the Protestant belief. Even the clothing of the clergy was stripped back – gone were the elaborate and beautifully-adorned copes traditionally worn by the Catholics, and instead plain white surplices, and less-elaborate copes and albs were worn in the deliverance of religious services. This was then followed by perhaps one of the most influential books of the day, the Book of Common Prayer, which enforced Protestantism even further across England, and extended the reach of the Protestant church all across the sixteenth century.

In 1553, all Protestant Reforms made under the rule of Edward VI were repealed by the Queen, Mary I, who restored Catholicism to England and encouraged her subjects to follow her 'true' religion. It meant that days were full of religious sermons and prayers, amounting to around five to six hours of religious service a day for the most devout of English Catholics. In the morning would be ceremonies of Matins, Lauds, and Lady Mass, followed by Prime, and then a High Mass. Often, most of these would be said before breakfast had even been eaten. Then, in the afternoon would be the Vespers, followed by Compline. For many of the Tudors in sixteenth-century England, therefore, religion was one of the most popular forms of entertainment. Elizabeth, however, favoured the recent Protestant reforms enacted by her brother in the years prior to her accession as Queen, which popularised the Anglican church and Anglicanism as a religion across sixteenth-century England.

Regardless of religious denomination, however, many saint's days, festivals, and Holy Days (where we get the term 'holiday'!) were celebrated throughout the Tudor calendar with much vigour and enthusiasm all across sixteenth-century England. Many of these holidays we would recognise today, but many have since fallen out of fashion, or were suppressed in the years following the Henrician Reformation of the 1530s. A calendar year was typically split into four quarters, with each quarter having its own defining celebration that the Tudors could look forward. In the first quarter was Lady Day, which fell on the twenty-fifth of March.[52] Unlike today, where our year begins on the first of January, the Tudors acknowledged the beginning of the new year on Lady Day, yet it was not considered a celebration.[53] Rather, it was a purely executive, legal holiday that marked the beginning of the economic calendar, and signalled the renewal of taxes and the payments of debts. However, according to the Tudors, the first of January was still a date to remember, for this was the day that Tudors would exchange gifts in a celebration of the circumcision of Christ.

In the second quarter of the year, the Tudors celebrated Midsummer, which fell on the twenty-fourth of June, and was an official celebration of the beginning of summer.[54] It was celebrated with plentiful feasts, music, and much merry dancing. In the third quarter, the Tudors would celebrate Michaelmas on the twenty-ninth of September to venerate St Michael.[55] During this period, the Tudors would enjoy lavish feasts made up of whatever had been harvested that autumn. It also provided farmers and labourers a chance to take stock of their animals and crops, and to prepare for the next year of sowing, rearing, and harvesting. The calendar year would come to a close with the fourth quarter in which Advent was celebrated, culminating in Christmas Day on the twenty-fifth of December.[56] The four weeks of Advent were marked with four different occasions, including Advent Sunday, the Nativity, Christmas Eve and Christmas Day. Unlike today, Advent was a stretch in which people fasted and abstained from specific foods including meats, cheese and eggs until the midnight mass celebrated on Christmas Eve, which signalled the beginning of feasting and festivities. The first of February was known as Candlemas Eve, and was marked by the removal of festive decorations. The Tudors believed that keeping the house decorated with festive ornaments after the Christmas period had ended allowed wicked spirits to enter the home and cause mischief. The end of the twelve days of Christmas was marked on the sixth of January, a date known as 'Plough Monday'.[57] This day was a day that many Tudors undoubtedly dreaded, for it marked the beginning of the working year, and signalled the return to manual labour and hard work.

Christmas was not too dissimilar from what we recognise today, and we get many of our traditions from the Tudors – there would be feasting, as well as turkeys (after they were introduced to England), communal family and community dinners, and a Yule log that would be set alight every Christmas Yuletide. Lady Day (as on New Year's Day) was also the Tax Day, the only day where it was marginally easier to be employed and negotiate rent! King Henry VII, known for his miserly attitude toward money and taxes, ordered cash audits of the country to be taken on the first of January every year.[58] These audits, which were conducted in the Royal Mint at the Tower of London, were collections of records of the fiscal wealth of every town across sixteenth-century England, and were stored in great storerooms in the basement of the White Tower. Taxes from the poor made up much of the Crown's revenue, so much so that it is estimated that around 40 per cent of the Crown's income during the reign of King Henry VII was sourced from the taxes of the poor.[59]

Gifts were given on Boxing Day, rather than on the twenty-fifth of December, for Christmas Day was intended to be a day dedicated entirely to faith and the Church. Traditional Christmas gifts were often handmade articles of clothing (the act of gifting socks has apparently never gone away!), children's toys or other longed-for implements like writing apparatus or a recently printed book straight from the presses of Fleet Street in London. Gifts were not in abundance, however, unlike in modern day, though houses certainly were not bare. Although the Tudors did not erect beautiful, crisp-smelling Christmas trees in their houses – that would be a Victorian custom – they would have hung stockings upon their fireplaces. The custom of gifting a stocking goes back to 300 AD, and it was a favourite amongst Catholics – both young and old alike – who searched excitedly through these sacks for odd gifts like citrus fruit, a wooden peg doll, or a newly-knitted pair of stockings. Chunks of coal for naughty children, it appears, did not appear in stockings until much later, in the nineteenth and twentieth centuries. Although it seems like a concept deriving entirely from the modern age, buffets, where serving carts known as 'voids' would be set up in the kitchens, parlours and dining halls of people all across sixteenth-century England, where guests were encouraged to help themselves to finger foods like sweetmeats and baked goods, and to enjoy the delicious treats that were often served only at festive periods. Voids were traditionally held on Twelfth Night and at Christmas, and would have traditionally held bowls of nuts, fruits and peels candied and iced with sugar, and spectacular items made from marchpane and spun sugar that would have wowed and entertained the hungry guests.

The first day of May, known then as is now, as May Day, was a day in which fertility, growth and new life were celebrated.[60] The arrival of spring was marked by processions and plays, pantomimes and pageantry, and by the erection of a May Pole, a large wooden pole to which long ribbons would be attached. Morris dancers would then dance around the pole with a ribbon in their hand, crisscrossing their partners until their ribbons were entwined. May Day was also marked by the naming of the May Queen, a position that many young girls and women in the village vied for. The May Queen reigned supreme over the festivities, often sitting upon carnival floats or at the head of feasting tables, with their heads and hair adorned with flower crowns and wreaths of ribbon placed around their necks.

On the thirteenth of October the Feast of St Edward the Confessor was celebrated, a day in which the Mayor of London would be chosen at the Guildhall in the city.[61] Hallowtide was a three-day group of celebrations which we would now consider Halloween. The first of these days was All Hallows' Eve, celebrated on the thirty-first of October, and was a day when the wandering spirits of the deceased were said to roam the earth, seeking out mischief and haunting the living. The next day, November the first, came All Saint's Day, which was also known as All Hallows' Day, or Hallowmas, and was believed by the Tudors to cleanse the earth of the tortured souls that had arrived the day prior; with the intercession of the saint's miraculous powers, the ghosts would be forced to return to Purgatory to continue to languish in their state of limbo. The festivities culminated on the final day, November the second, which was known as All Souls' Day, a day where the living would pile into church and offer prayers for the souls of all those departed from the mortal world.[62]

Francis Bacon once commented that of the three most defining inventions of the Elizabethan Age, it was the compass, the use of gunpowder, and the increase in printing and publication that defined the turning points in social advancement and progress in the sixteenth and early seventeenth centuries. With the use of gunpowder came advancements in military and martial understanding, which led to the shift away from physical armed combat, to allow for the use of cannons and pistols. The compass, the image that reflected the navigational advancements of the sixteenth century, was an all-important item, small as it was, and, quite literally, changed the course of worldwide history. Finally, the printing press; though it had had its grassroots in the Middle Ages, printing and publication on a mass scale only really began to take off in the sixteenth century, with a noticeable shift from illuminated manuscripts, to books and incunabula (early printed versions of books and pamphlets). Whereas manuscripts were difficult to access for the vast majority of society, slow to write and decorate, and written largely in Latin or Greek, books were easy to copy, easy to print, and easy to read. Soon, literature was not only reserved for the ecclesiastics; now, even labourers, women, and children could hope to learn to read. And indeed, the sixteenth century saw a marked increase in literacy rates, particularly for females, with more girls than not being able to at least understand the alphabet or sign their names by the end of the Tudor Age. The book, it should be said, was a device on which Elizabethan society depended. William Caxton's printing press, which had been established in Westminster in London in 1476 had bridged the gap between literacy and illiteracy, and had made literature available for all.

Chapter 9

Dangers in the Home

'at one of the clock of the morning, there happened to
break out, a sad and deplorable fire, in Pudding-lane neer
Fishstreet...in a quarter of the town so close built with
wooden pitched houses, spread itself so far before day'.
The London Gazette, Whitehall, September 8th 1666.[1]

On a morning in 1538, parishioners of St Margaret Pattens in London
awoke to walls of flames. The street, which housed the workshops of
local basket weavers, had caught alight, and the fire was spreading. The
contemporary chronicler, John Stow, wrote of the fire in his *Survey of
London*, describing it as:

a great fyre where were burnt and perished in three houres
above a dossin howses and 9 persons of men, women, and
children, cleane burnt to death.[2]

It was a tragic event, but the devastating fire at St Margaret Pattens was
certainly not unique. House fires feature prominently in the coroner's
reports and mortuary records of sixteenth-century England, and in
London alone there were at least seven devastating fires between 1485
and 1595, each destroying entire rows of houses and claiming the lives
of their inhabitants. House fires had been a problem which had plagued
London for a long while, with complaints of 'the frequency of fires' in
the city mentioned in chronicles dating as early as the twelfth century.[3]
Houses were flammable, particularly in the sixteenth century, where the
exteriors of buildings were typically supported by timber beams and
roofs were made from dried, densely packed straw. These thatched roofs
proved a significant problem in the event of fires, for they would be
entirely consumed by flames within minutes. This was especially true in
dense urban areas like cities and large towns, where townhouses were

tightly packed and jettied, and overcrowding was the norm. In these areas, regulations to control the spread of house fires were of top priority.

One London Assize in 1212 had paved the way for fire prevention in the city, and had instructed that all houses with thatched roofs in London be replaced with tiles in an effort to reduce flammability.[4] However, it was little enforced and little respected, and thatched houses continued to be built throughout the city in a direct violation of the law. Efforts persisted, and by the sixteenth-century law courts had put in place rulings intended to police the construction of thatched houses in densely populated areas of cities; the law dictated that buildings must be spaced at least twelve metres apart to prevent the spreading of embers.[5] Local sheriffs were sent out with instructions to strip the roofs of city residences of their thatch, instead replacing it with tiling or covering it with plaster so that it was no longer flammable. Although the actions of the city sheriffs had been successful to some extent, ultimately the use of thatch for roofing was just too appealing for Tudors, who appreciated its low cost and its pleasant aesthetic.

Further steps were taken by desperate city officials to prevent the spread of fires in areas under their jurisdiction. Timber framed townhouses and thatched cottages were being increasingly replaced by structures made of heat-resistant materials like brick and stone. But, yet again, these efforts were in vain; it was the interior of the household that now presented the biggest challenge in the fight against flammability.

The floors of the vast majority of houses in sixteenth-century England would have been covered with a carpet-like layer of matted rushes made from dried materials such as reed and straw, and would have been compacted tightly, similarly to roofing thatch, to form a suitable walking platform. These dry, fibrous mats were a great fire hazard, and would have been close to naked flames all throughout the Tudor home. Of course, the main form of light in the sixteenth century came from open fires and free-standing candles, which were often left to continuously burn throughout the evening while homeowners busied themselves in other pursuits. This lack of supervision could be fatal, and often was, for all it took was one stray ember to catch alight on the rushes upon the floor. Fireplaces too could be incredibly dangerous, for even though the hearth was contained by a lintel; it would take just one spark to reach a wall hanging, a carpet or a wooden item of furniture, and the whole house could be engulfed in flames. Fireplaces indeed commonly appear in mortuary records, particularly those of unfortunate children, who had wandered too close to open flames or whose loose clothes had been set aflame.

But just as dangerous as the open hearth was the chimney itself. A recent invention to the Tudors, chimneys were not fully understood. Many chimneys had been installed in houses all across England that were simply too short to sufficiently carry away the smoke from the fire, causing dangerous carbon monoxide to build up in excess within the chimney flue. Without sufficient apertures at the opening of these chimney flues, this noxious gas would continue to accumulate and the likelihood of carbon monoxide poisoning, or even of fireplace explosions, increased. According to Susannah Lipscomb, the Tudors did not clean their fireplaces or chimney flues, allowing for residual soot to build-up, happily unaware of the dangers it could cause.[6] However, by the close of the sixteenth-century knowledge of the dangers of fireplaces and of the importance of proper air circulation had certainly advanced enough that the numbers of recorded house fires had all but halved.

Indeed, although attempts at regulating the construction of thatched houses in dense, urban areas had been greatly overestimated by Tudor city officials, there does appear some evidence to suggest that the residents of cities had begun paying attention to their fire safety. While bakehouses and eateries continued to have roofs made of thatch and floors made from dried rushes, they were also frequently built with small portholes or niches cut out within the rafters and ceiling to expel excess smoke; and, it was largely successful. William Shakespeare took this idea one step further, ordering his Globe Theatre to be constructed with a thatched roof open entirely to the elements. It appeared to be a fool-proof plan, but, during a fateful performance in 1613 the whole building burned down to its foundations when an ember emitted by a stage prop caught the thatch alight.

It was a devastating blow for Shakespeare, who had to watch, helpless, as his legacy burned down around him. There was little anyone could do in cases of fire, other than sound the horns which signalled for an early predecessor of the modern-day fire brigade to be called. These crews of men would have tried desperately to extinguish the roaring flames with buckets of water extracted from nearby rivers, such as the Thames, and barrels of sand, but manpower was simply not enough to quell the raging fires. Once a house had caught alight, it would create a continuous chain of fiercely burning flames all throughout the surrounding area. It was a culmination of these factors - the thatched roofs, dry rush mats, and helpless fire crews - that resulted in perhaps one of the most devastating fires in the whole of English history; the Great Fire of 1666.

Although it would not occur until sixty-three years after the death of the last Tudor monarch, Elizabeth I, the Great Fire of London had had its shortcomings in the sixteenth century. Despite London citizens tirelessly attempting to quell the ferocity of the flames, the Great Fire continued to tear through houses and civic buildings for four entire days. It was only when men, armed with cannons, fired at surviving houses to create a break-fire, did the flames finally cease. The Great Fire of London left a lasting legacy on city building regulations, and even now districts under the jurisdiction of civic councils must abide by fire prevention laws that were no doubt influenced by the devastating instances of the sixteenth and seventeenth centuries.

Yet it was not only fires which presented a great risk to architectural structures in the sixteenth century. Building regulations were also imposed intended to police the construction of houses located near open water sources. Running water, such as streams and rivers, attracted people to build their houses nearby, lessening the long, arduous journeys that homeowners regularly had to make to transport heavy butts of water back to their homes. It seemed like a fool-proof plan; yet, in periods of excessively wet weather, these streams would swell and their banks would burst, flooding the nearby houses and resulting in fatalities. Weather conditions have little changed since the sixteenth century, and rain and stormy conditions were just as frequent then as they are now, and they could be fatal. On the fifteenth of January 1506, a storm described as a 'tempest' uprooted trees, killed roaming livestock, and dislodged whole tiles from house roofs, as well as snapped the weather vane from the roof of St Paul's Cathedral.[7] The storm had been a catastrophic event, and many people across the country got severely injured or killed in its midst. The walls of houses toppled, and soaked thatched roofs caved in under the weight of accumulated water. Household historian Barbara Hanawalt wrote that houses constructed from wattle and daub were particularly victim to the wind and rain, for it would beat holes and cracks into the foundations, as well as cause leaks to drip through its ceilings.[8]

Houses constructed from wattle and daub, so insubstantial that men could apparently knock down entire walls with little effort, were not the only types of building that buckled under the elements.[9] Brick, a relatively modern invention to the Tudors, had not yet been fully refined, and as such was full of impurities. Because of this, brick was prone to crumbling, and, since walls had often been built up in layered stacks rather than in interlaced patterns, many brick houses had very little structural reinforcement. This was particularly concerning for those who lived in coastal areas, where strong gusts of wind and rock falls would have been a constant worry. Houses were restricted from being built too close to cliff edges, and required additional supports to be added to buildings in the hopes of strengthening their foundations. These measures certainly did lessen the risk of weather-induced accidents to an extent, as did the eventual installation of fences, flood defences, and dedicated water pumps throughout the sixteenth century.

Yet structural advancements could not protect the Tudors from every kind of element, and just as stormy weather could be fatal in the sixteenth century, so too could the cold. Bitter frosts and heavy snowfalls, such as the one that occurred in England in 1517, led to many families living in freezing conditions.[10] Thatched roofing would collapse under the weight of the compacted snow, and cracks in foundations began to appear. As the snow melted, timber structural framing got damp and turned to rot, and house collapsing became increasingly likely. Water pumps froze and thin window panes shattered, and firewood had to be kept in dry storage or else run the risk of not igniting.

Dangers were present in the summer months too, with intense droughts and periods of prolonged dry weather resulting in a serious risk of starvation and lack of proper nutrition. One particular drought, which lasted from September 1516 to May of the next year, led to alarming levels of emaciation across sixteenth-century England, and the entire period of 1594 through to 1597 was marked with famines fatal to Tudor society.[11] Children conceived during this period were born small and ailing, their mothers unable to receive and produce the proper nutrients their bodies required. These children in turn failed to thrive, and there was a significant increase in child mortality directly linked to the bad harvests of the late 1590s.

Poor harvests also meant a lack of employment security, and many agricultural labourers who had once relied on the land were forced to find work elsewhere. However, many of these labourers had never experienced civic duties, and agriculture was all that they had known.

Their fathers and grandfathers before them had worked upon the land, and they too had been prepared for a similar life. As such, many of the poorest members of sixteenth-century society were ill-equipped for other lifestyles, and desperation began to rise. The loss of employment amongst the poorest classes had led to a sharp rise in thievery, beggary, illegal poaching, violence and even murder. These methods were some of the only ways in which the poor could find food for themselves and for their families, and were often the only avenues to which they could turn.

Of course, these were not without significant risk. Beggary and thievery were outlawed in the sixteenth century, and were punishable by harsh penalties that included heavy fines, imprisonment, and even execution. The theft of just thirteen pence worth of goods in sixteenth-century England (a little more than five pounds today) could result in the death penalty, and many thieves could be distinguished by amputated fingers or hands, or slits cut deep into their nose. It did little to deter criminals, however, and reprimands of house burglars and petty thieves are frequent throughout sixteenth-century records.[12]

Even the establishment of 'Keepers of the Peace', who were established in 1400, did little to stop criminal gangs. Under the Tudors, these Keepers of the Peace evolved into local 'Justices of the Peace' who set the precedent for policemen and law enforcement, and who would report to local sheriffs any crimes that had occurred in that locality. Interestingly, there was a significant increase in crime rates in areas where adolescents and young men resided, most notably in London, Cambridge and Oxford, where the high student population resulted in riots, burglary, prostitution, homosexual debauchery, and drunkenness. In fact, according to Barbara Hanawalt, taverns located near universities and schools were ordered to close earlier than those elsewhere, especially on holidays, 'to discourage drunken brawling'![13]

The punishments of these crimes, although shocking and extreme to our modern eyes, were commonplace in sixteenth-century England. In one such punishment, a sharp stone would be placed upon the ground, and the accused would be forced to lie naked upon it, their spine aligned with the sharp lip of the rock. Another heavy rock would then be placed on the thief's abdomen, crushing their bodies until either they had learned their lesson, or until they died. It could take as long as twelve hours to die in this way, and was perhaps one of the most painful and prolonged methods of execution in the sixteenth century. Most thieves were lucky however, and they were reprimanded with less horrific punishments. Unruly criminals would often be taken to pillories (or 'stocks'), which were typically located within communal areas such as market squares and street corners. Here, their hands, heads, and often feet, would be locked to a wooden post, and local residents would be encouraged to pelt them with rotting meat and produce. It was a humiliating – and smelly – punishment if nothing else, and would have been extremely uncomfortable, especially since many of those who found themselves in the pillories would have been locked in overnight, and left to the whim of the outdoors and the elements. Still, it was a better outcome than death.

The punishment of crimes was largely dependent on the crime itself. In cases of thievery and beggary, the accused's hand would be lopped off, or their ears and noses cut. Illegal prostitution could result in the shaving of one's head, and poisoners would be boiled alive in vats of oil and water, just like the cook of Bishop Fisher who was executed in 1530 for attempting to poison his master's dinner guests. Criminals could be executed without a fair trial, assaulted, tortured or thrown in 'gaol', a sort of halfway prison. Prisoners would languish in these cold, damp gaols until 'gaol delivery' would take place, where a local law court would determine the outcome of a trial. However, these deliveries only occurred five times a year, by which point, much physiological and psychological damage had already been done.

The establishment of Houses of Correction in 1576 did alleviate the sufferings of prisoners to some extent, and allowed the incarcerated to appeal for fair trials. Houses of Correction also served as more permanent depositories of criminals, who were more likely to spend their lives languishing there, instead of meeting their fates at the hands of executioners. The medieval Clink prison in Southwark, for example, had housed both male and female prisoners whose crimes ranged from petty theft to murder. Ultimately, however, the criminal justice system of the sixteenth century still had a long way to go, and, according to Barbara Hanawalt, crime rates were just as high in sixteenth-century England as they are today.[14]

Indeed, daggers and other small, sharp implements were common possessions in the sixteenth century, and would have been worn on the belts of men, women and even children alike. It is traditionally believed that the Tudors carried these daggers as a form of weapon and for self-defence, but, in the vast majority of cases, these daggers would have simply been intended for personal use, especially as an eating implement as part of a cutlery set. No attempt was made to conceal these daggers, and they are even prominent in the portraiture of the time. Daggers in portraiture became a symbol of wealth, power and even sexual potency, and could be ornamental or beautifully inscribed, furthering the idea that they were intended for personal use, and certainly not as weapons.

The majority of weaponry in sixteenth-century England would have been too large and cumbersome to be carried upon the body, especially concealed under clothing. In an inventory of the ill-fated shipwreck, the *Mary Rose*, large weapons of many different calibres were found, including pikes (a long spear that would be thrust into the body of an enemy), halberds (spears that were topped with a small axe, as well as an extremely sharp point), longbows and arrows, and culverins, small, portable cannons that were the predecessor of the musket and the modern-day gun.[15] The culverins on board the *Mary Rose* were particularly special, for each had been inscribed with the names of its owner, carved by the hands of a Mr Robert and a Mr John Owen.[16] Hundreds of shots (or bullets) for these culverins were found, as were cannonballs and arrowheads, as well as small moulds that would be filled with molten metal for their manufacture.

Regimental life, particularly on-board ships, was a dangerous lifestyle that many sought to avoid. Although in 1513, the household inventory of the *Mary Rose* recorded only one hundred and twenty mariners, two hundred and fifty-one soldiers, thirty-six servants, twenty gunners, two pilots and five trumpeters, by the time of its sinking three decades later in 1545, it was estimated that at least five hundred men had lost their lives with the ship.[17] The *Mary Rose* had been constructed using the clinker building technique, where planks of sturdy wood were overlapped and waterproofed to form the hull and the decking platforms.[18] Although the nails that had held the ship together had been made from oak, there is also evidence of 'lands' being used during its construction, an ingenious technique in which small notches were cut into the timber planks to help form and connect the clinkers.[19] Although this technique sounds precarious, particularly in the stormiest of seas, it was largely effective, and its puzzle-style system allowed for the tight interlocking of materials. Ultimately, however, even the King's most expensive and sumptuously-built warship could not avoid the risk of sinking – after all, the adequacy of the builders little mattered, for the survival of Tudor ships and their crews were entirely dependent on the weather and the sea.

Regardless of where one lived or worked in the sixteenth century, danger was at every turn. In an age where even small bone fractures could be lethal, accidents in the home and at work were to be carefully avoided. This, of course, was not always possible, and many accounts of individuals dying from fractures and broken bones appear in sixteenth-century mortuary records. Once broken, a bone would often fail to heal in the sixteenth century, unlike in modern day where plaster casts are commonly used to reset bones and allow them to refuse. This often meant that fracture wounds would get inflamed and infected, and increased a person's chances of causing further injury. Many excavated sixteenth-century skeletons have shown evidence of bone fractures and clean cuts during their lifetimes, particularly those of men who worked heavy manual labouring jobs, or served in military regiments. Women too were also at risk of bone breakage and fracture in their daily lives, and one particular case from 1560 still baffles historians today.

The curious case of Amy Robsart, the wife of a favourite of Queen Elizabeth I, Robert Dudley, has never been fully understood. One day in September 1560, Amy had sent away all the servants of the household to enjoy festivities taking place in the nearby town. When they returned later that day, they were horrified to find their mistress's body at the foot of a small flight of stairs. Her neck had been broken, and her head was gashed with wounds. Immediately, speculation arose as to the true nature of Amy's death – was it suicide, murder, or simply just a genuine accident? Many contemporaries and modern commentators alike believed that Amy's death had been conducted by her own husband in order to rid himself of his wife and marry the Queen, for whom his desires and passions were well-known. Others ruled it a suicide, but the length of the flight of stairs seemed inconceivably capable of breaking Amy's neck. Ultimately, Amy's death had been ruled as an accident, with the coroner reporting that:

> the aforesaid Lady Amy was found there and then without any other mark or wound on her body; and thus the jurors say on their oath that the aforesaid Lady Amy in the manner and form aforesaid by misfortune came to her death.[20]

Amy's supporters were furious. How could such a short flight of stairs result in such a death? Although modern historians still continue to assert, just like her contemporaries, that Amy had been wrongfully killed, it is important to remember that stairs in the households of the sixteenth century were occasionally too tall, too steep, too worn, too shallow, uneven, or utterly entirely warped. Visitors of authentic sixteenth-century houses will understand the trip hazards that these crooked staircases present, particularly if they had been constructed with a characteristic Tudor bend. Although the staircases of the wealthy were typically levelled and straight (one flight of stairs at Windsor Castle was so apparently so wide that a fully grown man on horseback could ride up it), for the vast majority of multi-storied Tudor homes, staircases would have been built to fit the natural shape of the house. As such, bends in staircases were customary, and differed between every household.

Additionally, staircases could be very dangerous and slippery, for they were often constructed with wooden beams or stone. The introduction of runners (thin cuts of rug) would be trailed up them, intended to prevent household occupants from slipping on their ascent and descent. But, without proper tacking, these runners often caused more harm than good, and as such, many Tudors faced great injury, or even their deaths, because of them. Staircases were not just dangerous for adults. There were no such things as baby gates and child locks in the sixteenth century, and as such many children were recorded as getting into serious, often life-threatening accidents while climbing the stairs, particularly if they were unstable on their feet and had not yet learnt properly to walk.

The Tudor home was dangerous, and so was the world around it. Almost every death in sixteenth-century England had occurred within the home in some manner, and the threat of danger and death had never been too far away.[21]

143

Chapter 10

Death and Dying

'Death, a necessary end, will come when it will come.'
William Shakespeare, *Julius Caesar*:
Act 2, Scene 2., 1599.[1]

The life expectancy for the average person in the sixteenth century was estimated at just a measly thirty years old, and it is traditionally accepted in historiography that the vast majority of Tudors would die before they reached middle age at around forty.[2] But to what extent was this a true reflection of mortality in sixteenth century England?

In actuality, there are plentiful recorded instances of people, most often women, reaching advanced ages in sixteenth-century England. Queen Elizabeth I reached the age of 69, and her great-grandmother, Lady Margaret Beaufort reached the age of 66. Even commoners could reach impressive ages – one widow, Elizabeth Menson, who had lived in Norwich in 1570, lived until she was eighty years old and had continued her profession in spinning and wool-winding despite suffering from numerous strokes in later life.[3] Mary Arden, the mother of William Shakespeare, died in her mid-seventies in 1608. One remarkable tale even survives of a so-called Thomas 'Old-Tom' Parr, who was believed to have lived from 1482 to 1635, putting his age at around 153 years. 'Old Tom' was an enigma who captured the imaginations of Tudor society, and supposedly told tales of his rambunctious sex life that had lasted well into his centenary years.[4] 'Old Tom' accredited his impressive age to a strict diet of 'subrancid cheese and milk in every form, coarse and hard bread and small drink [and] generally sour whey'.[5] Although modern historians, scientists and sceptics have since discredited the story of the supercentenarian 'Old Tom', instead putting his age at death at around ninety years old, he nonetheless reached an impressive age that was all the more extraordinary given the time in which he lived. Ultimately, mortality rates in the sixteenth century were much lower than they are today, though not as low as is traditionally accepted. Significant factors including a high rate of infant mortality, conflict and war, and natural disasters like famine and pandemics devastated large portions of the population of sixteenth-century England. The plague in particular was completely unforgiving, and anyone could be its victim; man, woman or child.

The bodies of those who had died from infectious diseases, particularly of the plague or of the sweating sickness, were buried with haste, often mere hours after they had died. These infectious corpses were traditionally buried at night, not only to lessen the risk of contagion, but also to spare onlookers the unpleasant sight – and smell – of bursting pus-filled buboes and hideous, erupting skin rashes. Whereas the majority of bodies in sixteenth-century England would be cleaned, dressed, and wrapped in linen shrouds in preparation for burial inside sturdy wooden caskets or coffins, the corpses of plague victims were often just placed within open holes or communal pits and left to decompose.[6] These burial sites were known as 'plague pits', and it was not wholly uncommon for entire communities to be buried within them if they had been particularly ravished by the infectious disease.[7] In central London alone, there were at least thirty-five different plague pits estimated to have been filled by the bodies of around 100,000 victims.[8] Ultimately, mass burials in plague pits were the only option available to parish councillors desperate to remove the rapidly decaying bodies of the dead; individual burials would have taken up too much precious time and space, and cremation was entirely discouraged, for it was believed that any noxious or contagious fumes (or 'miasmas') would infect the air and the living around them.

In many cultures today, cremation of the deceased is a popular way of laying the dead to rest. However, the cremation of corpses was banned in the sixteenth century, for it was believed that the mortal body had to be fully intact in order for the soul to ascend to the afterlife. If a body was biologically destroyed through cremation, argued the Catholic Church, the soul of the deceased would not enter into Heaven. This proved a problematic point for those who had died in fires, or those whose bodies had been inaccessible at death (as in the case of shipwrecks and drowning). Yet, the Church reiterated its teachings – without an intact body, the soul would be denied entry to the afterlife.

It is for this reason that the torturous deaths of criminals through burning, as well as through hanging, drawing and quartering, were particularly brutal. Not only was it a horrific ordeal to endure in the mortal world, but it also took away the chance for the soul of the accused to reach spiritual redemption in the afterlife. On this issue, both the Church and common law allowed cremation through the burning at the stake, a form of execution typically reserved for religious heretics and women, particularly those suspected of being a witch. Since it was believed that these criminals, heretics and witches had immoral and corrupt souls – or even no soul at all – it did not matter which manner of death they were ordered to suffer.

Criminals were buried in 'deviant burials', which were located away from community cemeteries. At deviant burial sites, graves were usually shallow, uneven or entirely too small for the corpse, and required unceremonious and rough handling by undertakers to ensure that the body would fit. Sometimes criminals would be buried in communal pits, especially near execution sites such as Tyburn Hill near the Tower of London.[9] Even the remains of Queens Anne Boleyn, Catherine Howard and Jane Grey were thrown into unmarked, insufficient graves beneath the flagstones of St Peter ad Vincula in the Tower of London, with no funerary service or prayers sung for their souls due to the nature of their deaths as traitors to the Crown. If the highest ladies in the land could be treated in such a way, prospects for the majority of criminals looked exceptionally bleak.

The death penalty did not discriminate, and was ordered even for the most petty of crimes. If a thief had been caught stealing anything over the value of twelve pennies (around fifteen pounds in sterling today), they would be issued with an execution warrant.[10] Even children as young as ten could be executed, and there certainly are records of these such executions occurring in the fifteenth and sixteenth centuries.[11] Hanging was the most common form of execution, while beheadings were reserved for the wealthiest of prisoners. The remains of these criminals would then be displayed to the public as a warning to abide by the law – the corpses of executed criminals would be hung from tree branches and gallows (such as the one at Tyburn in London, which was known as 'Tyburn Tree', while severed heads would be dipped in tar for preservation purposes, and placed on spikes along bridges. The most infamous location where these morbid displays occurred was that of London Bridge, where pedestrians and barge-travelling Tudors who crossed beneath it could see for themselves the heads of famous felons.

Visiting the severed heads of London Bridge even became a sort of tourist attraction, where Tudors could come (literally) face-to-face with notaries whose stories they had heard of in news stories, and plays, and gossip.[12]

One of the most famous residents of London Bridge was that of the head of Thomas Cromwell, which had been horrifically hacked away at, since the executioner reportedly took three 'ragged and butcherly' attempts to sever his skull from his shoulders.[13] Cromwell's head had been dipped in black tar to slow the decomposition process, and must have been a deeply unpleasant and distressing sight for the Tudors. Another famous severed head, that of Sir Thomas More, was parboiled and impaled upon a pike after his execution.[14] Desperate to award her father some dignity in death, Thomas's daughter, Lady Margaret Roper, bribed the keeper of the Bridge to remove the head. Placing the head in a velvet bag, Margaret later preserved it with spices and kept it at her home until her own death in 1544, where it was nestled in her arms in her coffin.[15] Years later, curious Victorian thrill-seekers opened Margaret's tomb and removed More's head, placing it on public display at St Dunstan's Church, Canterbury, where it still belongs today.[16]

The remains of other famous criminals were not so lucky. On 28 June 1497, the accused traitor James Tuchet, 7th Baron Audley, 'was drawn from Newgate through the places of the city to the place of punishment near the Tower'.[17] There, 'his head was struck off [...] his body was, by the King's grace, buried in the Preachers, but his head was fixed on London Bridge', where it was pelted at by passers-by and wrapped in paper printed with his family coat of arms.[18] The tradition of displaying the severed heads of criminals continued well into the seventeenth century, but by the close of the sixteenth century, another use for criminal corpses was becoming increasingly popular: medical experimentation.

With the emergence of humanism during the Renaissance of late-sixteenth century England, interest in anatomy and the human body peaked. Until then, the dissection of corpses had been entirely banned in England, unless performed in secret by morbidly-curious surgeons and practitioners. By the 1600s, however, a royal warrant allowed the Company of Barber-Surgeons to source cadavers of murderers, thieves and criminals from execution sites, for use of dissection, experimentation and study, as well as the practice of surgical procedures. There was just one issue – the majority of executed criminals in the sixteenth century were male, with female dissection greatly discouraged on account of their 'gentle sex'.[19] This meant that knowledge of the female human body was greatly lacking, and certainly lagged behind understanding of the anatomy of males. Although pioneers such as Leonardo da Vinci had conducted studies into the anatomy of female sex and reproductive organs as early as the 1510s, ultimately, understanding of the female form would not truly be established until well into the seventeenth and even eighteenth centuries.

*

Suicide was a taboo matter in Tudor England, and it was expressly discouraged. To take someone's life through murder was bad enough, the Tudors believed, but to take your own was just as heinous. 'For the heinousness thereof', wrote the contemporary Michael Dalton in 1628, 'it is an offense against God, against the king, and against Nature' to commit suicide.[20] Indeed, the Tudors believed that both the mortal bodies and souls of those whose deaths occurred by their own hands, were unworthy of spiritual salvation. Those who died by suicide were not buried within the same graveyards and cemeteries as those who had died a natural death, but rather, their corpses were taken to the edges of crossroads and buried, for a very peculiar reason.

The Tudors believed that the bodies of the suicidal were vessels which carried tortured souls. Sixteenth-century thought asserted that, for the vast majority of people, once their physical body had expired, their souls would go on toward Purgatory, before advancing toward their final destinations in either Heaven or Hell. Tortured souls, however, did not advance to Purgatory, and instead, the Tudors believed, were forced to remain on earth in a perpetual cycle of suffering and agony; these souls were known as ghosts.

To prevent the ghosts of suicide victims returning to haunt the mortal world, the Tudors buried their dead at crossroads in order to confuse the souls. It was believed that, upon returning to Earth, the tortured souls of the departed would be unable to determine their locations, since they had been buried between village borders, and as such would be unable to haunt the families, friends or the properties they had frequented in life. Even more distressing, some Tudors even believed that in order to prevent the spirits of tortured souls from reanimating and rising as ghosts, a stake should be thrust through their hearts, or that they should be buried facing the ground.[21]

Although Protestants did not believe in the existence of ghosts (the Protestant reformer Robert Wisdom had written eruditely in 1543, 'souls departed do not come again and play boo-peep with us'[22]), many, if not most Catholics did. According to Catholic doctrine, only the most devout of believers reached Heaven, while everyone else remained in a middle-state called Purgatory, a place where souls were intended to be purified until they reached a state of enlightenment which permitted their entrance into Heaven. That souls wandered in Purgatory for an unspecified stretch of time led Tudors to ponder the existence of ghosts trapped between the mortal world and the immortal. This belief in ghosts and the supernatural rippled rapturously through sixteenth-century English society, and even folkloric tales, literature and theatre came to embody supernatural elements. One only has to turn to Shakespeare's *Macbeth* or *Richard III* to witness the mysterious and unnerving undead characters which undoubtedly scared unwitting sixteenth-century theatregoers and thrill-seekers in search of a bone-chilling story alike.

The poem *Cumner Hall*, written by William Mickle in the mid-1700s describes an eery, supernatural event in which the titular hall is supposedly haunted by the owners past:

> Thus sore and sad that lady griev'd,
> In Cumner Hall so lone and drear,
> And many a heartfelt sigh she heav'd,
> And let fall many a bitter tear.
> And ere the dawn of day appear'd,
> In Cumner Hall so lone and drear,
> Full many a piercing scream was heard,
> And many a cry of mortal fear.
> The death-bell thrice was heard to ring,
> An aerial voice was heard to call;
> And thrice the raven flapp'd its wing
> Around the tow'rs of Cumner Hall.
> And in that manor now no more
> Is cheerful feast and sprightly ball;
> Forever since that dreary hour
> Have spirits haunted Cumner Hall.[23]

It was essential then, that the Tudors attain a sense of a 'good death', the belief asserted by Catholics that the process of dying directly influenced the experience of the afterlife. To achieve a 'good death', the dying would receive the late rites (the presentation of a crucifix and a candle), would confess their sins and receive absolution, as well as take Holy Communion, which was also called the viaticum; finally, the dying would receive the extreme unction, or the anointment of holy oils to the body. Although the excessive and elaborate death rituals of sixteenth-century Catholics must have been uncomfortable and even distressing in the final few moments of life, ultimately the thought of eternal damnation was more terrifying than death and of the unknown itself. Regardless of Christian denomination, the majority of English society in the sixteenth century were united in their beliefs that perpetual peace and happiness in the afterlife were worth the (hopefully) brief discomfort of the process of death, and as such the confession of sins, performance of charitable acts, and the making amends with those of whom they had wronged in life were inherently vital to the 'good death'.

No Tudor wanted to spend an eternity in Purgatory, a place of limbo where thoughts and feelings were believed to be uncomfortable, and a deep reflection of one's life was encouraged. Masses for the soul said in church by members of the clergy and of the congregation following a person's death, ensured that the soul would spend less time in the state of Purgatory, and would instead move on to Heaven. As such, it was not uncommon for sixteenth-century wills to include instructions regarding masses on behalf of the dying, with many requesting that as many masses be said for their soul as often as possible. Some Tudors, if they had the money to do so, requested that masses be said for their soul years, even decades, after they had died, their families continuing to pay post-mortem sums to the church in order to keep the names of the deceased in the mass roster. Most often, when masses were read, the priest would read over the person's name or include it in a long list of deceased members of the congregation, and thus they would receive reverence in that way.

When a person died in the sixteenth century, their families mourned deeply just as we do today. In the 1500s, the ending of marriage was typically through death, not divorce, and as such, the majority of Tudor couples stayed married until one predeceased the other. Typically, the husband would be the first to die, due to factors such as war and a more gruelling physical lifestyle; their widows, who were often considerably young and wealthy, having inherited their husband's estates, were expected to remarry with haste. Although there was a distinctly higher percentage of widows than of widowers in sixteenth-century society, with many, if not all, of these women expected to marry again soon after the deaths of their husbands, that does not mean that they mourned little for their loved ones. Rather, the opposite was the case, with many widows paying great sums for the memorialisation of their husbands, as well as the erecting of expensive tombs, and the provisions of funerary arrangements.

It is important to remember that death was much more commonplace in sixteenth-century society than it is today, no-less exacerbated by a lack of adequate healthcare and medical understanding, as well as a frequency of conflicts and natural social disasters like pandemics. However, unlike in today's society, the Tudors did not shy away from death, nor treat it as an unspeakable subject. Rather, the Tudors popularised the concept of *memento mori,* or the reminder of the eventual mortalities that would come for us all. *Memento mori* proliferated in sixteenth-century art and literature throughout Europe, particularly within ecclesiastical spheres, where tombs and death monuments like headstones would often be inscribed with skeletal and skull motifs, cadavers carved from stone and resembling a putrid, festering body in an advanced stage of decomposition, or even life-sized wooden and wax effigies of the deceased which sat, rather disturbingly, atop their own graves. In an age where death was ever-present, and always just around the corner, one would expect sixteenth-century society to be fearful of it. Yet, the understanding and acceptance that death will eventually come for all, instead sparked intelligent and informed discussions of the body and the soul, as well as intense philosophical and scientific debates that formed the nucleus of medical advancements toward dissection and knowledge of human biology. After all, every Tudor mother would have undoubtedly worried about the fragile life growing within her womb, and many would have faced the reality of stillbirth or infant death. Many siblings grew up hyperaware that their brother or sister was there one day, but gone the next. Parents outlived their children; children became orphans while they were still in the cradle. Death was indiscriminate and unforgiving, but, it was also an expected part of life.

*

One of the most dangerous jobs a man could have in Tudor England was that of a sailor. The construction of ships and sailing vessels was often complex and of such a grand scale that accidents and injuries, or even death, was common. Paired with sailing itself upon vast open waters in a time before the invention of lifejackets and safety passenger boats, if a ship had capsized, collided with rocks or another ship, or had been tossed in stormy seas, then it was likely that many of the crew would not survive. Additionally, the lack of knowledge about the importance of fresh produce and hydration to the diet meant that many sailors also developed scurvy, a painful, slow-moving disease that affected the bones of those unable to absorb the rich vitamins of such things as spinach and citrus. In a letter to Lord Burghley dated 10 August 1588, the commander of the Armada fleet, Lord Howard of Effingham, described the extent of how severely diseases could quickly affect all men onboard:

> The Elizabeth Jonas, which hath done as well as ever any ship did in any service, hath had a great infection in her from the beginning, so as of the 500 men which she carried out, by the time we had been in Plymouth three weeks or a month there were dead of them 200 and above.[25]

Even seasoned sailors were acutely aware of the dangers seafaring could bring. In a letter to his wife Bess sent from Guiana in November 1595 while on his voyage to discover the lost golden city of El Dorado, Sir Walter Raleigh wrote:

> Sweet Heart, Can yet write unto you but with a weak hand, for I have suffered the most violent Calenture for fifteen days, that ever man did, and lived […] We have had two most grievous sicknesses in our Ship, of which fourtie two have died, and there are yet many sick […] I hope we shall recover them.[26]

Further, pirates and smugglers too proliferated the seas in the sixteenth century, particularly around areas of Cornwall and Portsmouth where trade was lucrative, and sailing in times of war (such as during the attack of the Spanish Armada in 1588) could increase the chances of attack, capture and death tenfold. In fact, around 83% of all sailors in sixteenth-century England died while at sea.[24]

For those who died at sea, no proper burial of the body could occur, and as such, many funerals took place on dry land with empty coffins and graves. For the most part, however, the burial of the dead would take place imminently. The corpses of those who had died a natural death would most likely be buried within the same day as the death had occurred, or a few days after at most. This was a period before embalming; a period where mortuary preservation techniques were still greatly lacking. Although bodies would not decompose within a matter of days, they were, quite frankly, too unpleasant to have lying around the Tudor home. Bodies would quickly stiffen after the flow of blood had ceased within their veins, and would prove entirely unmovable; it was, therefore, best to move the body as quickly as possible after death had occurred.

There was no such thing as a dedicated funeral director in the sixteenth century, and as such, the cleaning and embalming of a cadaver would have been carried out by any member of the local community who had even an ounce of anatomical knowledge. Barber-surgeons, apothecarists, and even midwives were commonly tasked with the duty of preparing the dead for burial, or sometimes even the very family of the deceased. Embalming, the process in which a body is injected with preserving chemicals in order to slow the process of decomposition, was a luxury only the richest of sixteenth-century society could afford. Embalming came with the added advantage of allowing mourners extended periods of time in which they could pay their respects to the deceased, as well as making it easier for the body to be transported if needed, especially in cases where death had occurred a great distance from the desired burial place. This was the case of Arthur, the Prince of Wales, whose untimely death from tuberculosis in the April of 1502 at Ludlow Castle required that his corpse be washed, embalmed and transported back to the Royal Family at Greenwich. Transporting a body in the sixteenth century was no easy feat, particularly when many had to be carried on unstable, rickety carts across unlevelled, rural and derelict roads. Even short journeys could take a long amount of time to travel, and thus, by embalming the body, the corpse would remain in relatively good condition until the time came for its burial.

The process of embalming in the sixteenth century was largely similar to that of today, though of course with much more rudimentary items and utensils. Just like today, the corpse of the deceased would be washed and stripped naked, before their body cavities were eviscerated and their internal organs removed. In some cases, a long metal pole that was tipped with a sharp point, known as a trocar, would be inserted into the chest cavity through an incision near the heart.[27] The trocar was carefully moved around, purposely puncturing the internal organs, which were then drained of blood and disinfected upon opening the body cavity. This was not always the norm, however. In some cases, such as in the case of Queen Jane Seymour, who died in 1537, the internal viscera would be buried separately from the physical body, with hearts and entrails buried in capsule-like caskets at places that the individual held particularly dear. Jane Seymour's heart, for example, is buried at Hampton Court Palace, the place where she had died after a long, exhausting labour giving birth to the future King Edward VI.

The reasoning for the burials of viscera is not always clear, and presumably depends on the capabilities available at the location in which the deceased had died, as well as the wishes of the deceased individual. For some, the symbolic burial of the heart in the place that they loved most was intended to be seen as a reflection of their deep love and affinity to that particular location; other times, the viscera of the deceased would be buried separately to the skeletal remains on account of any infectious diseases that were believed to spread if left to decompose within the body cavity. Further still, in instances where it was wholly unpractical to transport a whole deceased body across the country, it was ultimately decided that only the viscera would be transferred so that the individual could still have some semblance of a 'proper' burial. Although the physical body was important to the Tudors, they were simply perceived as vessels in which souls would be carried; they held no purpose after death, and little thought was given, therefore, to the discarding of the physical remains. The flesh was simply the *mortal* body; it was the spirit and the soul that really mattered, the Tudors believed. However, in the vast majority of cases, most people in sixteenth-century society would have been buried with their internal viscera still within their bodies, and even in modern day, embalmers and funeral directors place internal organs back inside the body after embalming in preparation burial.[28]

After evisceration came the disinfecting of the body cavity. Aromatic herbs, flowers and spices such as clove and lavender would be added to a mixture of oils and beeswax before being spread on the inside and outside of the corpse. These fragrant liquids would assure that the cadaver would remain sweet-smelling for days and was almost akin to pickling the body, allowing for a prolonged duration before burial. The chest cavity would then be filled with sawdust, wool or another form of stuffing, intended to dehydrate and desiccate the body. This would essentially dry out the corpse, and resulted in a form of mummification, drawing the skin taught and close to the bones.[29] Toward the latter end of the sixteenth century, advancements in embalming were making great strides, and there emerged a market for dedicated funerary implements, including specific instruments, such as the trocar, as well as other fragrant powders, creams and fluids aimed at the preservation of the deceased.[30]

After embalming came the burial. In most cases, the deceased were buried in coffins made from pliable wood, which were topped with a lid in which either their names, initials or a brass likeness of themselves would be carved. These funerary brasses were important features for those who could not read, and aided in identifying the deceased inside. Many funerary brasses have survived, and commonly appear in archaeological excavations of sixteenth-century osteological remains today. The body would be wrapped in a shroud, a sort of oversized linen bag, in which the deceased would be fitted snugly, before being tied at the head. It was then wrapped in layers of cerecloth, a waxed cloth usually made from beeswax and principally used by the Tudors in the preservation of meats and cheese. Now that the corpse resembled a sort of Egyptian mummy, wrapped in layers of adhesive cloth, it was then lowered gently into a box made of supple wood such as oak, before sheets of lead were placed at its edges. The vast majority of people in the sixteenth century were buried in consecrated ground, whether it be within a graveyard or a cemetery, or within a church itself. It was believed in the sixteenth century that the closer one was buried to the altar within a church, the closer one's spirit was to God. As such, members of the community fought over spots closest to church altars, desperate to consolidate their piety and eager to prove their devotion to their faith.

For those who did not wish to be buried within a simple church or chapel, there was always the option of burial within monasteries, abbeys and other such ecclesiastical buildings for those who could afford it. Henry VIII's youngest sister, Princess Mary Tudor, the Dowager Queen of France, was buried within the Benedictine monastery at Bury

St Edmunds, Suffolk following her untimely death at just thirty-seven years old in 1533. Burial in a monastery seemed like the best possible decision for those wishing for their remains to be as close to God as was mortally possible on earth, yet by the time of the Dissolution of the Monasteries in the mid-1530s, it had fallen greatly out of fashion. In fact, burials in monasteries had completely ceased, for there were simply no monasteries left to be buried in across England.

Yet, not every person in sixteenth-century England had the fortune of being buried within a monastery, or even within a coffin at all. In certain cases where the family of a deceased individual may have had insufficient funds to pay for a full funeral, the bodies of the deceased would simply be placed inside a coffin briefly, before being taken out again and buried within the ground simply in their shrouds. This must have been particularly distressing for the families of the deceased, who often had little choice but to keep the corpses of their loved ones in their shrouds within their homes until burial.[31] Considering that many of the houses of the poorest members of Tudor society were tiny, poky houses, it must have been a truly disturbing sight indeed.

*

Headstones and memorials for the deceased varied greatly depending on the wealth and social standing of the individual. In some cases, particularly in instances where the individual was particularly poor, the deceased were buried with simple grave markers most often made from wood and constructed to resemble a crucifix. The next step up from these rudimentary markers were small stone plot markers that were effectively rocks inscribed with the name or initials of the deceased. These were particularly used in cases of infant and child burials, and would sometimes even be off-cuts of stone from masonry construction that had been recycled and repurposed for memorialisation. More decorative still were gravestones, which were often just sheets of stone that had been carved and laid flat above a burial plot or erected to stand upright. Over time these stones have been lost to history, consumed by the overgrowth of vegetation in cemeteries and graveyards, or destroyed by the weather. The gravestones that do remain, however, are often rudimentary and simple, inscribed with the iconography of skulls and crossed bones, as well as of sand timers that represented the eventual and imminent arrival of death. Aside from these motifs, very little else marks the identity of those who lay beneath. Free-standing mausoleums would not become popular until the seventeenth and eighteenth centuries.

Unlike the poor, the richest and noblest of sixteenth-century society could afford burial markers that would have been elaborately carved and intricately decorated, painted with colourful varnish that was intended to catch the eye. Above-ground tombs of the deceased were the most popular form of death memorial for the richest of Tudor society, and were favoured by clergymen, wealthy merchants and their families, and anyone who had a link to the nobility. These tombs would be inscribed with motifs including statuettes of the family of the deceased in a state of mourning, a physical (and somewhat excessively performative) reminder of the perpetual reverence toward the deceased. These statuettes were known as 'weepers', for they commonly depicted family members in a state of distress and overcome with emotion. Ultimately, the existence of weepers on tombs showcased not only the familial love between the deceased and their family, but also served as a reminder of the successful familial lineages the deceased had come from, or created for their own.[32] For an individual's legacy to be depicted upon a tomb was very important indeed for those who could afford it in the sixteenth century, for it proved to the living that their lives had been well lived, and their jobs had been well done.

Statuettes of other figures would also be carved upon a death monument, most notably of the Catholic saints, particularly those that the deceased had personally revered. Interestingly, many individuals chose to have depicted on their tombs saints with whom shared their names, and as such, references to many St Marys or St Thomases can be found in surviving sixteenth-century tombs. As well as shared names, many individuals chose saints who patronised a particular ailment or occupation that the deceased had experienced in life. As well as these statuettes, the tombs of the rich and wealthy in sixteenth-century England would often be carved with animals, foliage, or items such as books (to symbolise intellect, piety and studiousness) and swords (to represent martial strength, prowess and masculinity). The inclusion of animals in some form in a sixteenth-century tomb was common, with statuettes often lying at the feet of the monument. The most popular of these animals were dogs or lions, symbolising loyalty and bravery; and, it would not be too far of a stretch to imagine that an individual who was particularly close to a canine companion in life wanted their likeness perpetually with them in death.

Indeed, Tudor death monuments can tell us much about the identities of the deceased. Whereas men tended to be personified with motifs that ascribed to their masculinity, women were depicted alongside icons that served as a reminder of their roles as daughters, mothers and wives. Commonly, the tombs of Tudor women would feature such animals as swans and pelicans, birds revered for their gentleness and piety, purity and representation of motherhood. Additionally, women who had died in childbirth were often depicted in brass monuments, wall paintings and stone effigies as holding an infant to their breast. Many were also depicted with 'Puttis', child-sized stone carvings of angelic cherubs.

Children are depicted in death less commonly than adults, though this does not mean that they were completely left out of memorialisation and reverence. In the sixteenth century, it was believed that stillborn children had no soul, since they had not been baptised, and as such did not require a full, Christian burial ceremony. Babies who had been born still were therefore often wrapped in shrouds and placed alongside their mothers who had died in childbirth with them, or even within the coffins of other members of the community who had died around the same time.[33] The infant did not have to have any sort of familial relationship with a deceased individual; nor did they have even lived in the same community. All that mattered was that the infant had adult company who could lead them from the world of the living to the world of the dead, assisting them and helping them so that they would not get lost, lonely or scared.[34]

Older children would be buried within graves of their own, or within family plots. Sometimes, the pre-existing coffins of long-deceased family members would be cracked open so that the body of the child could be placed alongside it, but, in the vast majority of cases, most children were buried in their own, personal graves.[34] The only exception to this was in the case of children who had died after contracting the plague or some other infectious disease, who were often placed with other unfortunate souls in communal burial pits.[35] The bodies of most children in sixteenth-century England were not embalmed, unless they belonged to the wealthier class of society; rather, they were buried as soon after death as possible. For the nobility, however, no expense was spared in the funerary arrangements and burials of their children. In the case of young Henry and Charles Brandon, the two adolescent sons of Charles Brandon, 1st Duke of Suffolk, who had died on the same day from sweating sickness in 1551, the boys were embalmed and laid to rest in a chapel of rest for an entire month. This was known as a 'month's mind', a funerary ceremony which typically took place an entire month after the death of an individual.

It is commonly believed in historiography that the parents of the past cared little for their children; however, in my own study of the parent-child relationships of Late Medieval England, I discovered that this was simply not the case.[36] Many historians support their argument of a lack of parental affection in the sixteenth century through the analysis of Tudor funerary customs, in which parents were dissuaded from attending the funerary ceremonies of their children. This was the case of little Prince Henry, the Duke of Cornwall, the firstborn child of King Henry VIII and his first wife Katherine of Aragon. The body of Henry, who had died just fifty-five days after his birth, was placed inside a tiny coffin which was taken, in ceremonious grandeur, down the River Thames and buried in a vault at Westminster Abbey. Although his parents were dissuaded from attending the funeral, the procession of Henry's coffin had been accompanied by 'official mourners', a group of select men made up of nobility and knights, as well as servants and around two hundred paupers who had gathered outside the Abbey for the ceremony. It would be unfair to argue that the King and his Queen had not been devastated by the loss of their son, and indeed there is plentiful evidence to support the fact that both King Henry and Queen Katherine were devastated at the deaths of their subsequent children.[37] And indeed, it was no different for the children of the working classes of sixteenth-century England, whose families mourned and prayed both privately and publicly, calling upon the prayers of the community and relying on the goodwill of their kin in the harrowing time that came after the loss of those they held so dear.[38]

*

Tudor coffins and death monuments, particularly those of the rich, were often topped with full-sized, life-like statuettes of the deceased known as effigies. These effigies would be made from painted wood or moulded wax, and many have survived today, including the effigies of Elizabeth of York, King Henry VII's queen, and Queen Mary I.

A particularly haunting example of a Tudor wooden effigy is that of King Henry VII himself, which had been carved in exquisite detail from a plaster cast that had been taken of his face immediately after death, known as a 'death mask'. These death masks allowed for every inch of detail of the individual's face to be seen, every wrinkle and blemish, and, as was famously muttered during the process of producing the death mask of Oliver Cromwell in 1658, 'warts and all'. Death masks, such as Henry VII's, give us a glimpse into the true appearances of those people we consign only to the annals of history; we forget that once these people were living too.

Death masks would be created from a thick mixture of plaster and gauze spread evenly upon the face (similarly to papier-mâché) and left to set and harden. It would then be removed and painted to resemble the flesh of the deceased. False beards would be set upon the death mask in an added sense of realism, as were moustaches, eyebrows and wigs – Queen Elizabeth I had had her characteristic bright orange tresses piled around the head of her effigy at her funeral procession.

Effigies were not only afforded to the wealthiest of society, however, and even the middling classes could afford to have their own likenesses placed upon their coffins and tombs after they had died. Wealthy merchants, such as the case of John Baret, paid for their body measurements to be taken, often still while they were alive, in preparation for the carving of their effigies.[39] These would then be worked upon by skilled carpenters and stonemasons, before being placed atop the long, oblong monuments of the deceased. In some cases, the effigies of the deceased would take on an entirely new form. Instead of depicting the individual as they had appeared in life, plump of flesh and youthful in glow, they would be depicted as little more than skeletons or corpses in an advanced stage of decay.

'Cadaver tombs', which were also known as 'transi tombs', were popular in the Late Middle Ages and continued to be so well into the sixteenth century. Many examples of cadaver tombs still survive across England today, such as in the cloisters of Lincoln Cathedral and in private chapels such as the Fitzalan Chapel at Arundel Castle in Sussex. If an individual could not afford to have their entire decaying body reproduced in intricate and graphic detail, then they would settle for certain body parts such as skulls or specific limbs to be depicted as skeletal instead. The purpose of the sixteenth cadaver tomb was not wholly to spook or scare the living, but rather to remind them, while they sat at Sunday religious services in Church just inches away from tombs, of the imminent and inescapable deaths that awaited them all. *Memento mori, memento vivere*, the Tudors believed; remember that we must die, so remember that you *must* live.

*

Funeral ceremonies were entirely dependent on the social status, prestige and fiscal wealth of a family in the sixteenth century. If the deceased had played a prominent part in society, it was customary for their funeral processions to be excessive public affairs in which whole communities would gather to pay their respects. With the tolling of church bells, the family and friends of the deceased led a procession behind the coffin, which would have been transported upon a hearse of a wagon or cart and covered with a pall of velvet, often in black or dark colours. As they passed through the community, additional mourners would join the fray, including guildsmen, clergy, scholars and any other individuals of prominence and social standing. But so too would children join, caught up in the excitement of a bustling, growing crowd, as would paupers hoping for charitable alms or donations of food that the family of the deceased would give to the crowds that had gathered.

Once at the church, torches and candles would have been supplied, one for each mourner (if funds allowed), or to simply stand at each of the four feet of the coffin, as was more likely during the funerals of poorer Tudors. Oftentimes, these candles were specially measured in advance, and intentionally matched the length of the body of the deceased. A length of string running alongside the corpse of the deceased was cut, then repeatedly dipped into vats of wax to form a candle the exact height of the dead. These candles would be lit at the funeral and would be allowed to burn until they had entirely melted away, symbolising the fading of a life. Sometimes, excess candle tapers, coins or offerings of food would be handed out after the funeral had ceased, a way in which the families of the deceased could offer thanksgiving for the prayers the crowds had said for the soul of the dead. Churches would have been hung or decorated with black palls of rich cloth, often made from velvet or silk, during funeral ceremonies. Wall paintings would be covered, as would mirrors and artworks depicting positive, light-hearted subjects.

161

It was believed that the covering of a mirror following the passing of a deceased loved one would help a soul on its way to the afterlife, else it would get trapped inside the glass and would have been unable to progress to Purgatory. Windows too were thrown open immediately following the death of a loved one, for it was believed in the sixteenth century, much as it is in many cultures today, that shut windows trapped and oppressed the souls, and forced them to languish in a state of despair between the mortal world and the afterlife. The opening of the windows of the home, therefore, symbolised the releasing of a soul, and no doubt had practical effects also, to provide some much-needed fresh air for the embalmers who had just spent the prior moments eviscerating, sluicing and desiccating the internal organs of the deceased.

In 1537, John Mason, a glover who lived in York, requested in his will to be buried 'beside my father and my mother in Saint Thomas' closet within my parish church of the Trinities in Micklegate'.[40] The fact that John had requested to be buried with his parents presumably suggests that he had never married, nor sired any children. Even in death, sixteenth-century English communities were close-knit and familial. The sixteenth century, often characterised as a period remembered for its harsh executions and bloodthirsty monarchs, actually placed great emphasis on achieving the 'good death', and of revering the deceased. The Tudors respected death, and they recognised its importance in the grand circle of life. Death to the Tudors was just like birth; nothing more than a transitory moment, and a chance to start a new life.

Postscript

On the morning of 24 March 1603, the ailing and elderly Queen Elizabeth I lay slumped in a nest of pillows on the floor. She had refused to move and to take any food, and had resisted the attempts of her devoted ladies-in-waiting to coerce her to bathe. Her hair, once a mass of gorgeous red-gold curls, had now all but fallen out, only orange wisps left to cover her skull. Her skin, famed for its purity, had now grown translucent and painfully taut.

The Tudor dynasty had ended with the whispers of a woman once famed for her power and ostentation, her intelligence and her pride. And with Elizabeth died the hopes of her forefathers before her. The Tudor Age had lasted a period of just one hundred and eighteen years, yet it had seen the introduction of the printing press, the discoveries of new worlds, and the heralding of an utterly dazzling Golden Age. However short their reigns had been, the Tudors had truly left their marks on England.

As the casket of Queen Elizabeth I was being lowered into her vault at Westminster Abbey, change began brewing on the horizon. A young king still in the prime of his life was preparing to take the throne of a country he had scarcely known.

The Age of the Tudors had ended. The Stuart Era was about to begin.

Notes

Money Conversion

1. The National Archives, *Currency Converter: 1270 – 2017*. Available online at https://www.nationalarchives.gov.uk/currency-converter/#currency-result.

Introduction

1. P. Williams, *The Tudor Regime*. (Oxford: Clarendon Press, 1979), p. 154.
2. R. Goodman, *How To Be a Tudor: A Dawn-to-Dusk Guide to Everyday Life*. (London: Penguin Books, 2016), Introduction IX.
3. R. Goodman, *How To Be a Tudor: A Dawn-to-Dusk Guide to Everyday Life*. (London: Penguin Books, 2016), Introduction X.
4. Michael Wood, *Shakespeare's Mother: the Secret Life of a Tudor Woman*. (Documentary Series: Aired 2015).
5. S. Thurley, *Houses of Power: The Places that Shaped the Tudor World*. (London: Penguin & Random House, 2017), p. 181.

Chapter 1: Building the Tudor Home

1. William Harrison, *The Description of Elizabethan England, 1577*. (Washington D.C., Folger Shakespeare Library, 1994).
2. P. Williams, *The Tudor Regime*. (Oxford: Clarendon Press, 1979), p. 156.
3. S. Thurley, *Houses of Power: The Places that Shaped the Tudor World*. (London: Penguin & Random House, 2017), p. 346.
4. Ibid, p. 346.
5. I. Mortimer, *The Time Traveller's Guide to Medieval England*. (London: The Bodley Head, 2008), p. 22.

6. John Stow, *A Survey of London: Written in the Year 1598 by John Stow*. (Gloucestershire: Sutton Publishing, 2005).

7. Thomas More, *The Complete Works of St. Thomas More: The History of King Richard III*, ed. S. Sylvester (London: Yale University Press, 1961).

8. S. Porter, *Everyday Life in Tudor London*. (Gloucestershire: Amberley Publishing, 2016), p. 20.

9. William Harrison, *The Description of Elizabethan England, 1577*. (Washington D.C., Folger Shakespeare Library, 1994).

10. P. Brimacombe, *Tudor England*. (Gloucestershire: Pitkin Publishing, 2011).

11. John Stow, *A Survey of London: Written in the Year 1598 by John Stow*. (Gloucestershire: Sutton Publishing, 2005).

12. I. Mortimer, *The Time Traveller's Guide to Elizabethan England*. (London: Vintage Books, 2013).

13. S. Thurley, *Houses of Power: The Places that Shaped the Tudor World*. (London: Penguin & Random House, 2017).

14. British History Online, *Letters and Papers, Henry VIII*. Court Petition, 1538. Available online at: https://www.british-history.ac.uk/.

15. William Harrison, *The Description of Elizabethan England, 1577*. (Washington D.C., Folger Shakespeare Library, 1994).

16. I. Mortimer, *The Time Traveller's Guide to Elizabethan England*. (London: Vintage Books, 2013).

17. Ibid.

18. S. Thurley, *Houses of Power: The Places that Shaped the Tudor World*. (London: Penguin & Random House, 2017).

19. Ibid.

20. Historic England. Available online at: https://historicengland.org.uk/.

21. I. Mortimer, *The Time Traveller's Guide to Elizabethan England*. (London: Vintage Books, 2013), p. 292.

22. Ibid, p. 292.

23. S. Thurley, *Houses of Power: The Places that Shaped the Tudor World*. (London: Penguin & Random House, 2017), p. 75.

24. Ibid, p. 125.

25. Ibid, p. 126.

26. P. Williams, *The Tudor Regime*. (Oxford: Clarendon Press, 1979), p. 37.

27. R. Suggett, 'The Interpretation of Late Medieval Houses in Wales', in *From Medieval to Modern Wales* (Cardiff: University of Wales Press, 2004), p. 87.

28. S. Thurley, *Houses of Power: The Places that Shaped the Tudor World.* (London: Penguin & Random House, 2017), p. 245.
29. Ibid, p. 245.
30. Ibid, p. 126.
31. Ibid, p. 130.
32. Ibid, p. 170.
33. S. Porter, *Everyday Life in Tudor London.* (Gloucestershire: Amberley Publishing, 2016), p. 21.
34. S. Thurley, *Houses of Power: The Places that Shaped the Tudor World.* (London: Penguin & Random House, 2017), p. 329.
35. I. Mortimer, *The Time Traveller's Guide to Elizabethan England.* (London: Vintage Books, 2013).
36. M. Whittock, *A Brief History of Life in the Middle Ages.* (London: Robinson Publishing, 2009), p. 36.
37. P. Brimacombe, *Tudor England.* (Gloucestershire: Pitkin Publishing, 2011), p. 67.
38. M. Whittock, *A Brief History of Life in the Middle Ages.* (London: Robinson Publishing, 2009), pp. 57-58.
39. Ibid, p. 39.
40. John Stow, *A Survey of London: Written in the Year 1598 by John Stow.* (Gloucestershire: Sutton Publishing, 2005).
41. S. Porter, *Everyday Life in Tudor London.* (Gloucestershire: Amberley Publishing, 2016), p. 15.
42. J. Webb, *The City of Portsmouth.* (London: Pitkin Pictorials, 1984), p. 3.
43. S. Porter, *Everyday Life in Tudor London.* (Gloucestershire: Amberley Publishing, 2016), p. 16.
44. S. Thurley, *Houses of Power: The Places that Shaped the Tudor World.* (London: Penguin & Random House, 2017), p. 6.
45. P. Williams, *The Tudor Regime.* (Oxford: Clarendon Press, 1979), p. 154.

Chapter 2: Life as a Tudor

1. Venetian Reporter, 'A Relation, or rather a True Account, of the Island of England', ed. V. Dillon (1922), in, The Journal of the Society for Army Historical Research, Vol. 1(5) (September 1922).

2. R. Goodman, *How To Be a Tudor: A Dawn-to-Dusk Guide to Everyday Life*. (London: Penguin Books, 2016).
3. R. Goodman, *How To Be a Tudor: A Dawn-to-Dusk Guide to Everyday Life*. (London: Penguin Books, 2016).
4. B. Watts, *'Children in the Home: Infant Wellbeing and Parent-Child Relationships in Late Medieval England, 1250 – 1500'*. (Unpublished Master's Thesis: University of Wales, Trinity Saint David, 2022).
5. B. Hanawalt, *Growing Up in Medieval London: The Experience of Childhood in History*. (Oxford: Oxford University Press, 1993).
6. John Russell, *'Sermons on the Role of the Lords'*, ed. S. B. Chrimes, in, English Constitutional Ideas in the Fifteenth Century. (Cambridge, 1936).
7. Edward Hall, *Hall's Chronicle*. (London: J. Johnson, 1809), p. 87.
8. John Stow, *A Survey of London: Written in the Year 1598 by John Stow*. (Gloucestershire: Sutton Publishing, 2005), p. 33.
9. M. Whittock, *A Brief History of Life in the Middle Ages*. (London: Robinson Publishing, 2009), p. 110.
10. I. Mortimer, *The Time Traveller's Guide to Medieval England*. (London: The Bodley Head, 2008), p. 36.
11. E. Amt, and K. Allen Smith, *Medieval England, 500 – 1500: A Reader*. (Ontario: University of Toronto Press, 2018), p. 415.
12. Ibid., p. 415.
13. R. Goodman, *How To Be a Tudor: A Dawn-to-Dusk Guide to Everyday Life*. (London: Penguin Books, 2016).
14. A. Strickland, *Lives of the Tudor Princesses: Including Lady Jane Gray and Her Sisters* (London: Longmans Green, 1868), p. 239.
15. Collections, *Shoe T.602-1913*. The Victoria and Albert Museum, (9 Dec 2004). Available online at: https://www.vam.ac.uk/.
16. Ibid.
17. Thomas More, *The Complete Works of St. Thomas More: The History of King Richard III*, ed. S. Sylvester (London: Yale University Press, 1961).
18. John Stow, *A Survey of London: Written in the Year 1598 by John Stow*. (Gloucestershire: Sutton Publishing, 2005).
19. Ibid.
20. Ibid.
21. William Harrison, *The Description of Elizabethan England, 1577*. (Washington D.C., Folger Shakespeare Library, 1994), p. 307.

22. S. Porter, *Everyday Life in Tudor London.* (Gloucestershire: Amberley Publishing, 2016).

23. Ibid.

24. The National Archives, Currency Converter: 1270 – 2017. Available online at: https://www.nationalarchives.gov.uk/currency-converter/#currency-result.

25. S. Porter, *Everyday Life in Tudor London.* (Gloucestershire: Amberley Publishing, 2016).

26. Ibid.

27. A. G. R. Smith, *Tudor Government.* (London: The Historical Association, 1990), p. 29.

28. John Stow, *A Survey of London: Written in the Year 1598 by John Stow.* (Gloucestershire: Sutton Publishing, 2005), p. 44.

29. Ibid., p. 45.

30. S. Porter, *Everyday Life in Tudor London.* (Gloucestershire: Amberley Publishing, 2016), p. 16.

31. S. Thurley, *Houses of Power: The Places that Shaped the Tudor World.* (London: Penguin & Random House, 2017), pp. 111 – 113.

32. Ibid, pp. 111 – 113.

33. Ibid, pp. 111 – 113.

34. S. Porter, *Everyday Life in Tudor London.* (Gloucestershire: Amberley Publishing, 2016).

35. M. Rule, *The Mary Rose.* (Portsmouth: The Mary Rose Trust, 1983), p. 12.

36. Ibid., p. 12.

36. P. Williams, *The Tudor Regime.* (Oxford: Clarendon Press, 1979), p. 135.

37. Desiderius Erasmus, *The Correspondence of Erasmus* (Toronto: University of Toronto Press, 2019).

38. Ibid.

Chapter 3: Health and Medicine

1. Edward Hall, *Hall's Chronicle*, 1518.

2. H. E. Salter, *'Registrum Annalium Collegii Mertonensis'*, ed. A. Pickering (2000), in *Lancastrians to Tudors: England 1450 – 1509.* (Cambridge: Cambridge University Press, 2005).

3. Ibid.

4. D. O'Sullivan, and R. Lockyer, *Tudor England 1485 – 1603: Longman Sources and Opinions*. (Essex: Longman Group UK Ltd, 1993), p. 13.
5. M. Whittock, *A Brief History of Life in the Middle Ages*. (London: Robinson Publishing, 2009), p. 119.
6. Ibid, p. 119.
7. Thomas More, *The Complete Works of St. Thomas More: The History of King Richard III*, ed. S. Sylvester (London: Yale University Press, 1961).
8. S. Porter, *Everyday Life in Tudor London*. (Gloucestershire: Amberley Publishing, 2016).
9. S. Thurley, *Houses of Power: The Places that Shaped the Tudor World*. (London: Penguin & Random House, 2017), p. 137.
10. I. Mortimer, *The Time Traveller's Guide to Medieval England*. (London: The Bodley Head, 2008), p. 190.
11. Susannah Lipscomb, *Hidden Killers of the Tudor Home*. (Documentary Series: Aired 2015).
12. R. Goodman, *How To Be a Tudor: A Dawn-to-Dusk Guide to Everyday Life*. (London: Penguin Books, 2016).
13. Samuel Pepys, *The Diary of Samuel Pepys*, ed. H. B. Wheatley (1893).
14. M. Rule, *The Mary Rose*. (Portsmouth: The Mary Rose Trust, 1983).
15. William Harrison, *The Description of Elizabethan England, 1577*. (Washington D.C., Folger Shakespeare Library, 1994).
16. David Starkey, *Henry VIII used his very own 'stairthrone' when the steps became too much, says Starkey*. Newspaper article in, *The Daily Mail*, 7 February 2009.

Chapter 4: The Bathroom

1. Girolamo Fracastoro, *Syphilis, or a Poetical History of the French Disease*, 1530.
2. S. Thurley, *Houses of Power: The Places that Shaped the Tudor World*. (London: Penguin & Random House, 2017).
3. John Stow, *A Survey of London: Written in the Year 1598 by John Stow*. (Gloucestershire: Sutton Publishing, 2005), pp. 38 - 39
4. Ibid, pp. 38 – 39.
5. Ibid, pp. 38 – 39.

6. I. Mortimer, *The Time Traveller's Guide to Elizabethan England*. (London: Vintage Books, 2013).

7. M. Whittock, *A Brief History of Life in the Middle Ages*. (London: Robinson Publishing, 2009).

8. The Anne Boleyn Files. Available online at: https://www.theanneboleynfiles.com/.

9. M. Whittock, *A Brief History of Life in the Middle Ages*. (London: Robinson Publishing, 2009).

10. R. Goodman, *How To Be a Tudor: A Dawn-to-Dusk Guide to Everyday Life*. (London: Penguin Books, 2016).

11. S. Bryson, 'Menstruation in the Tudor period'. The Tudor Society (2016). Available online at: https://www.tudorsociety.com/.

12. C. Rawcliffe, *Medicine & Society in Later Medieval England*. (Gloucestershire: Sutton Publishing, 1995).

13. S. Bryson, 'Menstruation in the Tudor period'. The Tudor Society (2016). Available online at: https://www.tudorsociety.com/.

14. Kyra Kramer, 'The Sad Reign of Mary I Comes to an End'. Kyra Cornelius Kramer (2017). Available online at: http://www.kyrackramer.com/.

15. Ibid.

16. I. Mortimer, *The Time Traveller's Guide to Medieval England*. (London: The Bodley Head, 2008), p. 199.

17. John Stow, *A Survey of London: Written in the Year 1598 by John Stow*. (Gloucestershire: Sutton Publishing, 2005).

18. Ibid.

19. M. Whittock, *A Brief History of Life in the Middle Ages*. (London: Robinson Publishing, 2009).

20. Public permanent exhibit on the history of toilets at The Science Museum at Kensington, London.

21. Collections, *A Set of Miniature Whistle Pendants*, LOAN: MET ANON.1-1984. The Victoria and Albert Museum, (27 March 2003). Available online at: https://www.vam.ac.uk/.

22. Samuel Pepys, *The Diary of Samuel Pepys*, ed. H. B. Wheatley (1893).

23. Venetian envoy to England, c. 1497, in, D. O'Sullivan, and R. Lockyer, *Tudor England 1485 – 1603: Longman Sources and Opinions*. (Essex: Longman Group UK Ltd, 1993).

24. R. Goodman, *How To Be a Tudor: A Dawn-to-Dusk Guide to Everyday Life*. (London: Penguin Books, 2016).

25. Ibid.

26. S. Bryson, 'Menstruation in the Tudor period'. The Tudor Society (2016). Available online at: https://www.tudorsociety.com/.

27. Susannah Lipscomb, *Hidden Killers of the Tudor Home*. (Documentary Series: Aired 2015).

28. John Stow, *A Survey of London: Written in the Year 1598 by John Stow*. (Gloucestershire: Sutton Publishing, 2005).

29. M. Whittock, *A Brief History of Life in the Middle Ages*. (London: Robinson Publishing, 2009).

30. William Camden, *The History of the Most Renowned and Victorious Princess Elizabeth Late Queen of England*. (Chicago: The University of Chicago Press, 1970).

31. British History Online, *Letters and Papers, Henry VIII*. Court Petition, 1538. Available online at: https://www.british-history.ac.uk/.

32. John Stow, *A Survey of London: Written in the Year 1598 by John Stow*. (Gloucestershire: Sutton Publishing, 2005), p. 35.

33. Ibid, p. 36.

34. Ibid, p. 40.

35. B. Watts, 'Children in the Home: Infant Wellbeing and Parent-Child Relationships in Late Medieval England, 1250 – 1500'. (Unpublished Master's Thesis: University of Wales, Trinity Saint David, 2022).

36. Collections. *Nit combs*. Unknown (England, c. 1545). The Mary Rose Trust (2022).

37. S. Porter, *Everyday Life in Tudor London*. (Gloucestershire: Amberley Publishing, 2016), p. 19.

38. R. Goodman, *How To Be a Tudor: A Dawn-to-Dusk Guide to Everyday Life*. (London: Penguin Books, 2016).

39. L. Alchin, *Tudor Hair*. June, 2014. Available online at: https://www.sixwives.info/.

40. R. Goodman, *How To Be a Tudor: A Dawn-to-Dusk Guide to Everyday Life*. (London: Penguin Books, 2016).

41. S. Porter, *Everyday Life in Tudor London*. (Gloucestershire: Amberley Publishing, 2016), p. 21.

Chapter 5: The Kitchen

1. William Harrison on Food and Drink, *The Description of Elizabethan England*, 1577.

2. T. Breverton, *The Tudor Kitchen: What the Tudors Ate & Drank.* (Gloucestershire: Amberley Publishing, 2015).

3. S. Thurley, *Houses of Power: The Places that Shaped the Tudor World.* (London: Penguin & Random House, 2017), p. 162

4. B. Watts, 'Children in the Home: Infant Wellbeing and Parent-Child Relationships in Late Medieval England, 1250 – 1500'. (Unpublished Master's Thesis: University of Wales, Trinity Saint David, 2022).

5. B. Hanawalt, *Growing Up in Medieval London: The Experience of Childhood in History.* (Oxford: Oxford University Press, 1993).

6. John Stow, *A Survey of London: Written in the Year 1598 by John Stow.* (Gloucestershire: Sutton Publishing, 2005).

7. Ibid.

8. Ibid, p. 8.

9. P. Williams, *The Tudor Regime.* (Oxford: Clarendon Press, 1979), p. 159.

10. Susannah Lipscomb, *Hidden Killers of the Tudor Home.* (Documentary Series: Aired 2015).

11. Sir Hugh Plat, *Delightes for Ladies.* (London: 1602).

12. Venetian Reporter, 'A Relation, or rather a True Account, of the Island of England', ed. V. Dillon (1922), in, The Journal of the Society for Army Historical Research, Vol. 1(5) (September 1922).

13. T. Breverton, *The Tudor Kitchen: What the Tudors Ate & Drank.* (Gloucestershire: Amberley Publishing, 2015).

14. Susannah Lipscomb, *Hidden Killers of the Tudor Home.* (Documentary Series: Aired 2015).

15. J. L. Matterer, *17th Century English Recipes.* Available online at: http://www.godecookery.com/engrec/engrec.html.

16. Susannah Lipscomb, *Hidden Killers of the Tudor Home.* (Documentary Series: Aired 2015).

17. B. Watts, 'The Middle Ages – a period where 'hygiene counts for nothing'?'. (Unpublished Undergraduate Thesis: University of Wales, Trinity Saint David, 2019).

18. S. Bryson, 'Menstruation in the Tudor period'. The Tudor Society (2016). Available online at: https://www.tudorsociety.com/.

19. S. Thurley, *Houses of Power: The Places that Shaped the Tudor World.* (London: Penguin & Random House, 2017), pp. 167 – 168.

20. S. Bryson, 'Menstruation in the Tudor period'. The Tudor Society (2016). Available online at: https://www.tudorsociety.com/.

21. M. Whittock, *A Brief History of Life in the Middle Ages*. (London: Robinson Publishing, 2009), p. 107.

22. Ibid, p. 109.

23. Ibid, p. 109.

24. John Stow, *A Survey of London: Written in the Year 1598 by John Stow*. (Gloucestershire: Sutton Publishing, 2005), p. 6.

25. Ibid, p. 6.

26. Thomas More, *The Complete Works of St. Thomas More: The History of King Richard III*, ed. S. Sylvester (London: Yale University Press, 1961).

27. R. Goodman, *How To Be a Tudor: A Dawn-to-Dusk Guide to Everyday Life*. (London: Penguin Books, 2016).

28. Ibid.

29. I. Mortimer, *The Time Traveller's Guide to Elizabethan England*. (London: Vintage Books, 2013).

30. John Stow, *A Survey of London: Written in the Year 1598 by John Stow*. (Gloucestershire: Sutton Publishing, 2005).

31. B. Hanawalt, *Growing Up in Medieval London: The Experience of Childhood in History*. (Oxford: Oxford University Press, 1993).

32. Ibid.

33. John Stow, *A Survey of London: Written in the Year 1598 by John Stow*. (Gloucestershire: Sutton Publishing, 2005).

34. *How to Behave Thyself in Serving the Table*, Francis Seager's School of Virtue, (1557), in, Frederick James Furnivall, *The Babees' Book*, ed. E. Rickert and L. J. Naylor. (Ontario: Cambridge University Press, 2000).

35. B. Hanawalt, *The Ties That Bound: Peasant Families in Medieval England* (Oxford: Oxford University Press, 1986).

36. *How to Order Thyself Sitting at the Table*, Francis Seager's School of Virtue, (1577), in, Frederick James Furnivall, *The Babees' Book*, ed. E. Rickert and L. J. Naylor. (Ontario: Cambridge University Press, 2000).

Chapter 6: The Bedroom

1. Richard Weste, *How Thou Oughtest to Prepare Thyself, When Thou Risest in the Morning*, 1619.

2. B. Watts, '*Children in the Home: Infant Wellbeing and Parent-Child Relationships in Late Medieval England, 1250–1500*'. (Unpublished Master's Thesis: University of Wales, Trinity Saint David, 2022).

3. R. Goodman, *How To Be a Tudor: A Dawn-to-Dusk Guide to Everyday Life*. (London: Penguin Books, 2016).

4. Ibid.

5. Ibid.

6. Venetian Reporter, '*A Relation, or rather a True Account, of the Island of England*', ed. V. Dillon (1922), in, The Journal of the Society for Army Historical Research, Vol. 1(5) (September 1922).

7. R. Goodman, *How To Be a Tudor: A Dawn-to-Dusk Guide to Everyday Life*. (London: Penguin Books, 2016).

8. *Ibid.*

9. *Ibid.*

10. I. Mortimer, *The Time Traveller's Guide to Elizabethan England*. (London: Vintage Books, 2013).

11. Frederick James Furnivall, *The Babees' Book*, ed. E. Rickert and L. J. Naylor. (Ontario: Cambridge University Press, 2000).

12. Venetian envoy to England, c. 1497, in, D. O'Sullivan, and R. Lockyer, *Tudor England 1485 – 1603: Longman Sources and Opinions*. (Essex: Longman Group UK Ltd, 1993).

13. B. Watts, '*Children in the Home: Infant Wellbeing and Parent-Child Relationships in Late Medieval England, 1250–1500*'. (Unpublished Master's Thesis: University of Wales, Trinity Saint David, 2022).

14. Ibid.

15. B. Hanawalt, *The Ties That Bound: Peasant Families in Medieval England*. (Oxford: Oxford University Press, 1986).

16. I. Mortimer, *The Time Traveller's Guide to Elizabethan England*. (London: Vintage Books, 2013).

17. Ibid.

18. M. Whittock, *A Brief History of Life in the Middle Ages*. (London: Robinson Publishing, 2009).

19. Ibid.

20. P. Williams, *The Tudor Regime*. (Oxford: Clarendon Press, 1979), p. 142.

21. Ibid.

22. Ibid.

23. C. Rawcliffe, *Medicine & Society in Later Medieval England.* (Gloucestershire: Sutton Publishing, 1995).
24. P. Williams, *The Tudor Regime.* (Oxford: Clarendon Press, 1979), p. 158.
25. John Stow, *A Survey of London: Written in the Year 1598 by John Stow.* (Gloucestershire: Sutton Publishing, 2005).
26. Ibid.
27. B. Hanawalt, *The Ties That Bound: Peasant Families in Medieval England.* (Oxford: Oxford University Press, 1986).
28. Ibid.
29. British History Online, *Letters and Papers, Henry VIII.* Court Petition, 1538. Available online at: https://www.british-history.ac.uk/.
30. I. Mortimer, *The Time Traveller's Guide to Elizabethan England.* (London: Vintage Books, 2013).
31. P. Williams, *The Tudor Regime.* (Oxford: Clarendon Press, 1979), p. 142.
32. William Close, in, F. Wallis, *Medieval Medicine: A Reader.* (Ontario: University of Toronto Press, 2010).
33. C. Rawcliffe, *Medicine & Society in Later Medieval England.* (Gloucestershire: Sutton Publishing, 1995).
34. British History Online, *Letters and Papers, Henry VIII.* Court Petition, 1538. Available online at: https://www.british-history.ac.uk/.
35. F. Wallis, *Medieval Medicine: A Reader.* (Ontario: University of Toronto Press, 2010).
36. J. Webb, *The City of Portsmouth.* (London: Pitkin Pictorials, 1984), p. 11.
37. M. Rule, *The Mary Rose.* (Portsmouth: The Mary Rose Trust, 1983), p. 10.

Chapter 7: The Nursery

1. William Shakespeare, *As You Like It: Act 2, Scene 7.*, 1599.
2. B. Watts, *'Children in the Home: Infant Wellbeing and Parent-Child Relationships in Late Medieval England, 1250 – 1500'.* (Unpublished Master's Thesis: University of Wales, Trinity Saint David, 2022).
3. Ibid.

4. *The Vaux Family Passional* (MS 482D). The National Library of Wales. Available online at: https://www.llyfrgell.cymru.

5. Michael Wood, *Shakespeare's Mother: the Secret Life of a Tudor Woman*. (Documentary Series: Aired 2015).

6. B. Watts, '*Children in the Home: Infant Wellbeing and Parent-Child Relationships in Late Medieval England, 1250 – 1500*'. (Unpublished Master's Thesis: University of Wales, Trinity Saint David, 2022).

7. Ventian Envoy to England, c. 1497.

8. Ibid.

9. B. Hanawalt, *Growing Up in Medieval London: The Experience of Childhood in History*. (Oxford: Oxford University Press, 1993).

10. B. Watts, '*Children in the Home: Infant Wellbeing and Parent-Child Relationships in Late Medieval England, 1250 – 1500*'. (Unpublished Master's Thesis: University of Wales, Trinity Saint David, 2022).

11. B. Hanawalt, *Growing Up in Medieval London: The Experience of Childhood in History*. (Oxford: Oxford University Press, 1993), p. 16.

12. Frederick James Furnivall, *The Babees' Book*, ed. E. Rickert and L. J. Naylor. (Ontario: Cambridge University Press, 2000).

13. B. Hanawalt, *Growing Up in Medieval London: The Experience of Childhood in History*. (Oxford: Oxford University Press, 1993).

14. Ibid., p. 125.

15. B. Hanawalt, *Growing Up in Medieval London: The Experience of Childhood in History*. (Oxford: Oxford University Press, 1993), p. 72.

16. Ibid, p. 72.

17. Ibid.

18. Frederick James Furnivall, *The Babees' Book*, ed. E. Rickert and L. J. Naylor. (Ontario: Cambridge University Press, 2000).

19. B. Watts, '*Children in the Home: Infant Wellbeing and Parent-Child Relationships in Late Medieval England, 1250 – 1500*'. (Unpublished Master's Thesis: University of Wales, Trinity Saint David, 2022).

20. Ibid.

21. Ibid.

22. Ibid.

23. Ibid.

24. Ibid.

25. Ibid.

26. Ibid.
27. B. Hanawalt, *Growing Up in Medieval London: The Experience of Childhood in History*. (Oxford: Oxford University Press, 1993), p. 139.
28. Anon., '*How the Goode Wife Taught Hyr Daughter*', in, *The Trials and Joys of Marriage*, ed. E. Salisbury (Michigan: Medieval Institute Publications, 2002), p. 75.
29. Frederick James Furnivall, *The Babees' Book*, ed. E. Rickert and L. J. Naylor. (Ontario: Cambridge University Press, 2000).
30. B. Hanawalt, *Growing Up in Medieval London: The Experience of Childhood in History*. (Oxford: Oxford University Press, 1993).
31. John Stow, *A Survey of London: Written in the Year 1598 by John Stow*. (Gloucestershire: Sutton Publishing, 2005), p. 7.
32. John Heywood, *The proverbs of John Heywood. Being the "Proverbes" of that author printed 1546. Ed., with notes and introduction* (London: George Bell and Sons, 1874).

Chapter 8: Fun, Games and Entertainment

1. Henry Howard, Earl of Surrey, *Private Letter* 1543.
2. M. Rule, *The Mary Rose*. (Portsmouth: The Mary Rose Trust, 1983).
3. I. Mortimer, *The Time Traveller's Guide to Elizabethan England*. (London: Vintage Books, 2013).
4. T. Breverton, *Everything You Ever Wanted to Know About the Tudors But Were Afraid to Ask*. (Gloucestershire: Amberley Publishing, 2015).
5. Francis Bacon, *The Reign of Henry VII*. (London: 1621).
6. Anon, *Little Jack Horner*. English, c. 1530s.
7. S. Thurley, *Houses of Power: The Places that Shaped the Tudor World*. (London: Penguin & Random House, 2017), p. 170.
8. S. Porter, *Everyday Life in Tudor London*. (Gloucestershire: Amberley Publishing, 2016), p. 15.
9. John Stow, *A Survey of London: Written in the Year 1598 by John Stow*. (Gloucestershire: Sutton Publishing, 2005).
10. R. Goodman, *How to Behave Badly in Renaissance Britain*. (London: Michael O'Mara Books Ltd, 2018).

11. Ibid.
12. William FitzStephen, *An Annotated Translation of the Life of St. Thomas Becket by William FitzStephen*, ed. L. T. Gourde. (Chicago: Loyala University, 1943).
13. Ibid.
14. J. Simkin, *The History of Football*. (Published Online: Spartacus Educational, 1997).
15. Ibid.
16. Ibid.
17. S. Thurley, *Houses of Power: The Places that Shaped the Tudor World*. (London: Penguin & Random House, 2017), p. 145.
18. Ibid.
19. Ibid.
20. The National Archives, Currency Converter: 1270 – 2017. Available online at: https://www.nationalarchives.gov.uk/currency-converter/#currency-result.
21. R. Goodman, *How to Behave Badly in Renaissance Britain*. (London: Michael O'Mara Books Ltd, 2018).
22. P. Brimacombe, *Tudor England*. (Gloucestershire: Pitkin Publishing, 2011).
23. R. Goodman, *How to Behave Badly in Renaissance Britain*. (London: Michael O'Mara Books Ltd, 2018).
24. S. Thurley, *Houses of Power: The Places that Shaped the Tudor World*. (London: Penguin & Random House, 2017), p. 147.
25. William Harrison, *The Description of Elizabethan England, 1577*. (Washington D.C., Folger Shakespeare Library, 1994).
26. Ibid.
27. Ibid.
28. Ibid.
29. S. Thurley, *Houses of Power: The Places that Shaped the Tudor World*. (London: Penguin & Random House, 2017), p. 103.
30. William Harrison, *The Description of Elizabethan England, 1577*. (Washington D.C., Folger Shakespeare Library, 1994).
31. Ibid.
32. The Anne Boleyn Files. Available online at: https://www.theanneboleynfiles.com/.
33. Ibid.

34. S. Thurley, *Houses of Power: The Places that Shaped the Tudor World*. (London: Penguin & Random House, 2017).
35. The Anne Boleyn Files. Available online at: https://www. theanneboleynfiles.com/.
36. S. Thurley, *Houses of Power: The Places that Shaped the Tudor World*. (London: Penguin & Random House, 2017).
37. William Harrison, *The Description of Elizabethan England, 1577*. (Washington D.C., Folger Shakespeare Library, 1994).
38. G. Elliot, *Cardinal Wolsey, Cat Lover*. Grace Elliot Author (2016). Available online at: http://graceelliot-author.blogspot.com/.
39. William Camden, *The History of the Most Renowned and Victorious Princess Elizabeth Late Queen of England*. (Chicago: The University of Chicago Press, 1970).
40. *The Earl of Southampton*. John de Critz [Oil on canvas] (England, c. 1603), and accompanying notes, held in the Private Collection of the Duke of Buccleuch and Queensbury.
41. Ibid.
42. Ibid.
43. John Stow, *A Survey of London: Written in the Year 1598 by John Stow*. (Gloucestershire: Sutton Publishing, 2005).
44. Ibid.
45. N. Williams, *Henry VII*. (London: Weidenfeld Nicolson, 1973).
46. S. Thurley, *Houses of Power: The Places that Shaped the Tudor World*. (London: Penguin & Random House, 2017).
47. Ibid, p. 92.
48. John Stow, *A Survey of London: Written in the Year 1598 by John Stow*. (Gloucestershire: Sutton Publishing, 2005).
49. Samuel Pepys, *The Diary of Samuel Pepys*, ed. H. B. Wheatley (1893).
50. Ibid.
51. Ibid.
52. M. Jones, and C. R. Cheney, *A Handbook of Dates: For students of British history*, 2nd edn. (Cambridge: Cambridge University Press, 2004).
53. Ibid.
54. Ibid.
55. Ibid.

56. Ibid.
57. M. Jones, and C. R. Cheney, *A Handbook of Dates: For students of British history*, 2nd edn. (Cambridge: Cambridge University Press, 2004).
58. S. Thurley, *Houses of Power: The Places that Shaped the Tudor World.* (London: Penguin & Random House, 2017), p. 81
59. Ibid, p. 45.
60. M. Jones, and C. R. Cheney, A Handbook of Dates: For students of British history, 2nd edn. (Cambridge: Cambridge University Press, 2004).
61. Ibid.
62. Ibid.

Chapter 9: Dangers in the Home

1. *The London Gazette*, Whitehall, September 8th 1666.
2. John Stow, *A Survey of London: Written in the Year 1598 by John Stow.* (Gloucestershire: Sutton Publishing, 2005).
3. William FitzStephen, *An Annotated Translation of the Life of St. Thomas Becket by William FitzStephen*, ed. L. T. Gourde. (Chicago: Loyala University, 1943).
4. Thatching Information Resource. Available online at: https://thatchinginfo.com/.
5. Ibid.
6. Susannah Lipscomb, *Hidden Killers of the Tudor Home.* (Documentary Series: Aired 2015).
7. S. Porter, *Everyday Life in Tudor London.* (Gloucestershire: Amberley Publishing, 2016).
8. B. Hanawalt, *The Ties That Bound: Peasant Families in Medieval England* (Oxford: Oxford University Press, 1986).
9. Ibid, p. 7.
10. S. Porter, *Everyday Life in Tudor London.* (Gloucestershire: Amberley Publishing, 2016).
11. Ibid.
12. B. Hanawalt, *The Ties That Bound: Peasant Families in Medieval England.* (Oxford: Oxford University Press, 1986).

13. B. Hanawalt, *Growing Up in Medieval London: The Experience of Childhood in History*. (Oxford: Oxford University Press, 1993).
14. B. Hanawalt, *The Ties That Bound: Peasant Families in Medieval England*. (Oxford: Oxford University Press, 1986).
15. M. Rule, *The Mary Rose*. (Portsmouth: The Mary Rose Trust, 1983), p. 10.
16. Ibid, p. 10.
17. Ibid, p. 10.
18. Ibid, p. 3.
19. M. Rule, *The Mary Rose*. (Portsmouth: The Mary Rose Trust, 1983), p. 10.
20. The National Archives, *Coroner's Report* (KB 9/1073/f.80). Available online at: https://www.nationalarchives.gov.uk/.
21. The University of Oxford, et al., *Everyday Life and Fatal Hazard in Sixteenth-Century England*. Available online at: https://tudoraccidents. history.ox.ac.uk/. For further reading of coroner's rolls, see, R. R. Sharpe, *Calendar of Letter-Books of the City of London*. Available online at: https://www.british-history.ac.uk/search/series/london-letter-books. (London: Richard Clay and Sons, 1913).

Chapter 10: Death and Dying

1. William Shakespeare, *Julius Caesar*: Act 2, Scene 2., 1599.
2. M. Whittock, *A Brief History of Life in the Middle Ages*. (London: Robinson Publishing, 2009).
3. Michael Wood, *Shakespeare's Mother: the Secret Life of a Tudor Woman*. (Documentary Series: Aired 2015).
4. T. Breverton, *Everything You Ever Wanted to Know About the Tudors But Were Afraid to Ask*. (Gloucestershire: Amberley Publishing, 2015).
5. Ibid.
6. B. Watts, '*Children in the Home: Infant Wellbeing and Parent-Child Relationships in Late Medieval England, 1250 – 1500*'. (Unpublished Master's Thesis: University of Wales, Trinity Saint David, 2022).
7. B. Johnson, *The Reputed Plague Pits of London*. Historic UK (2022). Available online at: https://www.historic-uk.com/.

8. Ibid.

9. John Stow, *A Survey of London: Written in the Year 1598 by John Stow.* (Gloucestershire: Sutton Publishing, 2005).

10. R. Goodman, *How to Behave Badly in Renaissance Britain.* (London: Michael O'Mara Books Ltd, 2018).

11. B. Watts, *'Children in the Home: Infant Wellbeing and Parent-Child Relationships in Late Medieval England, 1250 – 1500'.* (Unpublished Master's Thesis: University of Wales, Trinity Saint David, 2022).

12. J. Schofield, *'Thomas Cromwell and the 'ungoodly' executioner'.* The History Press. Available online at: https://www.thehistorypress. co.uk/.

13. Ibid.

14. The Love of History, *'The Head of Sir Thomas More'.* The Love of History (2011). Available online at: https://theloveforhistory. wordpress.com/.

15. Ibid.

16. Ibid.

17. H. E. Salter, *'Registrum Annalium Collegii Mertonensis'*, ed. A. Pickering (2000), in *Lancastrians to Tudors: England 1450 – 1509.* (Cambridge: Cambridge University Press, 2005), p. 92.

18. Ibid, p. 92.

19. The Royal College of Surgeons of England, *A History of Human Dissection* (London: The Royal College of Surgeons, 2004).

20. A. M. Lord, *'Four Perceptions of Suicide in Sixteenth- and Early Seventeenth-Century England'.* (Virginia: The College of William and Mary, 1990), p. 44.

21. Ibid, p. 44.

22. J. Matusiak, *A History of the Tudors in 100 Objects* (Gloucestershire: The History Press, 2019).

23. William Julius Mickle, *Cumner Hall,* in H. Wadsworth Longfellow, *Poems of Places: An Anthology in 31 Volumes*, Vol. I – IV. (London, 1876).

24. M. Rule, *The Mary Rose.* (Portsmouth: The Mary Rose Trust, 1983).

25. D. O'Sullivan, and R. Lockyer, *Tudor England 1485 – 1603: Longman Sources and Opinions.* (Essex: Longman Group UK Ltd, 1993).

26. Walter Raleigh, *The Works of Sir Walter Raleigh: Miscellaneous Works.* (Oxford: Oxford University Press, 1829).

27. C. Doughty, *Smoke Gets In Your Eyes and Other Lessons from the Crematorium* (Edinburgh: Canongate Books, 2016).
28. Ibid.
29. Ibid.
30. Ibid.
31. Ibid.
32. B. Watts, *'Children in the Home: Infant Wellbeing and Parent-Child Relationships in Late Medieval England, 1250 – 1500'*. (Unpublished Master's Thesis: University of Wales, Trinity Saint David, 2022).
33. Ibid.
34. Ibid.
35. Ibid.
36. Ibid.
37. S. Bryson, *'Childbirth in Medieval and Tudor Times'*. The Tudor Society (2016). Available online at: https://www.tudorsociety.com/.
38. B. Watts, 'Children in the Home: Infant Wellbeing and Parent-Child Relationships in Late Medieval England, 1250 – 1500'. (Unpublished Master's Thesis: University of Wales, Trinity Saint David, 2022).
39. See; *The Cadaver Tomb of John Baret* (Suffolk, 1463). Available online at Churches Conservation Trust, https://www.visitchurches. org.uk/.
40. The Borthwick Institute, York. Prob. Reg. II, f, 250v.

Bibliography

Primary Sources

Amt, E., and Allen Smith, K., *Medieval England, 500 – 1500: A Reader*. (Ontario: University of Toronto Press, 2018).

Andrew Boorde, *The Breviary of Helthe for all Manner of Sycknesses and Diseases*, 1547.

Anon., *A Relation, Or Rather a True Account, of the Island of England With Sundry Particulars of the Customs of These People, and of the Royal Revenues Under King Henry the Seventh, about the Year 1500*, trans. C. A. Sneyd (London: Camden Society, 1847).

Anon., 'How the Goode Wife Taught Hyr Daughter', in, *The Trials and Joys of Marriage*, ed. E. Salisbury (Michigan: Medieval Institute Publications, 2002).

Aughterson, K., *The English Renaissance: An Anthology of Sources and Documents*. (Oxford: Routledge, 2002).

Desiderius Erasmus, *The Correspondence of Erasmus* (Toronto: University of Toronto Press, 2019).

Edward Hall, *Hall's Chronicle*. (London: J. Johnson, 1809).

Francis Bacon, *The Reign of Henry VII*. (London: 1621).

Frederick James Furnivall, The Babees' Book, ed. E. Rickert and L. J. Naylor. (Ontario: Cambridge University Press, 2000).

George Owen of Henllys, *The Description of Pembrokeshire by George Owen of Henllys*, ed. D. Miles (Llandysul, 1994).

Henry Machyn, *The Diary of Henry Machyn, Citizen and Merchant-Taylor of London, 1550 – 1563*. (London: The Camden Society, 1848).

Henry VII, 'The Proclamation of Henry Tudor, 23 August 1485', ed. P. L. Hughes, and J. P. Larkin (1964), in *Medieval Worlds: A Sourcebook*, ed. R. Anderson, and D. A. Bellenger. (London: Routledge, 2003).

Sir Hugh Plat, *Delightes for Ladies*. (London: 1602).

_____, *The Jewell house of art and nature*. (London: 1594).

Lord Howard Effingham, 'Letter to Lord Burghley, 10 August 1588', ed. H. W. Hodges and E. A. Hughes (1922), in *Select Naval Documents*. (Cambridge: Cambridge University Press, 1927).

John Leland, *The Itinerary of John Leland 1535 - 1543*, ed. L. T. Smith. (London: George Bell & Sons, 1906).

John Russell, 'Sermons on the Role of the Lords', ed. S. B. Chrimes, in, *English Constitutional Ideas in the Fifteenth Century*. (Cambridge, 1936).

John Stow, *A Survey of London: Written in the Year 1598 by John Stow*. (Gloucestershire: Sutton Publishing, 2005).

Jones, M., and Cheney, C. R., *A Handbook of Dates: For students of British history*, 2nd edn. (Cambridge: Cambridge University Press, 2004).

Salter, H. E., '*Registrum Annalium Collegii Mertonensis*', ed. A. Pickering (2000), in *Lancastrians to Tudors: England 1450 – 1509*. (Cambridge: Cambridge University Press, 2005).

Samuel Pepys, *The Diary of Samuel Pepys*, ed. H. B. Wheatley (1893).

Strickland, A., *Lives of the Tudor Princesses: Including Lady Jane Gray and Her Sisters* (London: Longmans Green, 1868).

Thomas Dawson, *The Good Huswife's Jewell* (1596). (London: Edward White).

Thomas More, *The Complete Works of St. Thomas More: The History of King Richard III*, ed. S. Sylvester (London: Yale University Press, 1961).

Venetian Reporter, 'A Relation, or rather a True Account, of the Island of England', ed. V. Dillon (1922), in, *The Journal of the Society for Army Historical Research*, Vol. 1(5) (September 1922).

Walker, G., *The Oxford Anthology of Tudor Drama*. (Oxford: Oxford University Press, 2014).

Wallis, F., *Medieval Medicine: A Reader*. (Ontario: University of Toronto Press, 2010).

Walter Raleigh, *The Works of Sir Walter Raleigh: Miscellaneous Works*. (Oxford: Oxford University Press, 1829).

William Camden, *The History of the Most Renowned and Victorious Princess Elizabeth Late Queen of England*. (Chicago: The University of Chicago Press, 1970).

William FitzStephen, *An Annotated Translation of the Life of St. Thomas Becket by William FitzStephen*, ed. L. T. Gourde. (Chicago: Loyala University, 1943).

William Harrison, *The Description of Elizabethan England, 1577.* (Washington D.C., Folger Shakespeare Library, 1994).

Secondary Sources

Boulton, J., 'Food Prices and the Standard of Living in London in the 'Century of Revolution', 1580 – 1700', in *The Economic History Review*, Vol. 53(3) (2000).

Breverton, T., *The Tudor Cookbook: From Gilded Peacock to Calves' Feet Pie.* (Gloucestershire: Amberley Publishing, 2016).

_____. *The Tudor Kitchen: What the Tudors Ate & Drank.* (Gloucestershire: Amberley Publishing, 2015).

_____. *Everything You Ever Wanted to Know About the Tudors But Were Afraid to Ask.* (Gloucestershire: Amberley Publishing, 2015).

Brimacombe, P., *Tudor England.* (Gloucestershire: Pitkin Publishing, 2011).

Bryson, S., 'Menstruation in the Tudor period'. The Tudor Society (2016). Available online at: https://www.tudorsociety.com/.

_____., 'Childbirth in Medieval and Tudor Times'. The Tudor Society (2016). Available online at: https://www.tudorsociety.com/.

Chapman, E. R., *Children and child burial in medieval England.* (Cambridge: University of Cambridge, 2016).

Dockray, K., 'Patriotism, Pride and Paranoia: England and the English in the Fifteenth Century', in, *The Ricardian*, Vol. 8(110) (1990).

Findlay, J., *The Children of England.* (London: Meuthen & Co., 1923).

Fleming, P., *Family and Household in Medieval England.* (London: Palgrave, 2000).

Furtardo, P., *Plague, Pestilence and Pandemic: Voices from History.* (London: Thames & Hudson Ltd, 2021).

Gies, F., and Gies, J., *Life in a Medieval Village.* (New York: Harper Perennial, 1991).

Goodman, R., *How to Behave Badly in Renaissance Britain.* (London: Michael O'Mara Books Ltd, 2018).

Gunn, S. J., *Early Tudor Government, 1485-1558.* (Hampshire: Palgrave Macmillan, 1995).

Guy, J., *The Oxford History of Britain: The Tudor Age, 1485 – 1603.* (Oxford: Oxford University Press, 1984).

Hanawalt, B., *Growing Up in Medieval London: The Experience of Childhood in History*. (Oxford: Oxford University Press, 1993).

_____, *The Ties That Bound: Peasant Families in Medieval England* (Oxford: Oxford University Press, 1986).

Hunt, D., *Parents and Children in History*. (New York: Harper and Row, 1972).

Leyser, H., *Medieval Women: A Social History of Women in England, 450 – 1500*. (London: Phoenix Press, 1995).

Loades, D., *The Chronicles of the Tudor Queens*. (Gloucestershire: Sutton Publishing, 2002).

Mawhinney, S. E., *Coming of Age: Youth in England, c. 1400 – 1600*. (York: University of York Press, 2015).

McIntosh, J. L. *From Heads of Household to Heads of State: The Preaccession Households of Mary and Elizabeth Tudor, 1516 – 1558*. (New York: Columbia University Press, 2008).

Mortimer, I., *The Time Traveller's Guide to Medieval England*. (London: The Bodley Head, 2008).

O'Sullivan, D., and Lockyer, R., *Tudor England 1485 – 1603: Longman Sources and Opinions*. (Essex: Longman Group UK Ltd, 1993).

Pickering, A., *Lancastrians to Tudors: England 1450 – 1509*. (Cambridge: Cambridge University Press, 2005).

Platt, C., *The Parish Churches of Medieval England*. (London: Chancellor Press, 1995).

Rappaport, S., *Words Within Worlds: Structures of Life in Sixteenth-Century London*. (Cambridge: Cambridge University Press, 1989).

Rawcliffe, C., *Medicine & Society in Later Medieval England*. (Gloucestershire: Sutton Publishing, 1995).

Reeves, A. C., *Pleasures and Pastimes in Later Medieval England*. (Gloucestershire: Sutton Publishing, 1997).

Ridley, J., *A Brief History of the Tudor Age*. (London: Constable & Robinson, 1998).

Rule, M., *The Mary Rose*. (Portsmouth: The Mary Rose Trust, 1983).

Saunders, A., and Schofield, J., *Tudor London: A Map and a View*. (London: London Topographical Society, 2001).

Schofield, J., 'Thomas Cromwell and the 'ungoodly' executioner'. The History Press, available online at: https://www.thehistorypress.co.uk/.

Sharpe, R. R., Calendar of Letter-Books of the City of London. Available online at: https://www.british-history.ac.uk/search/series/london-letter-books. (London: Richard Clay and Sons, 1913).

Shephard, R. J., 'An Illustrated History of Health and Fitness, from Pre-History to our Post-Modern World', in, *Studies in History and Philosophy of Science*, Vol. 39(2015) (2014).

Shorter, E., *The Making of a Modern Family.* (London: Collins, 1976).

Simpson, J., and Roud, S., *A Dictionary of English Folklore.* (Oxford: Oxford University Press, 2000).

Simkin, J., *The History of Football.* (Published Online: Spartacus Educational, 1997).

Smith, A. G. R., *Tudor Government.* (London: The Historical Association, 1990).

Suggett, R., 'The Interpretation of Late Medieval Houses in Wales', in *From Medieval to Modern Wales* (Cardiff: University of Wales Press, 2004).

Watts, B., 'Children in the Home: Infant Wellbeing and Parent-Child Relationships in Late Medieval England, 1250 – 1500'. (Unpublished Master's Thesis: University of Wales, Trinity Saint David, 2022).

_____., 'Marriage and the Consolidation of Tudor Power, 1485 – 1603'. (Unpublished Undergraduate Thesis: University of Wales, Trinity Saint David, 2020).

_____., 'The Middle Ages – a period where 'hygiene counts for nothing'?'. (Unpublished Undergraduate Thesis: University of Wales, Trinity Saint David, 2019).

Webb, J., *The City of Portsmouth.* (London: Pitkin Pictorials, 1984).

Whittock, M., *A Brief History of Life in the Middle Ages*. (London: Robinson Publishing, 2009).

Williams, N., *Henry VII.* (London: Weidenfeld Nicolson, 1973).

Williams, P., *The Tudor Regime*. (Oxford: Clarendon Press, 1979).

van Zanden, J. L., 'Wages and the cost of living in Southern England (London) 1450 – 1700', in *International Institute of Social History*, Vol. 3(2) (1999).

Internet Resources

John Noorthouck, *A New History of London Including Westminster and Southwark.* Available online at: https://www.british-history.ac.uk/no-series/new-history-london.

The Anne Boleyn Files. Available online at: https://www. theanneboleynfiles.com/.

Beard, G., and Gilbert, C., *Dictionary of English Furniture Makers, 1660 – 1840*. Available online at: https://www.british-history.ac.uk/ no-series/dict-english-furniture-makers.

British History Online, *Feet of Fines, Tudor Yorkshire*. Available online at: http://www.british-history.ac.uk/feet-of-fines-yorks/vol1.

British History Online, *Letters and Papers, Henry VIII*. Available online at: https://www.british-history.ac.uk/.

Elizabeth I. Available online at: https://www.elizabethi.org/.

Historic England. Available online at: https://historicengland.org.uk/.

Matterer, J. L, *17th Century English Recipes*. Available online at: http:// www.godecookery.com/engrec/engrec.html.

The National Archives, Currency Converter: 1270 – 2017. Available online at: https://www.nationalarchives.gov.uk/currency-converter/#currency-result.

Thatching Information Resource. Available online at: https:// thatchinginfo.com/.

Tudors Dynasty. Available online at: https://tudorsdynasty.com/.

Tudor History. Available online at: https://tudorhistory.org/.

Tudor Times. Available online at: https://www.tudortimes.co.uk/.

The Tudor Society. Available online at: https://www.tudorsociety.com/.

The University of Cambridge, *Casebooks*. Available online at: https:// casebooks.lib.cam.ac.uk/.

The University of Oxford, et al., *Everyday Life and Fatal Hazard in Sixteenth-Century England*. Available online at: https://tudoraccidents. history.ox.ac.uk/.

The University of Winchester, et al., *Kingship, Court and Society: the Chamber Books of Henry VII and Henry VIII, 1485 – 1521*. Available online at: https://www.tudorchamberbooks.org/.

Select Reading

Forgeng, J. L., *Daily Life in Elizabethan England*. (Oxford: Greenwood Press, 2010).

Goodman, R., *How To Be a Tudor: A Dawn-to-Dusk Guide to Everyday Life*. (London: Penguin Books, 2016).

Mortimer, I., *The Time Traveller's Guide to Elizabethan England*. (London: Vintage Books, 2013).

Norton, E., *The Lives of Tudor Women*. (Croydon: Head of Zeus Ltd, 2016).

Plowden, A., *Tudor Women: Queens and Commoners*. (Gloucestershire: Sutton Publishing, 2003).

Porter, S., *Everyday Life in Tudor London*. (Gloucestershire: Amberley Publishing, 2016).

Sim, A., *Food and Feast in Tudor England*. (Cheltenham: History Press Ltd, 2005).

_____., *The Tudor Housewife*. (Cheltenham: History Press, Ltd, 2011).

Thurley, S., *Houses of Power: The Places that Shaped the Tudor World*. (London: Penguin & Random House, 2017).

Weir, A., and Clarke, S., *A Tudor Christmas*. (New York: Random House, 2018).

Weir, A., *Henry VIII: King and Court*. (London: Vintage, 2008).

About the Author

Bethan Catherine Watts is an historian of medieval and early modern history, and specialises in the lives of everyday people, particularly those of children and youths. Her other academic interests include health, hygiene, and the household.

Bethan holds both a Bachelor's and a Master's degree in Medieval History, of which she obtained First Class Honours for both. She is currently studying for a PhD in History at the University of Wales, Lampeter.

When not writing or reading about history, Bethan enjoys crafting and cooking.

This is her first book.

Index

Please note that the names of Katherine of Aragon, Catherine Howard and Kateryn Parr have each been spelled differently to avoid confusion.

Index